THE TRAIL OF LEWIS AND CLARK

1804-1904

VOLUME 1 OF 2

Captain Lewis, with Drewyer and Shields, meeting the Shoshone Indians, August 13, 1805, on the head-waters of the Snake (Lemhi) River, in Idaho.

From a water-color painting by C. M. Russell

The
Trail of Lewis and Clark
1804-1904

A story of the great exploration across the Continent in
1804-06; with a description of the old trail, based
upon actual travel over it, and of the changes
found a century later

By

Olin D. Wheeler

Member of the Minnesota Historical Society

Author of "6000 Miles through Wonderland," "Indianland and
Wonderland," "Wonderland 1900," etc.

Two Volumes

With 200 Illustrations

VOLUME I.

G. P. Putnam's Sons
New York and London
The Knickerbocker Press
1904

The Knickerbocker Press, New York

THE TRAIL OF LEWIS AND CLARK
1804-1904
By Olin D. Wheeler

VOLUME I

Vol. 1 Trade Paperback ISBN: 1-58218-725-8
Vol. 1 Hardcover ISBN: 1-58218-727-4

VOLUME 2

Vol 2 Trade Paperback ISBN: 1-58218-726-6
Vol 2 Hardcover ISBN: 1-58218-728-2

As Published in 1904

Digital Scanning and Publishing is a leader in the electronic republication of historical books and documents. We publish many of our titles as eBooks, as well as hardcover and trade paper editions. DSI is committed to bringing many traditional little known books back to life, retaining the look and feel of the original work.

Cover portraits of William Clark and Meriwether Lewis were painted by Charles Willson Peale (1741-1847), and are used with the permission of Independence National Historic Park, Philadelphia.

Published by DIGITAL SCANNING, INC. Scituate, MA 02066
781-545-2100 www.digitalscanning.com

©2002 DSI Digital Reproduction
First DSI Printing: 2002

I INSCRIBE THESE PAGES TO

CHARLES S. FEE

TO WHOSE WARM SYMPATHIES, INTELLIGENT CRITICISMS, AND
WISE SUGGESTIONS I AM GREATLY BEHOLDEN, AND WHOSE
UNSELFISH FRIENDSHIP THROUGH MANY YEARS HAS
BEEN ONE OF THE PRIVILEGES OF MY LIFE

PREFACE

THE genesis of these volumes is attributable to *Wonderland 1900,* an annual publication of the Northern Pacific Rail way.

An important part of the duties of the writer, for several years, has been the annual preparation of a new *Wonderland.* In the course of many journeys in connection with this work he travelled over extended areas of the Northwest and thus became personally conversant with much of the route pursued by Lewis and Clark on their wonderful exploration in 1804-06. When it was determined to make the leading chapter of the *Wonderland* for 1900 an abridged narrative of the journey of those explorers, it became necessary to more particularly visit many places that were important and critical points in their exploration. In further preparation for the present work, the writer has explored still other portions of the old Lewis and Clark trail and has also revisited many points. Such portions of the route as could not be followed by railway train or steamboat, and that were deserving of close inspection, were visited by private conveyance or pack train.

Nearly all of the more important or peculiarly interesting places, therefore, on "The Trail of Lewis and Clark" have been visited, and the changes which a century has wrought in the region which those men, the real pathfinders in the Northwest, were the first to traverse, are pointed out. The writer was accompanied on these journeys by professional photographers and at all times had with him the printed reports of Lewis and Clark.

In the attempt to solve the hitherto baffling problem of the crossing of the Bitter Root Mountains, the writer feels that he has been, with the valuable assistance of his friend Mr. W. H. Wright, far more successful than he had reason to expect.

The scope of the narrative covers, in some respects, a rather wide field. It was thought advisable to include a brief yet somewhat full account of the Louisiana Purchase, which was so closely related to the Lewis and Clark exploration. The opinions and conclusions expressed regarding the first great expansion of the United States are the result of careful reading and study, and if there be those who dissent from them, it is proper to add that the subject is a somewhat complicated and confused one and that certain aspects of it admit of honest differences of opinion.

Great interest now attaches to the lives of all who formed that immortal band of adventurers of a century ago, and some of those men are historic characters aside from their relation to the great exploration. An attempt has therefore been made to tell the story of each so far as possible. No apology is felt necessary for the space devoted to the discussion of the death of Captain Lewis, and the writer will be glad to receive additional and reliable information or documents regarding Lewis or any member of the Lewis and Clark expedition.

The manuscript as originally prepared contained copious extracts from the journals of Lewis and Clark and from the writings of later but early explorers of the West. This, however, so lengthened the narrative that it was deemed best to largely eliminate such quotations.

In the narrative proper it has been the aim, first, to recount the great epic story of Lewis and Clark; second, to

Preface

supplement this with such material, drawn from later explorers, as bears upon and emphasizes, or accentuates, the
achievements of the original pathfinders; third, to interpret,
amplify, and criticise such parts of the original narrative as
the studies and explorations of the writer, one hundred years
later, seemed to render advisable, thus connecting the exploration with the present time; fourth, to show, without
undue prominence, the agency of the locomotive and the
steamboat in developing the vast region that Lewis and
Clark made known to us; and fifth, to make plain that the
army of tourists and travellers in the Northwest unknow-
ingly see and visit many points and localities explored by
Lewis and Clark a century ago.

With these prefatory statements the narrative will, the
writer thinks, easily tell its own story. Whether anything
of permanent value has been added to the literature of the
subject is, of course, for others to determine. The writer
can fairly claim that he has endeavored to do his work carefully and conscientiously, and knowing that it cannot be
flawless, he will be glad to have his attention called to all
errors or defects discovered.

O. D. W.

St. Paul, Minn.
April, 1904.

"RENDER UNTO CÆSAR"

THE preparation of these volumes necessarily entailed much correspondence through which, and in other ways, I came under obligations for assistance rendered. Many of those to whom I am thus indebted are referred to in the narrative and the nature of the obligation is there more or less indicated.

To Mr. Nathaniel P. Langford, of St. Paul, Minn., himself a western explorer and a writer, I am indebted for the loan of his set of *Lewis and Clark,* edited by Dr. Coues; for the critical reading of my entire manuscript; and for many valuable suggestions and criticisms which have been embodied in the work.

To Mr. Reuben G. Thwaites, the eminent historical writer and Secretary of the Wisconsin Historical Society, Madison, Wis., I am also under great obligations for the loan of important and rare publications and for other favors. Mr. Thwaites, in connection with his own forthcoming work on the original journals of Lewis and Clark, came into possession of these original journals of the explorers. Through his courtesy I was not only privileged to examine these precious volumes, but was supplied with photographs of their pages and with such excerpts as I needed, and Dodd, Mead & Co., New York, are to be favorably mentioned in the same connection.

It is not easy to state, in a paragraph, the full nature of my indebtedness to Mrs. Eva Emery Dye, of Oregon City, Oregon, the author of *McLoughlin and Old Oregon* and of

The Conquest. Mrs. Dye, in her researches for material for *The Couquest,* secured much that she did not use but which was of value to me. With friendly consideration she placed this at my disposal. This material included old and valuable photographs and other matter relating to the members of the Lewis and Clark expedition, while many suggestions were made as to where additional information regarding Captain Lewis and his men might be sought, which resulted in valuable finds.

Mr. Peter Koch, of Bozeman, Mont., allowed me to retain for months his copy of the *Travels,* etc., of Maximilian, Prince of Wied, a rare work and a valuable one to all students of the Northwest.

Mr. Francis P. Harper, of New York, the well-known publisher of historical works, accorded me permission to draw fully from the writings of Major Chittenden and of Larpenteur.

To Hon. Ringer Hermann, late Commissioner of the General Land office, Washington, D. C., and now a member of Congress from Oregon, I am indebted for material and suggestions relative to the Louisiana Purchase.

Mr. Warren Upham and Mr. D. L. Kingsbury, Secretary and Assistant Secretary, respectively, of the Minnesota Historical Society, St. Paul, have rendered valuable cooperation.

To Major H. M. Chittenden I am under obligations for a set of the valuable maps of the Missouri River Commission, and for other courtesies.

Dr. Washington Matthews, of Washington, D. C., has kindly loaned me many old and rare photographs.

Dr. J. K. Hosmer, the writer on historical subjects, of Minneapolis, Minn., has been of no little assistance, and to Mr. T. B. Walker, of the same city. I am indebted for a photograph of the painting of Napoleon by David.

Mr. E. C. Lewis, of Nashville, Tenn., supplied me with photographs of Captain Lewis and the Lewis monument, and in other ways has rendered me his debtor.

Chas. M. Russell, of Great Falls, Mont., Ralph E. De-Camp, of Helena, Mont., and E. S. Paxson, of Butte, Mont., have added much to the value of this work by their paintings and drawings. Mr. DeCamp, is the artist of two historic scenes in the journey of Lewis and Clark, which, unfortunately, it has been impossible to reproduce in color, and his services as photographer and cartographer have been of distinctive value.

In my search for historical material I have been cordially aided by the officers of the Historical Societies. Special acknowledgments are due to George H. Himes, of the Oregon Historical Society, Portland, Ore.; F. A. Sampson, of the Missouri Historical Society, Columbia, Mo.; Horace Kephart, of the Mercantile Library, St. Louis, Mo.; Geo. W. Martin, of the Kansas State Historical Society, Topeka, Kansas; and the Buffalo Historical Society, of Buffalo, N. Y.

In the same connection I should mention Mr. Henry King, of the *Globe-Democrat,* St. Louis, Mo.; Mr. John H. Charles, Mr. F. L. Ferris, and Mr. Waltermire, of Sioux City, Iowa, for material and photographs relating to Sergeant Floyd; Mr. C. A. Lounsberry, of the *Record,* Fargo, N. D.; Albert Drouillard, of Windsor, Ontario, for the letter written by George Drouillard; Captain J. C. Painter, Walla Walla, Wash.; Forest H. Young, Park City, Mont.; the Bureau of Ethnology, and the United States Geological Survey, Washington, D. C.

Rev. C. L. Hall and Mr. H. E. Wilson, of Elbowoods, N. D., have rendered me valuable aid in my researches connected with the Mandan Indians and allied tribes, as has also Mr. F. F. Gerard, of Minneapolis, Minn., who was an intrepreter among them, and who served also as interpreter for

General George A. Custer, at the time he rode to his death at the battle of the Little Big Horn

I have to acknowledge also the kindly aid and interest of the descendants of the family of Captain Lewis. Representatives of the family from Virginia to Texas, have been most cordial in their co-operation. Besides those referred to in the text I may especially mention Mr. and Mrs. C. Harper Anderson, of Ivy Depot, Virginia, and Mrs. Ella Walker Rogers Wood, of Charlottesville, Virginia.

Acknowledgements are also due to John O'Fallon Clark, of St. Louis; L. W. Wakeley, General Passenger Agent, St. Louis, Keokuk and Northwestern Railroad, St. Louis, Mo.; E. L. Lomax, General Passenger and Ticket Agent, Union Pacific Railroad, Omaha, Neb.; John Francis, General Passenger Agent, Burlington and Missouri River Railroad in Nebraska, Omaha, Neb.; A. L. Craig, General Passenger Agent, Oregon Railroad and Navigation Company, Portland, Ore.; The Chief Engineer's Office, Northern Pacific Railway, St. Paul, Minn.; W. H. Whitaker, Detroit, Mich.; P. H. Noel, St. Louis, Mo.; J. E. Turner, Indianapolis, Ind.; W. H. Merriman, Butte, Mont.; Harry J. Horn, St. Paul, Minn.; D. Boyle, Livingston, Mont.; R. H. Relf, Assistant Secretary, Northern Pacific Railway, St. Paul, Minn.; Z. B. Brown, Park City, Mont.; W. J. Jordan, Lewiston, Idaho; Mrs. Mary C. Ronan, Missoula, Mont.; W. S. Alloway, Dalles City, Ore.; Dr. F. W. Traphagen, formerly of Bozeman, Mont., now of Golden, Colorado; Mrs. Martha O. Kibbler, San Francisco, Cal.; The Bureau of Engraving, Minneapolis, Minn.; L. S. Storrs, St. Paul, Minn.; Dr. D. A. Pease, Twin Bridges, Mont.; Emil E. Nelson, Roscoe A. Carhart, Jesse L. Pryor, and Robert Stultz, all of St. Paul, Minn.; Major Lee Moorhouse, Pendleton, Ore.; and Benjamin A. Gifford, Dalles City, Ore.

O. D. W.

CONTENTS

CHAPTER   PAGE

  I. – The Louisiana Purchase   1

 II. – Blazing the Way   2 7

 III. – Organization and Personnel of the Expedition 54

 IV. – Wood River to Fort Mandan   136

  V. – The Winter at Fort Mandan, 1804-1805 194

 VI. – Fort Mandan to Maria's River   273

VII. – Maria's River to Three Forks of the Missouri 301

ILLUSTRATIONS

PAGE

Captain Lewis, with Drewyer and Shields, Meeting the Shoshone Indians, August 13, 1805, on the Headwaters of the Snake (Lemhi) River, in Idaho.   *Frontispiece*
   From a water-color painting by C. M. Russell.

Thomas Jefferson   4

James Monroe   6

Barbe Marbois   12
   (From *The Louisiana Purchase,* by permission of Binger Hermann.)

"The Louisiana Purchase Napoleon,"   13
   Painted from life by David, presented by Napoleon to Marshal Davoust, and purchased from the descendants of Davoust by T. B. Walker, Minneapolis. It now hangs in the Minneapolis, Minn., Public Library.

The Louisiana Purchase after the Treaty of 1819   17
   (From *The Louisiana Purchase,* by permission of Binger Hermann.)

A Facsimile Page from one of the Lewis and Clark Journals   21
   (Codes "O" p. 128). Being part of a copy of a letter written by Lewis to Jefferson from Fort Mandan in 1805.

Commission of Meriwether Lewis as Captain 1st U. S. Reg. Infty., April 15, 1802   29
   Courtesy of B. R. A. Scott, Galveston, Texas.

Illustrations

PAGE

Meriwether Lewis, as Private Secretary of President
Jefferson   31

> From a painting by St. Memin, owned by C. H. Ander-
> son, Ivy Depot, Virginia, to whom it descended from
> Lewis's mother and only brother.

William Clark   35

> From the portrait in Independence Hall, Philadelphia.

House at Partlow's, Spottsylvania County, Va., in
which Captain Clark was Born   38

Jefferson's Letter of Credit to Lewis   41

Telescope Used by Lewis on the Exploration in 1804-6   45

> Now owned by C. H. Anderson, Ivy Depot, Virginia.

The Original Journals, or Codices, of Lewis and Clark   49

> Codex "A" open at pp. 18 and 19. There are two sizes
> of these Journals: the "Red" leather covered books
> 5" x 8", and the "Marbled" books, 4" x 6¾".

Meriwether Lewis, from an Original Portrait Belonging
to Meriwether Family   59

Moccasins and Shoe-buckle Used by Captain Lewis   63

One of the Drafts of Governor Lewis on James Madison, Secretary of State, which was Protested
for Non-payment by the State Department.
The Protest of this and Other Drafts was, Partially, the Occasion for the Trip of Lewis to
Washington, in the Course of which he Lost his
Life   70

Receipt Showing Payment of a Protested Bill of Governor Lewis's by General William Clark, after
the Death of Lewis   73

Monument of Captain Lewis   76

Illustrations xvii

PAGE

William Clark   79
> Supposed to be from an old portrait by Harding, made when Clark was Govenor of Missouri Territoy.

House of John Clark, Father of Captain Clark, near Louisville, Ky. Captain Clark Lived there in his Boyhood Days   82
> Photograph taken from an oil painting when the house was one hundred years old.

The Skull of Sergeant Charles Floyd   84

The Site of Sergeant Floyd's Grave before the Re-interment   87

The Stone Slab Placed August 20, 1895, Marking Final Resting-Place of Sergeant Floyd, on Floyd's Bluff   90

On the Jefferson River, near where Colter Escaped from the Blackfeet. The Beaver's-head on the Left   104

Facsimile of the Drouillard Letter (page 1)   107

Facsimile of the Drouillard Letter (page 2)   108

Facsimile of the Drouillard Letter (page 3)   109

The Discharge of William Bratton from the Lewis and Clark Expedition Signed by Captain Lewis   113

Housewife and Needle Used by George Shannon on the Lewis and Clark Expedition and now Owned by Mrs. Rev. J. P. Farmer, Shannon's Granddaughter, of Portland, Ore., This Housewife was of Red Leather, was Provided with Pockets, and Measured when open, 7 1/2 by 15 3/8 inches.   119

Alexander H. Willard and Wife   123

PAGE

Sacágawea, the Bird-woman   127
     From a drawing by E. S. Paxson.

Route of Lewis and Clark — Wood River to Heart
    River   139

"Burlington" Railroad Bridge across Missouri River,
    near the Point from which Lewis and Clark Be-
    gan their Exploration   145

The Indian Process of "Jerking" Meat on Scaffolds   150

A Page from the Journal of Sergeant Charles Floyd   153

The First Council with the Indians Held by Lewis and
    Clark   157
     From an old illustration in *A Journal of the Voyages and
     Travels of a Corps of Discovery,* etc., by Patrick Gass,
     published by Mathew Carey, Philadelphia, 1810.

Union Pacific Railroad Bridge across the Missouri
    River, between Omaha, Neb., and Council
    Bluffs, Iowa   159

Page 14 from Codex "B" — Clark — Regarding Sergeant
    Floyd's Illness and Death   165

Floyd Obelisk, Floyd's Bluff, Sioux City, Iowa   167

Bronze Plate Attached to Floyd Monument, Sioux
    City, Iowa   170

Bronze Plate Attached to Floyd Monument, Sioux
    City, Iowa   171

A Page of "Celestial Observations" from Codex "O" —
    Lewis   179

Northern Pacific Railway Bridge across Missouri River
    at Bismarck and Mandan, N. D. This Point Is
    an Old Bison and Indian Ford   187

Illustrations

PAGE

Site of Old Fort Abraham Lincoln, just below Mouth
of Heart River, North Dakota, from which General Custer Started on his Last Campaign, May
17, 1876. Lewis and Clark Camped at this Spot
October 20, 1801   189

Route of Lewis and Clark. Mouth of Heart River –
Bismarck to Mouth of Yellowstone River –
Fort Buford   193

Fort Clark, 1831 Opposite the Fort Mandan of Lewis
and Clark   197
  From *Maximilian's Travels*, etc.

Page 64 from Codex "C" – Clark – Noting Arrival
at Mandan Villages   201

Captain Clark and his Men Building a Line of Huts at
Fort Mandan, 1804   207
  From an old print from Gass's *A Journal of the Voyages
  and Travels*, etc.

A Winter Village of the Minnetaree, or Grosventre Indians   210
  From Maximilian.

A Mandan Village and "Bull-boats"   215
  From Maximilian

A Mandan Hut on the Fort Berthold Reservation in
1903. Primitive Ladder Reclines at Side of
the Covered Entrance   217

Two Chiefs and Daughter Relating the Story of the
Mandans   221

Mandan Indians of 1833   230
  From *Travels to the Interior of North America*, etc., by
  Maximilian.

Illustrations

PAGE

The Bison Dance of the Mandans   235
From *Travels to the Interior of North America,* etc, by
Maximilian.

Mandan Indian Graves in 1904, in the Hills near Fort
Berthold Indian Agency, North Dakota   239

Leggings, a Mandan Indian of 1904   241

A School Building, Teacher and Family, and Indian
Scholars on the Fort Berthold Reservation, in
1904   245

An Old Indian "Bull-boat" Made from a Buffalo-
hide Stretched over a Framework of Willow
Poles   214

Indians Hunting the Bison in the Days of Lewis and
Clark   249
From a water-color painting by C. M. Russell.

An Old French-Canadian Trapper   257
From a drawing by Paxson.

An Upper Missouri River Steamer in 1904   269

Map Showing Approximate Positions and Names of
Indian Villages at Fort Mandan in Time of
Lewis and Clark, 1804-5, also Names of Same
Villages According to Maximilian, 1833, and
Dr. Washington Matthews, 1870. River Laid
Down from Map of Missouri River Commis-
sion   .270

The Old Mandan Earth Lodge – in the Distance –
and the Newer Log Cabin, Fort Berthold Reservation, 1804 *vs.* 1904   271

Old Fort Berthold, Dakota Territory, in 1865   277
(Courtesy of Dr. Washington Matthews)

Illustrations

PAGE

Mandan Indian Ferry on the Upper Missouri River, Fort Berthold Reservation, 1904   278

Route of Lewis and Clark from Mouth of Yellowstone River to the Great Falls of the Missouri   280

Fort Union, at Junction of Missouri and Yellowstone Rivers, Built in 1828 or 1829
(Courtesy of Dr. Washington Matthews.)   282

Reverse Side of Discharge Paper of William Bratton   285

An Old Time Frontier Scout
From a drawing by Paxson.   291

The "White" or Grizzly Bear of Lewis and Clark –
Ursus Horribilis   294

The Remains of Old Fort Benton, Montana, Built in 1850   297

One of the Blackfeet – Siksika – Indians
From a drawing by Paxson.   300

The Great Falls of the Missouri Discovered by Captain Lewis, June 13, 1805   307

Route of Lewis and Clark from Maria's River to Traveller's-Rest Creek and Return and also Showing Route of Captain Lewis from White Bear Island to the Headwaters of Maria's River and Return to the Mouth of that Stream   313

Black Eagle Fall from Below, Showing the Island where the Eagle Had its Nest   317

The Wonderful Fountain near Great Falls, Montana, Discovered by Captain Clark on June 18, 1805, now Known as the Giant Spring   321

PAGE

Black Eagle Fall from Above. Showing the Smelter
and Chimney on the Hill Referred to in the
Text   325

Lewis and Clark's Map of the Region about the Great
Falls and Companion Cataracts, and Showing
the Line of Portage   329

Captain Clark, Chaboneau, Sacágawea, and Papoose
in the Cloud-burst near the Great Falls, on June
29, 1805   333
        From a drawing by Russell.

Captain Clark and his Men Shooting Bears   335
        From *A Journal of the Voyages and Travels,* etc., by
        Patrick Gass.

The White Bear Islands and the Missouri River above
the City of Great Falls. The Lewis and Clark
Portage from Below the Great Falls, Followed,
Approximately, the Line of Poles Seen at the
Left Centre of the Illustration   341

View from the Summit of Bear's-Tooth Mountain, just
below the Gates of the Rocky Mountains, Show-
ing the Missouri River   342

The Heart of the Gates of the Rocky Mountains   347
        (From a painting by De Camp.)

Hilger's Ranch, Montana, at Head of the Gates of the
Rocky Mountains. Source of Potts's Creek Is
just beyond the House, among the Trees   339

Cañon of the Gates of the Rocky Mountains   351

Head of the Gates of the Rocky Mountains, at Mouth
of Potts's Creek, near Hilger's Ranch Mon-
tana   355

PAGE

Cathedral Bluff, in the Canon of the Gates of the
    Rocky Mountains   359

Junction of Madison and Jefferson Rivers, Montana.
    The Madison on the Left, the Jefferson at the
    Right Centre   365

Gallatin River and Valley from Captain Lewis's Point
    of View of July 27, 1805   369

"Fort Rock" at Three Forks of the Missouri, Mon-
    tana, Looking South, the Gallatin River at the
    Left   371
        (From an oil painting by De Camp.)

Highest Knob of "Fort Rock" at Three Forks of the
    Missouri, from the South   375

Map of the Territory Crossed by Lewis and Clark in
    1804   378

THE TRAIL OF LEWIS AND CLARK

CHAPTER I

THE LOUISIANA PURCHASE

IN the year 1801, when Thomas Jefferson was inaugurated as the third President of the United States of America, the nation was ready for territorial expansion. Under the wise guidance of Washington, the hasty, patchwork confederacy of 1776 had grown into a homogeneous union, with a strong central government. Jefferson is chiefly remembered as the author of the Declaration of Independence, but he was also a leading figure in two later affairs which, as the years pass, seem destined to contribute almost equally to his fame. These were the purchase of Louisiana, and its later exploration by Lewis and Clark; the one consummated, the other initiated, in 1803.

It is not improbable that in history Jefferson's reputation will stand higher for the exploration than for the acquisition. The two are closely connected, but the exploration seems to have been peculiarly originated by Jefferson, whereas the purchase was the result of a combination of circumstances for which it is difficult to place the responsibility. Jefferson, Monroe, and Livingston, for the United States; Marbois, Talleyrand, and especially Napoleon Bonaparte, for France; all played important roles in the great international drama.

The province known as Louisiana became the property of France by the right of discovery. Robert Cavelier de la Salle was one of that band of hardy, brave, untiring, and unselfish explorers sent out in the seventeenth century to penetrate and possess the New World and to enlarge the boundaries of New France.

Starting from Fort Miami in December, 1681, and going by way of the site of the future city of Chicago, La Salle descended the Illinois and Mississippi rivers to the Gulf of Mexico. In April, 1682, with much pomp and ceremony, he erected a column and Cross and took possession of the country drained by the Mississippi and its western tributaries, in the name of Louis XIV. of France, and called it *La Louisianne.*

In 1684, with a large company, La Salle again sailed from France, this time to the Gulf of Mexico, bent upon founding a colony at the mouth of the Mississippi. He missed the river and finally landed at Matagorda Bay on the coast of Texas, where he built a fort and established a colony. Three years later, in March, 1687, while on a branch of the Trinity River, he was cruelly murdered by one of his followers.

Upon these operations of La Salle rests the claim of France to this country and upon the title of France depends that of the succeeding owners of Louisiana.

France retained possession of Louisiana until 1762. In that year, by a secret treaty, the text of which was not made known publicly in the United States until 1837, France conveyed Louisiana to Spain. It had been an expensive and troublesome province and France was glad to be rid of it. In 1800-01, nearly forty years later, Spain re-ceded the country to France, by the secret treaties of San Ildefonso. The fact of the attempted recession was virtually known in the United States late in 1801. The treaty, however, was not signed by the Spanish King until October, 1802. Napoleon had wished to have the transaction kept secret and had agreed on the part of France not to cede or alienate the province to any other nation without Spain's consent, a condition which was speedily broken. At the time of the recession the relations of the United States with both Spain and France were decidedly strained, the right of navigation of the Mississippi River being a particularly aggravating and momentous question.

Spain at no time had looked with favor upon the creation and growth of the Republic. Policy had compelled a certain amount of comity in her treatment of her new and lusty neighbors on the east and north, but there was no desire on her part, or at least on the part of her representatives in America, to exhibit international friendliness. On the contrary, intrigues had been carried on between Spanish and American officials looking toward annexation to Spain of that part of the United States bordering the Mississippi. These intrigues had proved fruitless, but the fact that the Mississippi River did not flow unvexed to the sea was a serious cause of trouble during the administration of Thomas Jefferson, as it was during that of Abraham Lincoln sixty years later.

Spain had held the island of New Orleans on both sides of the stream to its mouth. Treaty arrangements existed granting to Americans the free navigation of the river and the right of deposit in the Spanish storehouses at New Orleans, but the Spanish officials at length, presumably upon orders from Madrid, had denied these privileges. This obstructive policy caused great dissatisfaction on the part of the Western population of the United States, and even threatened national unity. Jefferson plainly saw that, to end the disputes, the United States should obtain possession of sufficient territory to control the mouth of the Mississippi and he made advances to Spain for the purchase of New

Orleans and the Floridas, but Spain, with the secret treaty of 1800 in her way, could only temporize and evade. War between Spain and the United States seemed imminent, when the treaty of San Ildefonso became known and it was discovered that the territory in question had become the

Thomas Jefferson

property of France. Negotiations for the purchase were then begun with that country, and Robert R. Livingston was sent out as Minister to France to treat of the affair. He had authority to pay $2,000,000, and if absolutely necessary, as much as $10,000,000 for the desired territory.

France, however, in the person of Napoleon, had her own views in regard to Louisiana and for a long time she virtually refused to consider the matter. Napoleon was boundless in his ambitions and his grand scheme of French colonial expansion literally embraced the ends of the earth. The first undertaking was a powerful expedition to San Domingo led by Napoleon's brother-in-law, General Leclerc. This West Indian island was a dependency of France, which in the days of the French Revolution had risen in successful revolt. Napoleon purposed to restore the supremacy of France, but between fate and yellow fever, his attempt was a gigantic failure. It had been his intention to follow up the San Domingo expedition with another which should land at New Orleans, possess Louisiana, and people it with French, annihilating the commerce of the United States which found its outlet down the Mississippi. But this campaign, planned with secrecy and energy during 1802, never started. Delay was caused by the deliberateness of the Spanish King in signing the act of transfer according to the treaty of San Ildefonso. When at last this matter was settled, the failure of the attempt to conquer San Domingo, with other disasters, ended Napoleon's dream of Western colonization.

The Peace of Amiens between France and England in March, 1802, seems to have been of the kind that ends one war only to pave the way for another. It was negotiated by Joseph Bonaparte, Napoleon's eldest brother, for the French, and by Lord Cornwallis, of Yorktown fame, for the English. It was utterly one-sided, the English giving up everything, the French gaining everything. Such an arrangement could not fail to create the greatest dissatisfaction in England, a feeling which was accentuated by subsequent events.

Napoleon himself had carefully coached Joseph and he kept a watchful eye on the negotiations during their progress. His actions afterwards were such as to incense and antagonize the English at every turn, making certain an early revival of hostilities. In March, 1803, at one of the ambassadorial receptions, Napoleon virtually insulted Lord Whitworth, the British Ambassador, and matters going from bad to worse, the Ambassador, on May 2d, demanded his passports. On May 12th he left Paris, and on May 16, 1803, Great Britain declared war.

Early in this year, Napoleon had seen that a conflict with England was imminent, and he realized that in such a struggle, the province of Louisiana would be a burden. His own plans for French expansion in the New World had failed. The province was the source of trouble with the United States and a cause of danger from England. All of the French outlying possessions would be at the mercy of England as mistress of the seas, and Louisiana would be the most vulnerable point.

The means for the solution of this difficulty were at hand. Robert R. Livingston, upon his arrival in France, late in 1801, had endeavored with persistence and assiduity to arrange with the First Consul, through Talleyrand, for the purchase of New Orleans. He had, however, made such small progress that he had become utterly discouraged. It is entirely probable that Talleyrand had little influence with Napoleon and knew next to nothing of his master's intentions.

Jefferson, in America, appreciated the emergency in French affairs, and when he saw that war was inevitable between France and England, he determined to reinforce Livingston with James Monroe as Minister Plenipotentiary and Envoy Extraordinary. Monroe was well fitted for his mission. He arrived in Paris April 12, 1803.

Before Monroe reached France, however, the sale of New Orleans had been practically decided upon. Napoleon, while splashing about in his bath, had a picturesque and now historic quarrel with two of his brothers, Joseph and Lucien, who favored the retention of the province. Lively discussions were held with his ministers and Napoleon quickly determined upon his course. Throwing sentiment, family remonstrance, and ministerial advice to the winds, he determined to thwart England by the only means in his power, and to sell, not the trifling piece of river land which Livingston hoped to obtain, but the entire province of Louisiana.

James Monroe

At one of the conferences at the Tuileries, Napoleon first indicated the bent of his mind in these words: "To emancipate nations from the commercial tyranny of England, it is necessary to balance her influence by a maritime power that may one day become her rival; that power is the United States."

To Decrès and Marbois, his Ministers of the Marine and of the Treasury, he said on April 10, 1803:

I know the full value of Louisiana, and I have been desirous of repairing the fault of the French negotiator who abandoned it in 1763. A few lines of a treaty have restored it to me, and I have scarcely recovered it when I must expect to lose it. But if it escapes from me, it shall one day cost dearer to those who oblige me to strip myself of it, than to those to whom I wish to deliver it. The English have successively taken from France, Canada, Cape Breton, Newfoundland, Nova Scotia, and the richest portions of Asia. They shall not have the Mississippi which they covet. The conquest of Louisiana would be easy, if they only took the trouble to make a descent there. I have not a moment to lose in putting it out of their reach. I know not whether they are not already there. It is their usual course, and if I had been in their place, I would not have waited. I think of ceding it to the United States. . . . They only ask of me one town in Louisiana. but I already consider the colony as entirely lost, and it appears to me that in the hands of this growing power, it will be more useful to the policy and even to the commerce of France, than if I should attempt to keep it.

At St. Cloud, upon the 11th of April, he continued, after receiving important information from London:

Irresolution and deliberation are no longer in season. I renounce Louisiana. It is not only New Orleans that I will cede. it is the whole colony without any reservation. . . . I renounce it with the greatest regret. To attempt obstinately to retain it would be folly. I direct you to negotiate this affair with the envoys of the United States. Do not even await the arrival of Mr. Monroe: have an interview this very day with Mr. Livingston: but I require a great deal of money for this war. . . . I will be moderate, in consideration of the necessity in which I am of making a sale. . . . I want fifty millions of francs, and for less than that sum I will not treat; I would rather make a desperate attempt to keep those fine countries.

When the proposition to buy this vast domain was presented to the American diplomatists they were naturally rather staggered. It was far beyond what they had asked for and they had no authority, as Napoleon supposed Monroe had, to negotiate for imperial domains. Talleyrand had once hinted to Livingston of the desire to sell Louisiana, but the latter believed it to be but another bit of clever trickery and gave it little or no serious consideration.

Napoleon was a man not to be trifled with at such a time. When he was in the mood quick action was advisable, and this was an epochal and critical moment in the national life of the United States. Monroe and Livingston at once rose to the occasion. In those days of slow-sailing ships and with no cables, they must themselves, unadvised by Jefferson and his Cabinet, assume the responsibilities of the moment and either accept or reject. Like brave patriots they accepted and closed the bargain. So long as our country endures, their memory should be held in grateful honor for the resolution and decision so signally displayed.

The result of the negotiations was extremely satisfactory to all immediately concerned. Livingston said: "We have lived long, but this is the noblest work of our whole lives." Napoleon, upon learning that the cession was an accomplished fact, expressed himself as follows: "This accession of territory, strengthens forever the power of the United States; and I have just given to England a maritime rival, that will sooner or later humble her pride."

In the negotiations for the purchase of Louisiana, Livingston bore himself superbly and did yeoman service for his country. Although he made little progress with Talleyrand, yet through Marbois, Bernadotte, and Joseph Bonaparte he managed to reach the First Consul, and there is reason to believe that at least some of certain "essays" that he wrote relative to the relations between France and the United States and to the Louisiana matter were read by Napoleon, who may well have been influenced by them.

Livingston's part and influence in these negotiations has been a subject for much discussion, but I believe the statement here made to be a true one. That he fairly deluged, and probably wearied, Talleyrand and others with the series of "essays" which he wrote – if they read them – and in which, somewhat didactically, he instructed the First Consul and his ministers as to their true course and interest regarding Louisiana, is undoubtedly true. But that he bore the brunt of the negotiations for the United States, whatever his real influence may or may not have been, is equally true, and he can hardly be blamed for being somewhat piqued that, at the end of it all, Monroe came in and, in popular estimation at least, completely overshadowed him. His reception of Monroe was manly, and if he acquired a somewhat exaggerated idea of the value of his own efforts, it is not surprising.

It seems now generally agreed that the treaty of cession was loosely and carelessly drawn – whoever deserves credit or discredit for it.

No one greatly influenced Bonaparte. He was, as his brother Joseph said, his own counsellor, and history abundantly proves that he was far in advance of his own family, ministers, Livingston, Monroe, and all others, in his ideas concerning the Louisiana country.

I have said that no man dreamed of purchasing Louisiana at the time. A partial modification of this should be made in Livingston's favor, to whom a glimmering of this idea came. In two or more communications he argues and argues to the point, that France might well afford, for her own strength and convenience, to sell to us all of Louisiana north of the Arkansas River. Nevertheless, when the proposition was made by Marbois to sell the whole of the province, he seems to have been astonished equally with Monroe.

On April 30th the treaty was signed transferring the entire province to the United States – and it was at once sent to Congress for ratification. Congress ratified it October 17, 1803, and on December 20th following the French colors came down at New Orleans and the Stars and Stripes went up in their stead. Then the Mississippi River ran its course to the sea wholly through American territory. The formal act of transfer of what was known as "Upper Louisiana" did not take place until March 10, 1804; both Lower and Upper Louisiana were, however, constructively in the possession of the United States from December 20, 1803.

We paid for Louisiana $15,000,000.

Napoleon asked fifty millions of francs, but Marbois, his negotiator, raised the price unknown to the First Consul, and maintained it. However, the United States virtually succeeded in reducing the amount, for it was finally agreed that twenty millions of the payment should be used in satisfying claims of American citizens against France, leaving sixty millions of francs as the net amount received by France for the territory, or ten millions more than Napoleon had himself demanded.

In the sale of the province from Spain to France, its value had been reckoned at one hundred millions of francs, so that France lost, on that basis, forty millions of francs in the sale made to us.

The amount that Napoleon demanded for Louisiana has been variously stated. Henry Adams appears to figure it at one hundred millions of francs exclusive of the American spoliation claims, and Dr. Hosmer, in his *The History of the Louisiana Purchase,* seems to follow Adams, but this figure, mentioned by Napoleon in one of his preliminary talks with Marbois, seems to have been an amount named offhand, without any intention of seriously demanding it. Marbois immediately told the First Consul that it was an exorbitant amount and it does not appear to have again been named.

Napoleon, on April 11th, as already stated, when he formally instructed Marbois to begin negotiations, named fifty millions of francs as his price.

Marbois distinctly states in his *History of Louisiana* that:

The First Consul, supposing that he carried his valuation very high, had said that he calculated on fifty millions. The French plenipotentiary, without entering into any explanation with him, considered this estimate a good deal too low, and, as soon as the price became the subject of conference, stated that it was fixed at eighty millions, and that it would be useless to propose a reduction.

There was some haggling over the price, Livingston thinking that thirty millions was enough for the country, but Marbois held firm and eighty millions it remained.

Monroe, in one of his private letters published after his retirement from the Presidency, names one hundred and twenty millions of francs as the amount suggested to be paid for the country, but upon Marbois calling his attention to the error, he writes from Oakhill, Va., on April 4, 1828, admitting the mistake and adds, "You only asked the eighty millions that are stipulated in the treaty." It would seem that the agreement of Marbois and Monroe as to this sum ought to be conclusive in the matter.

It is an actual and historical truth that Marbois, a personal friend and admirer of Monroe, and also a warm friend of our country, was a most important factor in the Louisiana negotiations. While a true and tried Frenchman, he was a just and honorable man and diplomatist, not one of the

Barbé Marbois.
(From "The Louisiana Purchase,"
by permission of Binger Hermann)

Talleyrand type. There can be little doubt that, because of his known probity and integrity, Napoleon delegated to him instead of to Talleyrand, whom, probably, no man could greatly trust, the French part of the Louisiana negotiations, and that the ostensible reason assigned by the Consul, "that being an affair of the treasury," it came within Marbois's province, was merely a subterfuge.

Marbois had been attached to the French legation in the United States, and had married a Philadelphia lady. His experience in America and his judicial habit of mind enabled him to understand the young Republic, and to foretell her future with remarkable accuracy. He was peculiarly fitted to act diplomatically between the nation to which he owed allegiance and another to which he was strongly bound by ties of marriage and friendship, and he acquitted himself honorably.

It has been seen that in the real and final analysis of the matter Napoleon Bonaparte is the man to whom the United States owes its domain of Louisiana and the one who forced the Republic into its first great territorial expansion, when it obtained possession of the grandest part of its magnificent country.

An interesting aspect of this subject is given by Henry Adams, who argues that Napoleon's real reason for forcing

The Louisiana Purchase "Napoleon," painted from life by David, presented by Napoleon to Marshal Davoust, purchased from the descendants of Davoust by T. B. Walker, Minneapolis. It now hangs in the Minneapolis, Minn., Public Library

13

Louisiana upon the United States was that the transfer of this province might eventually prove to be of the same sort of benefit that the Grecian horse was to the Trojans, and "prove their ruin," owing to the additional ground which it would furnish for jealousies, dissensions, and ultimate disintegration of the Union. When one recalls the part that Missouri, Nebraska, and Bleeding Kansas played in the events that led up to the Civil War, this forecast, for such it virtually was, of Napoleon becomes a most interesting historical item.

After all, Adams concludes, "the real reasons which induced Bonaparte to alienate the territory from France remained hidden in the mysterious processes of his mind."

Among the Americans there were not wanting alarmists in those days, those who saw not the substance but only the shadow, and there were croakings, dismal forebodings, and direful prophecies. The treaty was ratified by Congress, but not until ultimate disunion, disintegration, and general demoralization had been predicted.

And what of this country – what were its boundaries, what its physical characteristics, what its possibilities?

The boundaries of Louisiana were loosely defined in the treaty simply because no one could state them with exactness, and they were, as has been well said, "incapable of any other than a forced solution."

There had been, originally, much obscurity and uncertainty regarding them, and the various cessions between France, Spain, and England certainly had not made the situation more clear. The truth is that there was ground, as Marbois intimates, for reasonable and honest doubt, but the United States, probably influenced largely by Talleyrand, made claims which Spain disputed with energy. Without going into details, the United States claimed, to the east, the country about the lower Mississippi to the region between

Mobile River and Pensacola; to the west, the country drained by the Mississippi River and its tributaries, which, under La Salle's discoveries and occupation, extended to the Rio Bravo or Rio Grande del Norte; and thence northbound from its sources to the summit of the Rocky Mountains, the mountains being the western limit of the Purchase.

This included the greater part of Texas – to which the claim of the United States would seem to have been a righteous one – west of the Great River; and what was then known as West Florida, east of the Mississippi, regarding the validity of which there was some question.

This contention as to West Florida was an afterthought on Livingston's part, based, admittedly, upon ambiguities of language in the treaties of 1762 and 1763, – for these two should be construed together, – wherein France intended to cede to Spain the Louisiana country *west* of the Mississippi, together with New Orleans, etc., and to Great Britain all the territory she owned east of that river south of the river Iberville. The idea was ingenious, but was based upon a quibble; it meant, really, a perversion of the plain intent and understanding of those treaties, and it was scarcely creditable to Livingston or to the country that it was insisted and acted upon by the United States, and, it must be said, with beneficial results in the ultimate acquirement of West, Florida after long contention and wrangling with Spain.

The contention between Spain and the United States ran on, becoming more and more acrimonious, but the United States took possession of Florida, though there was never any formal and joint statement of boundaries until the treaty of 1819, in which Spain ceded all of East and West Florida, and all country west of the Mississippi north of the forty-second degree of latitude and westward to the Pacific, to which she claimed ownership, while the United

States ignored and relinquished any claims to Texas. Therefore, whatever the justice of the original contention as to Texas, it was distinctly abandoned at the first formal opportunity of stating it, in 1819, and the United States is now certainly barred, technically, in making any claim to it in present-day discussions.

There was really, it would seem, no substantial ground upon which Spain could claim any part of the Texas country, after the recession to France, nor, as a matter of fact, does it appear that there really was any such claim. Spain was angered at the lack of faith shown by France toward her in selling Louisiana to the United States, and made some show of bluster toward the United States in opposition to the sale, but there was nothing serious in it. Had the United States made no claims to the Floridas nothing would have been heard, in all probability, of Spain's adverse pretentions to Texas. As for the reasons for surrendering Texas in 1819, they seem involved in obscurity, and there is a general feeling that Spain got the best of the transaction. But it must be remembered that the United States received as an equivalent, therefor Spain's title to the territory on the Pacific coast north of the forty-second parallel – in other words, a quit claim to Washington, Oregon, Idaho, and parts of Montana and Wyoming in return for the quit claim to Texas.

The general weight of opinion agrees, at the present time, that the Louisiana Purchase *did not* include the Oregon country, although an ingenious mind may, perhaps, still construct a plausible argument to the contrary. Marbois says: "The shores of the Western Ocean were certainly not included in the cession." The moral effect, at least, of Spain's relinquishment of the Oregon region, in the treaty of 1819, was subsequently very great.

The claim of the United States to Oregon was based upon

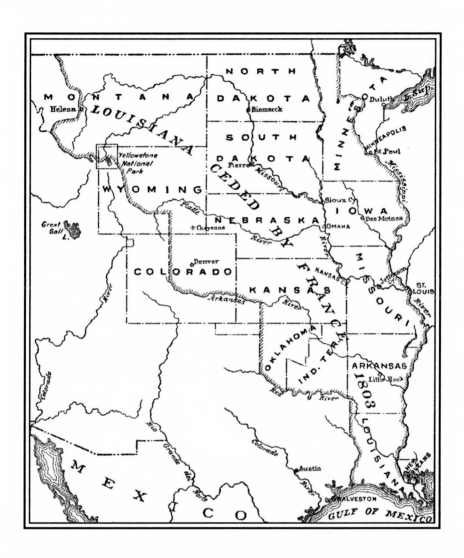

The Louisiana Purchase, after the Treaty of 1819.
(From "The Louisiana Purchase," by permission of Binger Hermann.)

Captain Robert Gray's discovery of the Columbia River in 1792; Lewis and Clark's exploration in 1805-06, and the Astorian settlement in 1811; and it was clinched by obtaining Spain's title in 1819.

It will thus be seen that the Lewis and Clark exploration, extending across both the Louisiana Purchase and the Oregon territory, became an interesting and important connecting link between the two, and doubtless led to some confusion, in thought, as to the western boundary line of the Old Louisiana. As finally determined, the boundaries of the Purchase were: on the east, from the Gulf of Mexico just east of Lake Pontchartrain, around the southern shores of Lakes Pontchartrain and Mauripas and up the river Iberviller[1] to the Mississippi, then up this stream to its source, and thence directly north to the forty-ninth parallel, where it meets the western side of the Lake of the Woods; on the north, the forty-ninth parallel to the Rocky Mountains; on the south, the "Gulph of Mexico" from east of Lake Pontchartrain to the mouth of the Sabine River; on the west, from the mouth of the river Sabine "continuing north along the western bank of that river to the thirty-second degree of latitude; thence by a line due north to the degree of latitude where it strikes the Rio Roxo of Nachitoches or Red River; then following the course of the Rio Roxo westward, to the degree of longitude 100 west from London and 23 from Washington; then crossing the said Red River and running thence, by a line due north, to the river Arkansas; thence following the course of the Arkansas to its source, in latitude 42 north"; thence along that parallel to the Rocky Mountains, and thence along the summit of the Rockies to the forty-ninth parallel.

Ex-United States Land Commissioner Binger Hermann,

---

[1] In the far North the Louisiana of La Salle was bounded by the dividing line between the Mississippi River and the Red River of the North.

in his admirable monograph, *The Louisiana Purchase,* published by the United States Government, gives the area of the Purchase as 883,072 square miles, or 565,166,080 acres, an area somewhat less than that of the original thirteen States, and it cost us, therefore, something less than three cents an acre.

The Louisiana Purchase was larger in area than Great Britain, France, Spain, Germany, Portugal, and Italy thrown into one. Out of it have been carved entire, Arkansas, Missouri, Iowa, Nebraska, North and South Dakota, and Indian Territory; nearly all of Louisiana, Oklahoma, Kansas, Wyoming, and Montana; about two thirds of Minnesota and one third of Colorado.

An idea of its present political importance may be gathered from the following statement:

At the time of the Purchase four additional States, Vermont, Kentucky, Tennessee, and Ohio, had been admitted into the Union, making seventeen in all. These, of course, supplied thirty-four United States Senators. Out of the Louisiana Purchase there have been formed, to the present time, in whole or in part, twelve States and two Territories, having a total of twenty-four United States Senators, with at least two more, from Oklahoma, yet to come. In other words, the territory which we purchased from Napoleon in 1803 will, virtually, soon have precisely the same numerical representation in the United States Senate that the original thirteen States had at the time of the cession, one hundred years ago.

It is an interesting fact that in the discussion in the United States Senate, in 1902, regarding the disposition to be made of the Philippine Islands, Senators from States formed from the Louisiana Purchase who strongly opposed territorial expansion in that direction would probably never have had an opportunity of voicing such opposition in that august forum had it not been for our first great expansion a century before.

This suggests the further thought that, as at the present time, so in 1803, awful calamities were foretold as the result of annexation. These predictions were not realized. As Henry Ward Beecher has said, the prophecy may have been all right, but the fulfilment was lacking, and instead we have gone on from great to greater splendor.

Without impugning the motives of those seers who now cry "Lochiel, Lochiel, beware of the day," the American whose patriotism is coupled with faith in an overruling Providence who has safely led us through a hundred wonderful years will feel, with Patrick Henry, that the experiences of the past are safe guides for the future.

As N. P. Langford has well said in *The Louisiana Purchase,* published by the Minnesota Historical Society:

> The doleful predictions of a century ago, like those we are hearing to-day, when our land is teeming with the spirit of acquisition, were born of a fear and timidity which are inimical to great progress; and they represent a mental attitude which is not fitted to grapple with new problems. This Nation is no longer an infant, but a giant. The sun never sets on the land over which now float the Stars and Stripes, and we have need to expand our ideas of our destiny as we have expanded our territory. The present is no time for faint-heartedness in the councils of the Republic.

It is quite doubtful if there was much known at the time of the Purchase of the physical character of this great acquisition, or that its probable politico-economical value was more than half suspected. It was, of course, known that the Mississippi rolled along its eastern border almost from one to the other of its extreme parallels of latitude; that the region was drained by the mighty tributaries of the Father of Waters, among them the Red, Arkansas, and the Missouri rivers and their feeders; that west of the

This river we suppose to be the S. fork of the Columbia, and the fish the Salmon, with which we are informed the Columbia river abounds. — This river is said to be rapid but as far as the Indian informants are acquainted with it is not interrupt=ed with shoals. its bed consists principally of sand and gravel. —

The waters of the Missouri are transparent at all seasons of the year above the falls.

With respect to other rivers, and their subsidiary streams, and their connection with other rivers and streams, the map which is herewith forwarded, will give you a more perfect idea, than a detailed discription of them would do. — the mountains, salines, trading establishments, and all other remarkable places, so far as known to us, are also laid down on this map. —

Meriwether Lewis Capt
1st U.S. Regt. Infty.

A facsimile page from one of the Lewis and Clark Journals (Codex 0, p. 128), being part of "A Summary View of the Rivers and Creeks which discharge them[selves] into the Missouri," etc.

Mississippi stretched the great plains and beyond rose the whitened, storm-drenched summits of the Shining or Rocky Mountains, and that these streams and plains harbored vast numbers of fur-bearing animals and Indians. The details of the topography were unknown. The grandeur of the Colorado and Montana Rockies, the unparalleled wonders of the Yellowstone Park, the wild, sombre majesty of the Black Hills, these and a thousand scarcely lesser bursts of scenic glory were yet to be revealed.

It was not until after Lewis and Clark returned to civilization that the fur traders and adventurers began to push boldly into the treeless, tireless spaces beyond the frontier and, returning, unfolded their border tales of the marvellous land which Napoleon had insisted that the United States should add to its national domain.

As to the possibilities of this region, what man is there that even now would dare to hint at them? How much more then was it a sheer impossibility for those of a century ago to form the remotest conception of the transformation to be effected in the new possessions! Was there any reason that they should foresee that the tremendous herds of bison, antelopes, deer, and elk that covered the great plains should, in the comparatively short space of a hundred years, be wiped out of existence or driven to the remotest recesses of the mountains, and that in their places bellowing cattle, bleating sheep, and neighing horses would be found? Could they reasonably have been expected to foretell that a century would see the tepee and wickiup of the Indian virtually swept from sight, his picturesque villages of buffalo skins supplanted by the thickly placed homes, palaces, and cities of the white man, and his children's children learning to read from the white man's primer? What an item of interest it would be, if we could know whether there came into the minds of any of Lewis and

Clark's men, as they sat around their camp-fires on the upper Missouri, about the Three Forks, or along the Yellowstone or Columbia rivers, the merest suggestion of a thought that they were the advance party of a railway engineering corps!

I may be pardoned for somewhat specifically, but briefly, pointing out the material contrasts of a hundred years by references to United States Census reports or other authorities. In doing this I shall not confine myself to the Louisiana Purchase, but include the Oregon country as well; it being so intimately related to the former and forming, also, equally as important a part of the territory traversed by Lewis and Clark.

In 1860, fifty-seven years after the purchase of Louisiana, fourteen years after the settlement of the Oregon question, William H. Seward stood upon the steps of the Capitol of Minnesota in St. Paul, just outside the limits of the Louisiana Purchase, – the Mississippi River being the eastern boundary and the main portion of the city being on the east side of the river, – and uttered this prophecy:

I find myself for the first time upon the high land in the centre of the continent of North America, equidistant from the waters of Hudson Bay and the Gulf of Mexico. Here is the place, the central place, where the agricultural products of this region of North America must pour out their tributes to the world. I have cast about for the future and ultimate seat of power of North America. I looked to Quebec, to New Orleans, to Washington, San Francisco, and St. Louis for the future seat of power. But I have corrected that view. I now believe that the ultimate last seat of government on this great continent will be found somewhere not far from the spot on which I stand, at the head of navigation of the Mississippi River.

Let us now, forty years afterwards, see what progress has been made in this region along the lines of Seward's prediction.

In 1800 – second census – the total population of the United States was, in round numbers, 5,308,000. From the census of 1900 – twelfth census – we can make three groupings of population, in round numbers, from the region under consideration, either of which exceeds that of the entire country in 1800.

These are:

1.

Louisiana	1,382,000
Arkansas	1,312,000
Missouri	3,100,000
Total.	5,794,000

2.

Missouri	3,107,000
Iowa	2,232,000
Total.	5,339,000

3.

Kansas	1,470,000
Iowa	2,232,000
Minnesota.	1,751,000
Total	5,453,000

The remaining States and Territories formed from the Louisiana and Oregon territory and not named in these groups had, in 1900, a population in excess of 4,500,000 and the total population of this portion of the country was, roundly speaking, 15,800,000. There were, in 1900, twenty-five cities having a population of 25,000 or more, each, within this area.

St. Louis, which had 925 population in 1800, according to Chittenden, had in 1900, 575,000; Portland, in Oregon, and Seattle, on Puget Sound in Washington, had respectively 90,000 and 80,000; Butte, Montana, had 30,000; Denver, Colorado, 133,000; Minneapolis, Minnesota, 202,000.

In 1800, the centre of population was eighteen miles from

Baltimore, Maryland. In 1900, it was six miles southeast from Columbus, Indiana. It has, therefore, moved westward nearly five hundred miles in one hundred years, across the States of Maryland, West Virginia, Ohio, and about one half of Indiana, a silent, moving instance, indeed, of the steady, resistless flow of population into the almost boundless spaces west of the Mississippi.

In 1800, there was not one Representative in the National House of Representatives from beyond the Father of Waters; in 1900, there were eighty Representatives from the Louisiana and Oregon region alone, considerably more than one half of the whole number constituting the entire lower House of Congress in 1800.

The growth of the agricultural interests in this quarter illustrates forcibly the progress of a century. There was, of course, in 1800 no agriculture worth mentioning. In 1900, there were reported to the Census authorities nearly 1,600,000 farms, having a total valuation of $7,200,000,000.

The value of agricultural implements on farms is returned at $270,865,000. There were nearly 4400 grist mills, having a capital of $70,000,000, employing 12,000 wage-earners, and they ground up 246,000,000 bushels of wheat into flour, which was worth $190,500,000.

If, at the time that Livingston signed the treaty of 1803, he could have known that in 1900 there would be, in the region for which he bargained, 1,300,000 farms upon which there were 29,400,000 cattle valued at $709,000,000; that 26,000,000 sheep, worth $75,000,000, would be grazing there; that there would be raised, among other products, 375,-000,000 bushels of wheat, 1,250,000,000 bushels of corn, 1,670,000 bales of cotton, 78,000,000 bushels of potatoes, and 1,200,000 pounds of tobacco, he would have felt truly enough that he had just finished "the noblest work" of his life.

After Texas, which was really a part of *La Louisianne,* Iowa, Kansas, and Nebraska lead the country in the number of cattle raised, and the highest average value of dairy cows is found in Montana, while Minnesota supplies the finest butter in the Union. In sheep raising, Montana stands first in the United States, Wyoming is second, Idaho sixth, and Oregon seventh.

The lumber industry is a very important one in the region bequeathed to us by Jefferson, Monroe, and Livingston. The census returns show that in the year 1900 there were 5,400 lumber establishments, having a combined capital of $154,000,000, and that their product was valued at $153,-000,000.

Could anything more forcibly show the clearness of Berkeley's vision or the fulfilment of his time-honored prophecy,

"Westward the course of Empire takes its way"?

CHAPTER II

BLAZING THE WAY

I HAVE said that the idea of this transcontinental exploration was original with Thomas Jefferson. He explicitly states in his memoir of Captain Lewis that when resident in Paris, he induced John Ledyard, a well-known citizen of Connecticut, to attempt an exploration across the Northwest. Ledyard was a natural-born and impecunious rover, ever ready for any adventure into unknown regions. He was with Captain Cook on his third voyage to the Pacific, and finally died in Cairo, in 1788, just as he was starting on a tour of African exploration. Ledyard seized upon Jefferson's scheme, through him obtained Russian credentials, and started across Russia and Siberia, whence he was to cross the Pacific to Nootka Sound and thence, via the Missouri, continue across the United States. After he was well started – having reached Yakutsk and Irkutsk – the Russian Government reconsidered its decision and unceremoniously compelled him to return.

In a letter dated Annapolis, December 4, 1783, to George Rogers Clark, Jefferson says:

I find they have subscribed a very large sum of money in England for exploring the country from the Missisipi [*sic*] to California. They pretend it is only to promote knolege [*sic*]. I am afraid they have thoughts of colonising into that quarter. some of us have been talking here in a feeble way of making the attempt to search that country, but I doubt whether we have enough of that kind of spirit to raise the money. how would

27

you like to lead such a party? tho I am afraid our prospect is not worth asking the question.

In 1792, Jefferson enlisted the American Philosophical Society in the matter, and although Captain Lewis then begged the privilege of going, a French botanist, Andre Michaux, was selected. He started on the journey, and went as far as Kentucky, when *he* was recalled by the French Minister, and thus ended the second attempt.

In January, 1803, before the purchase of Louisiana, Jefferson sent a confidential message to Congress which resulted in an appropriation of $2500 for this exploration, largely across the country of a foreign power — at that time France. Within about three months the country belonged to the United States, so that, actually, the exploration became one of its own territory. This fact was, however, not known publicly until July, and Jefferson's instructions regarding the expedition were drawn up upon the theory that the country belonged to France. This applies, of course, to the region east of the mountains. The country west of the Rockies was claimed by the United States under Gray's discovery of 1792.

Jefferson's message to Congress dated January 18, 1803, is worth reading in connection with this exploration. It was in relation to the renewal of the act for establishing trading houses among the Indians. Affairs were in such condition that it was deemed advisable to procure title to additional lands along the eastern bank of the Mississippi River in the Chickasaw country between the Ohio and Yazoo rivers; but the Indians were loath to sell. The idea was to establish Government trading posts among the Indians and by this means "place within their reach those things which will contribute more to their domestic comfort than the possession of extensive but uncultivated wilds," and in so doing seduce them from their old manner of life and open the way to a purchase of their lands. But, in doing this, private

Commission of Captain Lewis as Captain 1st U. S. Reg. Infty., Dated
April 15, 1802.
(Courtesy of B. R. A. Scott, Galveston, Texas.)

traders already established would be forced out, an injustice and hardship which the President proposed to remedy by providing another and more lucrative field for them in the trans-Missouri country. The message then continues:

The river Missouri and the Indians inhabiting it are not as well known as is rendered desirable by their connection with the Mississippi, and consequently with us. It is, however, understood that the country on that river is inhabited by numerous tribes, who furnish great supplies of furs and peltry to the trade of another nation, carried on in a high latitude through an infinite number of portages and lakes shut up by ice through a long season. The commerce on that line could bear no competition with that of the Missouri, traversing a moderate climate, offering, according to the best accounts, a continued navigation from its source, and possibly with a single portage from the Western Ocean, and finding to the Atlantic a choice of channels through the Illinois or Wabash, the Lakes and Hudson, through the Ohio and Susquehanna, or Potomac or James rivers, and through the Tennessee and Savannah rivers. An intelligent officer, with ten or twelve chosen men, fit for the enterprise and willing to undertake it, taken from our posts where they may be spared without inconvenience, might explore the whole line, even to the Western Ocean, have conferences with the natives on the subject of commercial intercourse, get admission among them for our traders as others are admitted, agree on convenient deposits for an interchange of articles, and return with the information acquired in the course of two summers. Their arms and accoutrements, some instruments of observation, and light and cheap presents for the Indians would be all the apparatus they could carry, and with an expectation of a soldier's portion of land on their return would constitute the whole expense. Their pay would be going on whether here or there. While other civilized nations have encountered great expense to enlarge the boundaries of knowledge by undertaking voyages of discovery, and for other literary purposes, in various parts and directions, our nation seems to owe to the same object, as well as to its own interests, to explore this the only line of easy communication across the continent, and so directly traversing our own part of it. The interests of commerce place the principal object within the constitutional powers and care of Congress, and that it should incidentally advance the geographical knowledge of our own continent, cannot but be an additional gratification. The nation claiming the territory, regarding this as a

Meriwether Lewis, as private secretary to President Jefferson, from a painting by St. Memin, owned by C. H. Anderson, Ivy Depot, Virginia, to whom it descended from Lewis's mother and only brother.

literary pursuit, which it is in the habit of permitting within its dominions, would not be disposed to view it with jealousy, even if the expiring state of its interests there did not render it a matter of indifference. The appropriation of $2,500 "for the purpose of extending the external commerce of the United States," while understood and considered by the Executive as giving the legislative sanction, would cover the undertaking from notice, and prevent the obstructions which interested individuals might otherwise previously prepare in its way.

There was here, evidently, a deliberate attempt, on the part of the President and Congress, at deception, probably justifiable, if deception be ever justifiable. It was intended to cover the real animus of the expedition under the title of a "literary pursuit." This effort at concealment of the real design may or may not have succeeded, but as France soon parted with the country, this feature became immaterial as far as Spain and France were concerned. England was the country, evidently, which it was particularly intended to deceive, but the real intention of the expedition was to be concealed from the American public as well. Lewis, in a letter to Jefferson, dated Lancaster, Ohio, April 20, 1803, states that to John Connor, a prospective interpreter, he has communicated "the real extent and objects of our mission, but with strict injunctions to secrecy," but in statements in general to the public he mentions its objects as those "which we [Jefferson and Lewis] agreed on as most proper to be declared publicly."

Jefferson, in writing to Lewis on April 27, 1803, uses these words: "The idea that you are going to explore the Missisipi [sic] has been generally given out; it satisfies public corosity [sic] and masks sufficiently the real destination."

But – all this was *before* the Purchase!

Congress having granted the appropriation as previously stated, the result was the first and, all things considered, the greatest exploration the United States ever attempted – that of Lewis and Clark.

The estimate for expenses upon which the appropriation was based is in Lewis's handwriting and was probably his own idea of what would be needed. It is as follows:

Mathematical instruments.	$217
Arms and accoutrements extraordinary	81
Camp equipage.	255
Medicine and packing.	55
Means of transportation.	430
Indian presents.	696
Provisions extraordinary.	224
Materials for making up the various articles into portable packs	55
For the pay of hunters, guides, and interpreters.	300
In silver coin, to defray the expenses of the party from Nashville to the last white settlement on the Missouri,	100
Contingencies.	87
Total.	$2,500

In planning for the leadership of this immortal expedition, Jefferson had, this time, no hesitancy in granting Captain Lewis's request to be entrusted with its direction. As Jefferson's private secretary, Lewis's qualifications for the chieftainship were now thoroughly known to the President. The tribute to him, found in Jefferson's *Memoir,* is worthy of reproduction here for more reasons than one:

I had now had opportunities of knowing him intimately. Of courage undaunted; possessing a firmness and perseverance of purpose which nothing but impossibilities could divert from its direction; careful as a father of those committed to his charge, yet steady in the maintenance of order and discipline; intimate with the Indian character, customs, and principles; habituated to the hunting life; guarded, by exact observation of the vegetables and animals of his own country, against losing time in the description of objects already possessed; honest, disinterested, liberal, of sound understanding, and a fidelity to truth so scrupulous that whatever he should report would be as certain as if seen by ourselves, – with all these qualifications, as if selected and implanted by nature in one body for this express purpose, I could have no hesitation in confiding the enterprise to him. To fill up the measure desired, he wanted nothing but a greater familiarity with the technical language of the natural sciences and readiness in the astronomical observations necessary for the geography of his route. To acquire these he repaired immediately to Philadelphia, and placed himself under the tutorage of the distinguished professors of that place, who, with a zeal and emulation enkindled by an ardent devotion to science, communicated to him freely the information requisite for the purposes of the journey. While attending, too, at Lancaster, the fabrication of the arms with which he chose that his men should be provided, he had the benefit of daily communication with Mr. Andrew Ellicot, whose experience in astronomical observation, and practice of it in the woods, enabled him to apprise Captain Lewis of the wants and difficulties he would encounter, and of the substitutes and resources offered by a woodland and uninhabited country.

It was wisely determined that a substitute leader was an indispensable feature of the enterprise, and William Clark, a tried friend of Lewis, was selected for the position of second in command, and the judgment shown in this selection was splendidly vindicated.

It is generally supposed that Clark was an army captain, as was Lewis, but this was not the case. It would seem that it was intended that he should be so commissioned, but in some manner not disclosed, when his commission was issued, March 26, 1804, it was as a second lieutenant of artillery, not a captain of engineers, as Clark had expected. From a military point of view, therefore, he was quite subordinate to Lewis, but in the conduct of the expedition he was co-equal with him, as Lewis had promised that he should be. Clark manfully subordinated any feelings that he might naturally have had in the matter, accepted the commission when received, and, on the return of the expedition, promptly resigned, and returned it. He had formerly been a captain of militia, so it is stated, and if so, the title still clung to him, which has added to the confusion as to relative rank in this connection. If *this* Wm. Clark ever was a captain of militia I have seen no definite and indisputable proof of it.

William Clark, from the Portrait in Independence Hall, Philadelphia.

A Wm. Clark was made a captain of militia by Governor St. Clair, but it does not appear to have been this one.

Jefferson's instructions to Captain Lewis were lengthy and comprehensive. They evince not only a deep regard for the complete technical success of the enterprise, but also a most fatherly interest for the comfort and safety of those engaged in it.

I give them nearly in full as worth preservation in a work of this nature:

To Meriwether Lewis, esquire, captain of the first regiment of infantry of the United States of America:

Your situation as secretary of the president of the United States has made you acquainted with the objects of my confidential message of January 18, 1803, to the legislature; you have seen the act they passed, which, though expressed in general terms, was meant to sanction those objects, and you are appointed to carry them into execution.

Instruments for ascertaining, by celestial observations, the geography of the country through which you will pass have been already provided. Light articles for barter and presents among the Indians, arms for your attendants, say for from ten to twelve men, boats, tents, and other travelling apparatus, with ammunition, medicine, surgical instruments, and provisions, you will have prepared, with such aids as the secretary at war can yield in his department; and from him also you will receive authority to engage among our troops, by voluntary agreement, the number of attendants abovementioned, over whom you, as their commanding officer, are invested with all the powers the laws give in such a case. . . .

Your mission has been communicated to the ministers here from France, Spain, and Great Britain, and through them to their governments, and such assurances given them as to its objects as we trust will satisfy them. The country of Louisiana having been ceded by Spain to France, the passport you have from the minister of France, the representative of the present sovereign of the country, will be a protection with all its subjects; and that from the minister of England will entitle you to the friendly aid of any traders of that allegiance with whom you may happen to meet.

The object of your mission is to explore the Missouri River, and such principal streams of it as, by its course and communication with the waters of the Pacific ocean, whether the Columbia, Oregan, Colorado, or any other river, may offer the most direct and practicable water-communication across the continent for the purposes of commerce.

Beginning at the mouth of the Missouri, you will take observations of latitude and longitude at all remarkable points on the river.

The interesting points of the portage between the heads of the Missouri, and of the water offering the best communication with the Pacific ocean, should also be fixed by observation, and the course of that water to the ocean in the same manner as that of the Missouri.

Your observations are to be taken with great pains and accuracy. . . . Several copies of these, as well as of your other notes, should be made at leisure times, and put into the care of the most trustworthy of your attendants to guard, by multiplying them, against the accidental losses to which they will be exposed. A further guard would be that one of these copies be on the cuticular membranes of the paper-birch, as less liable to injury from damp than common paper.

You will therefore endeavour to make yourself acquainted, as far as a diligent pursuit of your journey shall admit, with the names of the nations and their numbers;

The extent and limits of their possessions;

Their relations with other tribes or nations;

Their language, traditions, monuments;

Their ordinary occupations in agriculture, fishing, hunting, war, arts, and the implements for these;

Their food, clothing, and domestic accommodations;

The diseases prevalent among them, and the remedies they use;

Moral and physical circumstances which distinguish them from the tribes we know;

Peculiarities in their laws, customs, and dispositions;

And articles of commerce they may need or furnish, and to what extent.

And . . . it will be useful to acquire what knowledge you can of the state of morality, religion, and information among them.

Other objects worthy of notice will be –

The soil and face of the country, its growth and vegetable productions, especially those not of the United States,

The animals of the country generally, and especially those not known in the United States;

The remains and accounts of any which may be deemed rare or extinct;

The mineral productions of every kind, but more particularly metals, lime-stone, pit-coal, and saltpetre, salines and mineral waters, noting the temperature of the last, and such circumstances as may indicate their character;

Volcanic appearances;

Climate as characterized by the thermometer, by the pro-

House at Partlows, Spottsylvania County, Va., in which Captain Clark was Born.

portion of rainy, cloudy, and clear days; by lightning, hail, snow, ice; by the access and recess of frost; by the winds prevailing at different seasons; the dates at which particular plants put forth or lose their flower or leaf; times of appearance of particular birds, reptiles, or insects.

Although your route will be along the channel of the Missouri, yet you will endeavour to inform yourself, by inquiry, of the character and extent of the country watered by its branches, and especially on its southern side. The North River, or Rio Bravo, which runs into the gulf of Mexico, and the North River, or Rio Colorado, which runs into the gulf of California, are understood to be the principal streams heading opposite to the waters of the Missouri, and running southwardly. Whether the dividing grounds between the Missouri and them are mountains or flat lands, what are their distance from the Missouri, the character of the intermediate country, and the people inhabiting it, are worthy of particular inquiry.

In all your intercourse with the natives, treat them in the most friendly and conciliatory manner which their own conduct will admit; allay all jealousies as to the object of your journey; satisfy them of its innocence; make them acquainted with the position, extent, character, peaceable and commercial dispositions of the United States, of our wish to be neighborly, friendly, and useful to them, and of our dispositions to a commercial intercourse with them; confer with them on the points most convenient as mutual emporiums and the articles of most desirable interchange for them and us. If a few of their influential chiefs, within practicable distance, wish to visit us, arrange such a visit with them, and furnish them with authority to call on our officers on their entering the United States, to have them conveyed to this place at the public expense. . . . Carry with you some matter of the kine-pox, inform those of them with whom you may be of its efficacy as a preservative from the small-pox, and instruct and encourage them in the use of it. This may be especially done wherever you winter.

. . . Your numbers will be sufficient to secure you against the unauthorized opposition of individuals or of small parties; but, if a superior force, authorized or not authorized by a nation, should be arrayed against your further passage, and inflexibly determined to arrest it, you must decline its further pursuit and return. In the loss of yourselves we should lose also the information you will have acquired. By returning safely with that, you may enable us to renew the essay with better calculated means. To your own discretion, therefore, must be left the degree of danger you may risk and the point at which you should decline, only saying, we wish you to err on the side of your safety, and to bring back your party safe, even if it be with less information.

Should you reach the Pacific ocean, inform yourself of the circumstances which may decide whether the furs of those parts may not be collected as advantageously at the head of the Missouri (convenient as is supposed to the waters of the Colorado and Oregan or Columbia) as at Nootka Sound, or any other point of that coast; and that trade be consequently conducted through the Missouri and United States more beneficially than by the circumnavigation now practised.

On your arrival on that coast, endeavour to learn if there be any port within your reach frequented by the sea vessels of any nation, and to send two of your trusty people back by sea, in such way as shall appear practicable, with a copy of your notes; and should you be of opinion that the return of your party by the way they went will be imminently dangerous, then ship the whole, and return by sea, by the way either of Cape Horn or the Cape of Good Hope, as you shall be able. As you will be without money, clothes, or provisions, you must endeavour to use the credit of the United States to obtain them, for which purpose open letters of credit shall be furnished you, authorizing you to draw on the executive of the United States, or any of its officers, in any part of the world, on which draughts can be disposed of, and to apply with our recommendations to the consuls, agents, merchants, or citizens of any nation with which we have intercourse, assuring them, in our name, that any aids they may furnish you shall be honorably repaid, and on demand.

On re-entering the United States and reaching a place of safety, discharge any of your attendants who may desire and deserve it, procuring for them immediate payment of all arrears of pay and clothing which may have incurred since their departure, and assure them that they shall be recommended to the liberality of the legislature for the grant of a soldier's portion of land each, as proposed in my message to congress, and repair yourself, with your papers, to the seat of government.

To provide, on the accident of your death, against anarchy, dispersion, and the consequent danger to your party, and total failure of the enterprise, you are hereby authorized, by any instrument signed and written in your own hand, to name the person among them who shall succeed to the command on your decease, and by like instruments to change the nomination, from time to time, as further experience of the characters accompanying you shall point out superior fitness; and all the powers and authorities given to yourself are, in the event of your death, transferred to, and vested in the successor so named, with further power to him and his successors, in like manner to name each his successor, who, on the death of his predecessor, shall be invested with all the powers and authorities given to yourself. Given under my hand at the city of Washington, this twentieth day of June, 1803.   THOMAS JEFFERSON,

President of the United States of America.

Dear Sir

Washington. U.S. of America. July 4. 1803.

In the journey which you are about to undertake for the discovery of the course and source of the Missisipi, and of the most convenient water communication from thence to the Pacific ocean, your party being small, it is to be expected that you will encounter considerable dangers from the Indian inhabitants. should you escape those dangers and reach the Pacific ocean, you may find it imprudent to hazard a return the same way, and be forced to seek a passage round by sea in such vessels as you may find on the Western coast. but you will be without money, without clothes, & other necessaries; as a sufficient supply cannot be carried with you from hence. your resource in that case can only be in the credit of the U.S. for which purpose I hereby authorise you to draw on the Secretaries of State, of the Treasury, of War & of the Navy of the U.S. according as you may find your draughts will be most negociable, for the purpose of obtaining money or necessaries for yourself & your men: and I solemnly pledge the faith of the United States that these draughts shall be paid punctually at the date they are made payable. I also ask of the Consuls, agents, merchants & citizens of any nation with which we have intercourse or amity, to furnish you with those supplies which your necessities may call for, assuring them of honorable and prompt retribution. and our own Consuls in foreign parts where you may happen to be, are hereby instructed & required to be aiding & assisting to you in whatsoever may be necessary for procuring your return back to the United States. And to give more entire satisfaction & confidence to those who may be disposed to aid you, I Thomas Jefferson. President of the United States of America, have written this letter of general credit for you with my own hand, and signed it with my name.

Th: Jefferson

To
Capt. Meriwether Lewis.

Jefferson's Letter of Credit to Lewis

The facsimile of Jefferson's letter of July 4, 1803, written subsequent to his letter of general instruction, will show still further the determination of the President that all that could possibly be done for the success and comfort of the party should be done.

Among the natural reflections, upon reading these estimates and instructions is, first, the apparent utter inadequacy of the appropriation. – $2500 for an exploration across half a continent and consuming nearly two and one half years of time! This would seem to be Jeffersonian simplicity and frugality with a vengeance. In comparison with congressional appropriations for similar purposes – so far as comparable – at the present time, it was a bagatelle. But this expedition being ostensibly only a "literary pursuit," the appropriation must be commensurate with such an undertaking.

The sum appropriated by Congress for 1899-1900 for use by the United States Geological Survey, into which the old Powell, Wheeler, and Hayden Surveys were merged in 1879, was $834,240.89. Congressional ideas certainly have expanded since Jefferson and Lewis and Clark engaged in exploration.

The paucity of the amount provided for Lewis and Clark was undoubtedly more apparent than real. In recent times, nearly, or quite all perhaps, of our Government expeditions, particularly those under control of the War Department, have been, in addition to the regular appropriation, materially assisted by the Quartermaster and Commissary Bureaus of the War Department. The second paragraph of Jefferson's letter of instructions of April, 1803, would indicate that such assistance may have been given Lewis and Clark. In addition, the pay of nearly all of their men, who were regularly enlisted as soldiers, was not charged against the appropriation of $2,500. In a letter to Lewis dated November 16, 1803, Jefferson states that by wintering at Cahokia or Kaskaskia, his men would draw their winter rations and thus save their regular stores; also, that he expects Congress will further appropriate[1] "10 or 12,000 D for exploring the principal waters of the Missipi & Missouri."

Again, the second paragraph of instructions discloses contradiction or discrepancy regarding the number comprising the expedition. Mr. Jefferson mentions "from ten to twelve men" as the number of "attendants" to be engaged "from among our troops," to accompany Lewis and Clark. When the expedition started up the Missouri it consisted of forty-five men, thirty-five of whom – including Lewis and Clark – appear to have been soldiers.

It is highly probable, too, that the purchase of Louisiana changed in many respects the plans and details of the enterprise, including the numbers of the party. The necessity for secrecy, which, originally, limited the party to the least number possible, having vanished, there was no longer objection to increasing the expedition to a size more commensurate with the labors and dangers it would encounter, and this probably explains this feature of the enterprise.

A part of a letter written by Jefferson to Captain Lewis, dated January 22, 1804, incidentally indicates the effect of the Purchase upon the expedition, and elaborates a little more fully, perhaps, his views regarding the Indians.

When your instructions were penned, this new position [the purchase of Louisiana and the occupation of the territory] was not so authentically known as to effect the complection of your

---

1 Congress, by statute, March 3, 1807, granted to Lewis and Clark each, sixteen hundred acres of land, and to those members of the expedition who went beyond Fort Mandan, inclu,ding Chaboneau, and also to Corporal Warfington and to Newman, the repentant mutineer, and to the heirs of Sergeant Floyd, three hundred and twenty acres each, and to each of these double pay was also given.

instructions. being now become sovereigns of the country, without however any diminution of the Indian rights of occupency we are authorised to propose to them in direct terms the institution of commerce with them. It will now be proper you should inform those through whose country you will pass, or whom you may meet, that their late fathers, the Spaniards have agreed to withdraw all their troops from all the waters & country of the Missisipi and Missouri, that they have surrendered to us all their subjects Spanish and French settled there, and all their posts & lands: that henceforward we become their fathers and friends, and that we shall endeavor that they shall have no cause to lament the change: that we have sent you to enquire into the nature of the country & the nations inhabiting it, to know at what places and times we must establish stores of goods among them, to exchange for their peltries: that as soon as you return with the necessary information we shall prepare supplies of goods and persons to carry them and make the proper establishments: that in the meantime, the same traders who reside among or visit them, and who are now a part of us, will continue to supply them as usual: that we shall endeavor to become acquainted with them as soon as possible and that they will find in us faithful friends and protectors. although you will pass through no settlements of the Sioux (except seceders) yet you will probably meet with parties of them. On that nation we wish most particularly to make a friendly impression, because of their immense power, and because we learn they are very desirous of being on the most friendly terms with us.

This letter would indicate that the policy of deception originally attempted was to be of universal application; that not only Spain, France, England, America, but even the Indians came within its purview.

These instructions were all comprehensive, and what a burden they placed upon Lewis and Clark! Not only were they to be the executive officers, the leaders, in an exploration that would thus alone tax their time and abilities, but they must needs be, also, astronomers, ethnologists, geologists, engineers, physicians and surgeons, mineralogists, diplomatists and statesmen, naturalists, botanists, geographers, topographers, and meteorologists. In a word, all

Telescope Used by Lewis on the Exploration in 1804-1806, now Owned by C. H. Anderson, Ivy Depot, Virginia.

that was to be done that would have a lasting value was, virtually, laid upon the backs of two men. Of soldiers, hunters, rowers or watermen, interpreters, there were enough, but not one man of the medical profession to bind up wounds, mend broken limbs, or cure fevers, was there sent along, nor was there a solitary man of scientific attainments provided to relieve the leaders of a portion of such work. With the extreme care that was taken in arranging for this expedition, it seems passing strange that such oversights or omissions occurred. That no more serious and unfortunate results ensued because of this, was owing to rare good luck and simply redounded the more to the credit of the two captains. The truth is that good luck was a most valuable asset of the Lewis and Clark exploration.

The lack of scientific men with the expedition was seriously felt when the report came to be written. Wonders had been accomplished in the line of natural history discovery, but there was no member of the party competent to discuss the scientific observations and results, and the consequence was that Lewis and Clark lost that credit for priority of discovery to which they were entitled in many things. When Biddle and Allen were preparing the general report, an arrangement was made by which Dr. Benj. S. Barton of Philadelphia was to prepare a volume on the natural history of the expedition, but his death prevented the carrying out of this plan and nothing further was done in regard to it.

The letter of credit was a very commendable effort to provide, to the remotest degree, for the wants of the expedition. As was probably expected at the time it was written, it turned out valueless, but this was, apparently, the fault of Lewis and Clark and not of the letter of credit. As will appear in the course of the narrative, a Boston brig put into the mouth of the Columbia River at the very time that Lewis and Clark were searching for a suitable spot for a camp during the winter of 1805-06, but the explorers were ignorant of that fact, and I have never seen it referred to in any account relating to the exploration.

Some writers have seemed disposed to refer to this letter of credit almost facetiously. One says: "A letter of credit directed to the Man in the Moon would have served quite as well." As a matter of fact it was a far-sighted action; and while it could work no harm, it might have proved of untold benefit. As a credential, simply, what could have been better, and certainly a paper of this nature in the handwriting of the President of the United States was a very proper document for the expedition to possess.

I have wondered, latterly, whether there may not have been, after all, a deeper, more subtle reason for this exploration in the mind of Jefferson. Remembering that the expedition was planned prior to the purchase of Louisiana; recalling the difficulties with Spain concerning the navigation of the Mississippi and the consequent and increasing restlessness of our people; knowing that the ownership of the Oregon country might loom portentously and unexpectedly upon the diplomatic horizon, is it not possible that the President felt that a knowledge of this vast region was necessary in order that no mistakes might be made when the supreme moment came?

It is not improbable, too, that Jefferson intended to forge another link in the chain of discovery and exploration begun by Gray, in 1792, at the mouth of the Columbia.

The exploration was a remarkable one, not more in its important achievements than in minor details, management, progress, and results. It may well be regarded as our "national epic of exploration," and time, instead of diminishing, has added to its lustre.

The expedition started from the mouth of Wood (Du Bois) River, opposite the mouth of the Missouri River, in Illinois, May 14, 1804, and reached St. Louis on its return September 23, 1806, thus consuming in its work two years, four months, and nine days. During this time not one disagreement or clash of authority occurred between the leaders, a remarkable record. Although there was much sickness, there was but one death, – an equally remarkable fact, – that of Sergeant Floyd on August 20, 1804. There was but one suggestion of mutiny, and that on the part of one man only, who, besides being promptly punished, afterward fully atoned for his fault.   There were two attempts at desertion, one of which was successful; in the other case the man was promptly disciplined and discharged from service.

Through all their vicissitudes and dangers there was but one really serious mishap, Captain Lewis being accidentally shot through the thigh when nearing home. He recovered before reaching St. Louis.

Although their route was through an Indian country entirely, and the Indians were in most instances the wildest of nomads, in some cases never having seen a white man, yet there was but one serious difficulty with them. Their almost uniformly kind reception by, and treatment of, the Indians, and their absolute and utter dependence upon them, time after time, for food with which to save themselves from starvation, and for animals and canoes with which to continue their journey, furnishes the most caustic criticism upon the Government's subsequent treatment of the red man.

Heroes are not all of the martial sort. It required, perhaps, a more sturdy type of heroism for these men to penetrate an unknown wilderness than for Wolfe to climb the Heights of Abraham, Thomas to hold on at Chickamauga, Pickett to charge Cemetery Ridge, or Dewey to steam past

The Original Journals, or Codices, Lewis and Clark, Codex "A" open at pp. 18 and 19. There are two sizes of these Journals: the "Red" leather covered books, 5" x 8", and the "Marbled" 4" x 6-3/4", in size.

Corregidor Island. It is one thing to be brave and heroic in spectacular situations, or when the world is known to be locking on; quite another when heroism is the quiet, simple, unpicturesque performance of duty as it comes to one day by day.

BRIEF ITINERARY OF LEWIS AND CLARK, TABULATED

Month	Year	Place	Miles from Mouth of Missouri River	Remarks
May 14,	1804	Left mouth of Missouri River............	o	
June 26,	1804	At mouth of Kansas River...	340	Kansas City, Mo.
July 21,	1804	At mouth of Platte River...	600	Below Omaha, Nebr.
July 30,	1804	At Council Bluff.......	650	Not Council Bluffs, Iowa.
Aug. 21,	1804	At Sioux City, Iowa...	850	Serg. Floyd's grave just below city
Sept. 20,	1804	At Big Bend of Missouri River............	1,172	Below Pierre, S. D.
Nov. 2,	1804	Arrived at Fort Mandan	1,600	Below Knife River, N D, on left bank of Missouri, where they passed the winter of 1804–5.
Apr. 7,	1805	Left Fort Mandan.... .	1,600	
Apr. 26,	1805	At mouth of Yellow-stone River....... .	1,880	Fort Buford just above.
June 2,	1805	At mouth of Marias River.......... .	2,521	Fort Benton short distance above.
June 16,	1805	At Portage Creek, Great Falls, Mont	2,575	City of Great Falls two miles below.
June 18,	1805	At White Bear Islands	2,595	
July 25,	1805	At Three Forks of Missouri River.......	—	Gallatin Valley, Mont.
Aug. 12,	1805	At headwaters of Missouri River........	3,096	"Fountain," or spring, at head of Jefferson Fork (Beaver Head) of Missouri River.
Sept. 9,	1805	At mouth of Lolo Creek....	3,338	Bitter Root Valley, Mont.

Month	Year	Place	Miles from Mouth of Missouri River	Remarks
Oct. 10,	1805	At mouth of Clearwater River..............	3,567	Lewiston, Idaho.
Oct. 16,	1805	At mouth of Snake River.............	3,721	
Oct 22,	1805	At Great Falls of Columbia....	3,873	{ Now known as Celilo Falls.
Oct. 30,	1805	At Cascades of Columbia River........	3,944	
Dec. 7,	1805	Arrived at Fort Clatsop...	4,135	{ On Netul, or Lewis and Clark River, Ore, where they passed the winter, 1805–6.
Mch 23,	1806	Left Fort Clatsop.....	—	
Apr. 27,	1806	At mouth of Wallawalla River............	—	Washington.
June 30,	1806	At mouth of Lolo Creek	—	Party divided.
Aug. 3,	1806	At mouth of Yellowstone River........	—	{ Captain Clark's party via Three Forks.
Aug. 7,	1806	At mouth of Yellowstone River........	—	{ Captain Lewis's party via Great Falls, Mont.
Sept. 23,	1806	Arrived at St. Louis...		

In this age of railway expansion it can readily be surmised that the route followed by Lewis and Clark is now largely paralleled or trans-sected by one or more of nearly all the prominent railway systems of the middle West and Northwest. Among these are the Atchison, Topeka, and Santa Fé; Chicago, Rock Island, and Pacific; Missouri Pacific; Chicago, Burlington, and Quincy; Chicago, Milwaukee, and St. Paul; Chicago and Northwestern; Union Pacific; Northern Pacific; Great Northern; Oregon Short Line; Oregon Railroad and Navigation Company, and Astoria and Columbia River Railroad lines.

The route of the explorers is virtually paralleled by the Great Northern Railway, from the great southern bend of the Missouri in North Dakota west of Minot, to Helena; by the Oregon Short Line, for a short distance along the Jefferson River near Dillon, Montana; while the Oregon Railroad and Navigation Company's tracks and steamers follow their trail from Lewiston, Idaho, along the Snake and Columbia rivers to Astoria, Oregon, and the mouth of the Columbia River.

The Northern Pacific Railway is the most intimately related, however, to the Lewis and Clark trails and exploration. From Bismarck and Mandan on the Missouri River in North Dakota, it parallels the explorers' line of travel along the Missouri, Yellowstone, Gallatin, and Jefferson rivers to Helena and Whitehall, and on a part of the Hellgate River to Missoula, Montana; its main lines again connect with it on the Columbia River in eastern Washington and also in Oregon.

Through its branch lines it meets or parallels their route on the Jefferson, Bitter Root, Clearwater, and Snake rivers, in Montana, Idaho, Washington, and Oregon. For mile after mile, at many points, the rails of this line follow the very ground that the land parties of Lewis and Clark trod in crossing the mountains or in following the streams. The same is true to a much less extent of the Great Northern Railway, the Oregon Short Line, and of a part of the line of the Oregon Railroad and Navigation Company.

The discerning traveller can see from the trains on some of these railways, points made historic by Lewis and Clark and easily recognized. On the Great Northern Railway, between Fort Benton and Helena, in the region about Great Falls, Montana, and the Dearborn River and cliffs adjacent thereto, such places are at once determinable. On the Northern Pacific, Pompey's Pillar on the Yellowstone, the Pass between Livingston and Bozeman, pointed out by Sacágawea to Captain Clark and used by him, the Three Forks of the Missouri, the Beaver's-head on the Jefferson,

Lolo – Traveller's-rest – Creek in the Bitter Root Valley, all in Montana, and the junction of the Clearwater and Snake rivers in Idaho, are a few of many points thus seen. On the trains of the Oregon Railroad and Navigation Company, and from the decks of the many steamers which now plough the noble Columbia, the river which affords the grandest river scenery in the United States, the entire panorama noted by Lewis and Clark – the Dalles, Cascades, Castle (Beacon) Rock, Multnomah Fall, Coffin Rock, Cape Disappointment, etc. – unfolds itself bit by bit.

It will be seen that the Lewis and Clark trails are pretty closely related to the travelling public. It is to be hoped that, in the renaissance of Lewis and Clark and the Louisiana Purchase now possessing the country, this exploration and its trails, may be taken closer to the hearts of the people and become more and more a real part of our life.

CHAPTER III

ORGANIZATION AND PERSONNEL OF THE EXPE-
DITION

It goes without saying that to conceive the detailed plans for such an enterprise as this, and then successfully to carry them through, required the highest order of executive ability.

At the very outset, and as the foundation upon which success must necessarily rest, came the problem of the wise and discriminative organization of the party, and aside from the omissions already pointed out, the preparations appear to have been carefully and wisely planned.

We know from documents found in the Jefferson Papers that the greatest of care was taken in the composition of this expedition. Men of at least fair intelligence and common sense, temperate, physically strong and healthy, cheerful, subordinate, courageous, fertile in expedient, disposed to get along well one with another, and able and willing to "rough it" to the utmost extent, were the only sort of men that could be considered for a moment for such work as was in prospect.

The expedition consisted of forty-five men in all, including Lewis and Clark themselves, when the boats cast off from the shore above St. Louis, on May 13, 1804. Some were regular soldiers of the United States army, selected for this exploration from volunteers at various army posts throughout the Western country. The others, save one, were carefully picked frontiersmen valuable for special qualities, and all these were regularly enlisted as privates, thus giving the enterprise a military form and better ensuring discipline and subordination.

The original plan, to leave St. Louis in the fall of 1803, had been thwarted.

Their original intention was to pass the winter at La Charette, the highest settlement on the Missouri. But the Spanish commandant of the province, not having received an official account of its transfer to the United States, was obliged by the general policy of his Government to prevent strangers from passing through the Spanish territory. They therefore encamped at the mouth of Wood River, on the eastern side of the Mississippi, out of his jurisdiction, where they passed the winter in disciplining the men, and making the necessary preparations for setting out early in the Spring, before which the cession [of Louisiana] was officially announced.

That this delay, undoubtedly trying to all concerned, was, after all, a benefit aside from the discipline enforced, is, I think, demonstrable. One who has had even a limited experience in the free-and-easy, open life of the plains and mountains, knows that nowhere else will the selfish, ugly, lazy, mean characteristics of men more quickly show themselves than there. The opposite of this proposition is also true, but possibly in less degree. The winter spent at the mouth of the Wood River, therefore, provided an opportunity for thorough acquaintanceship among the men and a consequent adjustment to each other's peculiarities, and it also afforded the leaders time to study their men, mark well the excellencies and failings of each, and learn upon whom to call for special service in times of emergency and danger. All this was most important to be learned, as far as it could be, before the active, arduous, racking, patience-trying work itself really began.

The narrative continues:

The party consisted [besides Lewis and Clark] of nine young

men from Kentucky; fourteen soldiers of the United States Army, who had volunteered their services; two French watermen [Cruzatte and Labiche]; an interpreter and hunter [Drewyer]; and a black servant [York] belonging to Captain Clark. All these, except the last, were enlisted to serve as privates during the expedition, and three sergeants [Floyd, Pryor, Ordway, were] appointed from amongst them by the captains. In addition to these [there] were engaged a corporal and six soldiers, and nine watermen, to accompany the expedition as far as the Mandan nation, in order to assist in carrying the stores, or repelling an attack, which was most to be apprehended between Wood River and that tribe.

In the *Life and Times of Patrick Gass,* J. G. Jacob states, upon authority of Gass, that several men who volunteered for this exploration relinquished the honor and privilege when the time came to start – in common phrase, they "backed out."

It is to be regretted that the members of this expedition, from the leaders down, could not have foreseen more accurately the interest which posterity would attach to their work, and have been, in consequence, more precise and particular, in many ways, in the chronicles of the exploration. The ambiguities of expression, the blundering, laughable orthography, and the almost utter disregard, now and again, of the rules of syntax and punctuation, while they were to be expected, are wofully unfortunate to say the least, and they have caused the editorial and interpretative work of Biddle, Allen, Coues, and Thwaites to be of the monumental kind.

Of the three accounts of the expedition which we have, – those of Lewis and Clark, Gass, and Floyd, – no two agree, except after studied analysis, as to the number and occupations of the members of the expedition. They have all been construed to reach the same conclusion as to numbers, by methods somewhat forced, in some instances, yet undoubtedly correct.

Of these forty-five men, sixteen were to return from the Mandan towns in the spring of 1805, leaving twenty-nine men in the permanent party, and of these sixteen, the name of only one is known, – that of Warfington, the corporal in command.

So far as the writer knows the records, they show that not one of the Lewis and Clark exploration was a married man at the time of the expedition, except Chaboneau. Old Dorion, who was with the party for a time, was married, and probably some of the watermen who returned from Fort Mandan to St. Louis were, but appearances indicate that it was intended to engage none but unmarried men for the enterprise, and this was undoubtedly a wise course of action. Chaboneau had three wives, one of whom accompanied the expedition.

There proved to be comparatively few lapses from duty, and the chronicles and results of the exploration show that the members were persons of manly, rugged character, generally – yes, even the squaw who subsequently joined them – and equal to situations of delicacy and responsibility. A perusal of the original journals shows that there were more breaches of discipline than the published accounts indicate.

The successful accomplishment of any great deed, act, or enterprise in which the public or world takes an interest attracts microscopic attention to the actor or doers. We see this in all walks of life, but especially, perhaps, where physical strength, endurance, or prowess comes into play joined to mental alertness and ability. The action then acquires a more dramatic flavor.

There are two kinds of bravery or heroism – one where, under the stimulus of great and temporary excitement, the mind, often in an almost mechanical, unreasoning way, spurs the individual on to really superb but unconscious action; –

the other where, after careful, deliberate reflection and weighing of dangers and obstacles, the person knowingly goes ahead coolly taking all risks and chances of life. The one is most often, perhaps, seen on the battle-field, the other, where men like Lewis and Clark and Livingston deliberately plunge into unknown lands and dangers, or where the noble physician, with Christ's love for mankind alive within him, calmly goes into the plague-stricken region to aid dying humanity. The one is a more or less superficial and physical heroism; the other a deeper and purer, a moral heroism.

The heroism of Lewis and Clark and their men was of the moral sort, and the world's interest in them, while, perhaps, lively enough at the time, has been necessarily, I think, a rather latent and growing one, and is now approaching the ripening stage.

It is doubtful whether, a century ago, except to a very few far-sighted individuals, the real importance and value of that great exploration were even half apparent to the world. It has required a hundred years of progress and perspective to perceive what, coupled with the Louisiana Purchase and Gray's discovery of the Columbia River, it really did mean. No apology is therefore necessary for devoting such attention as we may to the personality of this band of true and tried adventurers.

CAPTAIN LEWIS

First, of course, in referring to these men, come the leaders.

Captain Meriwether Lewis was a Virginian of distinguished Scotch ancestry, born in 1774, and, therefore, twenty-nine years of age when he assumed command of the expedition in 1803.

One of Lewis's uncles married a sister of George Washington, and two others served their country in the Revolution and against the Indians. His father's family and also his mother's – the Meriwethers – were among the best families of Virginia. His father died while Meriwether was quite young, leaving him, and also his brother, a reasonable competency.

Meriwether Lewis, from an Original Portrait Belonging to the Meriwether Family.
Property of the Historical Society of Tennessee, Nashville.

Between the ages of thirteen and eighteen years he was attending a Latin school; at twenty he joined the militia and was soon transferred to the regular army; at twenty-three he became a captain, and in 1801, at twenty-seven years of age, he became President Jefferson's private secretary, which post he relinquished to assume command of the expedition.

The early life of Lewis was of a nature to prepare him in several ways for the successful direction of such an exploration.

Jefferson, in his *Memoir,* mentions the fact of his going out alone, when only eight years of age, in the dead of night to hunt opossums and raccoons with his dogs, as an evidence of "enterprise, boldness, and discretion" on his part.

Mrs. Caroline D. M. Goodlett of Nashville, Tenn., a descendant of Captain Lewis's family, in an interesting letter to me regarding Lewis's ancestry and life, mentions another incident that shows his quick intuition of the right thing to do in an emergency:

I will relate a little incident that happened when he was nine years old: The settlement near Charlottesville, Va., was expecting to be attacked by some hostile Indians, and all the able-bodied men had gone in search of them, and the women and old men and children, afraid to stay in their houses, went down into a deep wood camp. While sitting around the fire an Indian arrow was shot into the camp; in an instant all was confusion, women screamed and clasped their children in their arms, for they knew that the Indians could see them and the darkness hid the Indians. Meriwether Lewis, with the foresight of an experienced Indian fighter, jerked up a bucket of water and put out the fire, and then they fired off their guns and drove the Indians off.

That this incident occurred seems well authenticated. Gilmer, however, in his *First Settlers of Upper Georgia,* places the scene in Georgia and the time between 1790-95, which would make Lewis much older and lessen the brilliancy of the exploit.

Lewis, in order to perfect himself in the details of certain scientific work necessary in connection with the exploration, repaired to Philadelphia and received scientific instruction, particularly in astronomical work.

He left Washington July 5, 1803, Harper's Ferry July 8th, and Pittsburg August 31st. At Pittsburg he experienced exasperating delay in the completion of a boat in which he was to navigate the Ohio River to Louisville. He passed Wheeling September 9th, was at Cincinnati from September 28th to October 3d, and reached St. Louis in December. He went overland from Louisville to St. Louis *via* Kaskaskia, while Clark went down the Ohio with his men and the boats.

That Lewis's journey down the Ohio was not altogether a picnic is shown by the fact that below Wheeling and at Marietta he was obliged to use oxen to drag his boat over the shoals. He says of these horned assistants: "I find them the most efficient sailors in the present state of navigation of the rivers, although they may be considered rather clumsy."

Lewis was present at the formal transfer of Upper Louisiana from the Spanish to the French, at St. Louis, March 9th, and from the French to the United States, March 10, 1804, and so probably were Clark and the others of the party.

Soon after the return of the Lewis and Clark expedition in 1806, Lewis was made Governor of Louisiana Territory, – March 3, 1807, – succeeding General and Governor James Wilkinson, "that faithless servant of his country," as Capt. H. M. Chittenden well characterizes him, and this position he held at the time of his death.

The most interesting question in connection with Lewis now is regarding his death. Did he commit suicide, or was he murdered?

I extract from Jefferson's memoir of Captain Lewis that which bears upon this subject:

Governor Lewis had, from early life, been subject to hypochondriac affections. It was a constitutional disposition in all the nearer branches of the family of his name, and was more immediately inherited by him from his father. They had not, however, been so strong as to give uneasiness to his family. While he lived with me in Washington, I observed at times sensible depressions of mind; but, knowing their constitutional source, I estimated their course by what I had seen in the family. During his Western expedition the constant exertion which that required of all the faculties of body and mind suspended these distressing affections; but, after his establishment at St. Louis in sedentary occupations, they returned upon him with redoubled vigour, and began seriously to alarm his friends. He was in a paroxysm of one of these when his affairs rendered it necessary for him to go to Washington. He proceeded to the Chickasaw Bluffs, where he arrived on the sixteenth of September, 1809, with a view of continuing his journey thence by water. Mr. Neely, agent of the United States with the Chickasaw Indians, arriving there two days after, found him extremely indisposed, and betraying at times some symptoms of a derangement of mind. The rumours of a war with England, and apprehensions that he might lose the papers he was bringing on, among which were the vouchers of his public accounts, and the journals and papers of his Western expedition, induced him here to change his mind, and to take his course by land through the Chickasaw country. Although he appeared somewhat relieved, Mr. Neely kindly determined to accompany and watch over him. Unfortunately, at their encampment, after having passed the Tennessee one day's journey, they lost two horses, which obliging Mr. Neely to halt for their recovery, the governor proceeded, under a promise to wait for him at the house of the first white inhabitant on his road. He stopped at the house of a Mr. Grinder [or Griner], who not being at home, his wife, alarmed at the symptoms of derangement she discovered, gave him up the house, and retired to rest herself in an out-house, the governor's and Neely's servants lodging in another. About three o'clock in the night he did the deed which plunged his friends into affliction, and deprived his country of one of her most valued citizens, whose valour and intelligence would have been now employed in avenging the wrongs of his country, and in emulating by land the splendid deeds which have honoured her arms on the ocean. It lost, too, to the nation the benefit of receiving from his own hand the narrative now offered them of his sufferings and successes, in endeavouring to extend for them the boundaries of science, and to present to their knowledge that vast and fertile country which their sons are destined to fill with arts, with science, with freedom and happiness.

To this melancholy close of the life of one whom posterity will declare not to have lived in vain, I have only to add that all the facts I have stated are either known to myself or communicated by his family or others, for whose truth I have no hesitation to make myself responsible; and I conclude with tendering you the assurances of my respect and consideration.

TH. JEFFERSON.

MR PAUL ALLEK, Philadelphia.

Dr. Coues discusses this matter very fully, giving, besides Jefferson's version, additional evidence upon both sides of

Moccasins and Shoe-buckle Used by Captain Lewis.

it, and he decides, very sensibly, that unless a more conclusive case can be made out, Lewis's name should no longer rest under the cloud that the suicide theory had cast upon it.

The old military road known as the "Natchez Trace," which had been, originally, an Indian trail and was, in 1801, expanded into a public road by the United States, extended from Nashville, Tenn., to Natchez, Miss., and beyond, and was one link in a system of "traces," or primeval roads, from the Atlantic coast settlements to the interior of the

West and South, in the earlier settlement of the country. The taverns or stations on those primitive roads were lonely, rude affairs, and in many cases were said to be kept by robbers and ruffians. Such was the case with the Grinder stand, some seventy odd miles southwest from Nashville, where Lewis died.

Besides Jefferson's statement, the act of suicide is based upon a story told in 1810 by Alexander Wilson, the ornithologist, which is an improbable tale told to him by Mrs. Grinder, wife of the tavern-keeper. Coues gives the letter as dated at Natchez, Mississippi Territory, May 28, 1811. In George Ord's "Life of Wilson," in *American Ornithology*, vol. i., now before me, I find the letter, dated Natchez, May 18, 1810, addressed to Alexander Lawson, and the part relating to Lewis is as follows:

Next morning (Sunday) I rode six miles to a man's, of the name of Grinder, where our poor friend Lewis perished. In the same room where he expired, I took down from Mrs. Grinder the particulars of that melancholy event, which affected me extremely. This house or cabin is seventy-two miles from Nashville, and is the last white man's as you enter the Indian country. Governor Lewis, she said, came hither about sunset, alone, and inquired if he could stay for the night; and, alighting, brought his saddle into the house. He was dressed in a loose gown, white, striped with blue. On being asked if he came alone, he replied that there were two servants behind, who would soon be up. He called for some spirits, and drank a very little. When the servants arrived, one of whom was a negro, he inquired for his powder, saying he was sure he had some powder in a canister. The servant gave no distinct reply, and Lewis, in the meanwhile, walked backwards and forwards before the door, talking to himself. Sometimes, she said, he would seem as if he were walking up to her; and would suddenly wheel round, and walk back as fast as he could. Supper being ready he sat down, but had eaten only a few mouthfuls when he started up, speaking to himself in a violent manner. At these times, she says, she observed his face to flush as if it had come on him in a fit. He lighted his pipe, and drawing a chair to the door sat down, saying to Mrs. Grinder, in a kind tone of voice, "Madam, this is a very pleasant evening." He smoked for some time, but quitted his seat and traversed the yard as before. He again sat down to his pipe, seemed again composed, and casting his eyes wistfully towards the west, observed what a sweet evening it was. Mrs. Grinder was preparing a bed for him; but he said he would sleep on the floor, and desired the servant to bring the bear skins and buffalo robe, which were immediately spread out for him; and it being now dusk the woman went off to the kitchen, and the two men to the barn, which stands about two hundred yards off. The kitchen is only a few paces from the room where Lewis was, and the woman being considerably alarmed by the behaviour of her guest could not sleep, but listened to him walking backwards and forwards, she thinks, for several hours, and talking aloud, as she said, "like a lawyer." She then heard the report of a pistol, and something fall heavily to the floor, and the words "*O Lord!*" Immediately afterwards she heard another pistol, and in a few minutes she heard him at her door calling out, "*O madam! give me some water, and heal my wounds.*" The logs being open, and unplastered, she saw him stagger back and fall against a stump that stands between the kitchen and room. He crawled for some distance, and raised himself by the side of a tree, where he sat about a minute. He once more got to the room; afterwards he came to the kitchen door, but did not speak; she then heard him scraping the bucket with a gourd for water; but it appears that this cooling element was denied the dying man! As soon as day broke and not before, the terror of the woman having permitted him to remain for two hours in this most deplorable situation, she sent two of her children to the barn, her husband not being at home, to bring the servants; and on going in they found him lying on the bed; he uncovered his side, and showed them where the bullet had entered; a piece of the forehead was blown off, and had exposed the brains, without having bled much. He begged they would take his rifle and blow out his brains, and he would give them all the money he had in his trunk. He often said, "I am no coward; but I am *so* strong, *so hard to die.*" He begged the servant not to be afraid of him, for that he would not hurt him. He expired in about two hours, or just as the sun rose above the trees. He lies buried close by the common path, with a few loose rails thrown over his grave. I gave Grinder money to put a post fence around it, to shelter it from the hogs, and from the wolves; and he gave me his written promise he would do it. I left this place in a very melancholy mood, which was not much allayed

VOL. 1-5.

by the prospect of the gloomy and savage wilderness which I was just entering alone.

Those who are inclined to accept Wilson's story, aside from Mrs. Grinder's relation to it, should first read Audubon's narration of his experience with Wilson in 1810, as given on pages 30-33 of the *Life of Audubon,* edited by his widow and published by G. P. Putnam's Sons, New York, in order to judge the better as to its entire reliability.

The various stories of this sad event are, naturally enough, widely discrepant in detail and conclusive of nothing. In all of them, Neely, the guardian, is absent hunting horses at the supreme moment and the so-called guardianship proves a farce.

Although Jefferson does not so state, it is understood that Lewis had a misunderstanding with the Government about his accounts, and this it is stated is what preyed upon his sensitive nature and mind and finally forced him to self-destruction.

It is a matter for regret that Jefferson did not particularize more as to his sources of information regarding Lewis's death and the precise reasons for his conclusion, for there is no doubt that the weight of his name alone has given the suicide theory a force it otherwise would not possess.

Mrs. Goodlett expresses the belief of the family, as follows:

Of course it will ever be shrouded in mystery, but my father, Mr. Charles Meriwether, visited his aunt, Meriwether Lewis's mother, about 1820. She was then eighty years old, but remarkably vigorous in mind and body, rode around the country on horseback like a girl, my father said, and was fond of talking of her son. She said his letters, written to her before starting on his trip home were full of love and affection, and so hopeful of a good time with his old friends, that *she never entertained the idea for a moment* that he had committed suicide. The theory that the family have ever advanced is that he was murdered by his Spanish servant who was traveling with him on horseback, to take charge of his baggage and to care for his horses. We suppose that traveling together for a long distance, it is probable that Meriwether Lewis, being of a social and confiding nature, had spoken to the Spaniard of the valuable papers and maps he was carrying to Virginia; — and knowing that the Governor of the State would not travel without plenty of money, that the avaricious and treacherous nature of the servant got possession of him and he determined to possess himself of what valuables Captain Lewis had. The servant was never afterwards heard from, nor were the papers.

Why should a man in the zenith of his glory, with everything to live for, looking forward to a visit to his beloved mother, sure of a warm welcome from his patron and dear friend, the President, and of the grateful appreciation of his countrymen, kill himself if he was sane? His family can attest to the fact that there was no insanity in his branch of the family.

R. T. Quarles of Nashville, Tenn., corresponding secretary of the Tennessee Historical Society, and also a descendant of the Lewis family, corroborates Mrs. Goodlett's statement that the family belief is that Lewis was murdered by his body servant, stating that not only did the Captain have in his possession quite a sum of money, but also family jewels of far greater value.

Mrs. Goodlett is, without doubt, I think, in error as to the servant and papers. In Jefferson's *Complete Works,*[1] there is a letter from Jefferson to the President of the United States dated Monticello, November 26, 1809. In this he refers to two trunks that "Maj. Neely," the Indian agent, has and to two more in care of Captain Russel, at Chickasaw Bluffs, belonging to Lewis. The first two contained "public vouchers, manuscripts of his Western journey and private papers"; the others, Pernier, Lewis's servant, said contained Lewis's private property. These came into Jefferson's

---

[1] Vol. v., p. 480.

possession. Pernier said that Lewis owed him $240 for un-paid wages.

Correspondence with B. R. A. Scott of Galveston, Texas, and his wife, and with Mrs. S. E. Shelton of Waco, Texas, has developed some facts of interest. Mrs. Shelton and Mrs. Scott are both great-nieces of Captain Lewis and Mr. Scott is more remotely related to him. After referring to the family belief that Lewis's servant had murdered him and disappeared with his personal effects, Mrs. Shelton adds:

> After a lapse of years, perhaps as many as thirty, he [the servant] sent a trunk of papers to my grandmother, Mrs. William H. Moore, née Mary Garland Marks, a half sister of Meriwether Lewis. In this trunk was a will, in which Lewis made her his heiress to lands, of the extent of which I am ignorant, but which are now in the midst of the city of St. Louis. Such a long time had elapsed before she recovered the papers that the property had passed into other hands and she compromised her claim for six thousand dollars. . . .

The late Chief Justice Moore of Texas, son of the Mrs. William Moore mentioned by Mrs. Shelton, informed Mr. Scott that his father, William Moore, had at one time, on the Mississippi River, recognized some personal property of Governor Lewis, a gold watch as he recalls it, in the pos-session of a man whom he supposed to be the Spanish servant who had travelled with Lewis, and that he secured the watch at once and Mr. Scott thinks that branch of the family still retains it.

Mrs. H. M. Conklin of Corpus Christi, Texas, and a great-niece of Captain Lewis, writes me that "the gun Uncle Meriwether used in the expedition was given to my father, Col. J. M. Moore. It was sunk in a boat with many other relics when the Federal gunboats attacked this place in 1862 ."

In 1843, the Tennessee Legislature formed Lewis County,

in Captain Lewis's honor, and, in 1848, it appropriated five hundred dollars to erect a monument over his grave. His remains rest in the centre of this county.

The "Report of the Lewis Monumental Committee" to the Tennessee General Assembly – 1849-50 – announcing the completion of the monument, says in part:

> The impression has long prevailed that under the influence of disease of body and mind – of hopes based upon long and valuable services – not merely deferred but wholly disappointed – Governor Lewis perished by his own hands. It seems to be more probable that he died by the hands of an assassin.

We thus have the opinions of the Lewis family and that of a committee of the Tennessee General Assembly directly opposed to that of the President.

On September 6, 1891, there appeared in the Nashville, Tenn., *American,* an article relating to the death of Captain Lewis by "John Quill," otherwise James D. Park, a lawyer of Franklin, Tenn., much of which is reproduced by Dr. Coues in his discussion of this subject. Through the kindness of Hon. E. C. Lewis of Nashville, I have been supplied with a reprinted galley proof of this Park communication, a copy of the *American* containing it being unobtainable. The *American* has since reprinted the article.

Mr. Park seems to have as thoroughly investigated the whole matter as was then possible and his conclusion was that Lewis had been murdered and robbed. He says in part:

> It has always been the firm belief of the people of this region that Gov. Lewis was murdered and robbed. The oldest citizens now living remember the rumors current at the time as to the murder, and it seems that no thought of suicide ever obtained footing here. The writer recently had an interview with Mrs. Christina B. Anthony, who lives some two miles from the Lewis grave, and has lived all her life of 77 years in the neighborhood. She says that old man Grinder kept a "stand" for travelers

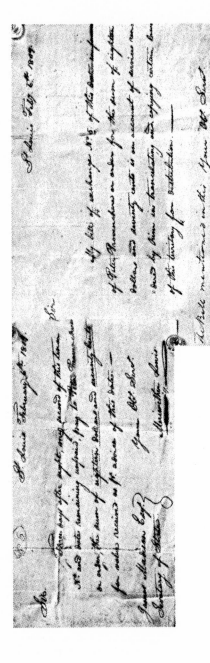

One of the drafts of Governor Lewis on James Madison, Secretary of State, which was protested for non-payment by the State Department. The protest of this and other drafts was, partially, the occasion for the trip of Lewis to Washington, in the course of which he lost his life.

on the Natchez Trace. Polly Spencer, whom she knew well before her death about forty years ago, was a hired girl at Grinder's, when Gov. Lewis was killed. Polly had often told the circumstances of the murder so far as she personally knew them.

She was washing dishes in the kitchen after supper with some of the females of the family when they heard a shot in the room where Capt. Lewis was sleeping. All rushed into the room and found him dead in his bed. Capt. Lewis being fatigued from his journey, had retired immediately after supper. His only companion, she said, was a negro boy, who was attending to the horses in the barn at the time. Old Grinder, who was of Indian blood, was at once suspected of the murder, ran away, was captured at Cane Creek, brought back and tried, but the proof not being positive, he was released. Only 25 cents was found on the person of Capt. Lewis after he was shot.

Old Grinder soon afterwards removed to the western part of the State, and it was reported in his old neighborhood had bought a number of slaves and a farm and seemed to have plenty of money. Before this he had always been quite poor.

Mrs. Anthony says the people always believed old Grinder killed Mr. Lewis and got his money. She had never heard of the theory of suicide until the writer mentioned it to her. Mrs. Anthony was a young married woman, boarding with the father of Polly Spencer when Polly told her these circumstances. Mrs. Anthony thus heard an ear-witness, so to speak, relate the story of the murder, which is pretty direct evidence. She is a bright, active, and intelligent old lady, and has for many years kept the little hotel at the hamlet of Newburg, the county seat of Lewis County, which is just two miles east of the monument.

Others living in Lewis and adjoining counties have been conversed with, who remember the general belief at the time, that Grinder killed his guest for the purpose of robbery. He must have observed that Capt. Lewis was a person of distinction and wealth; that he was almost alone, and that he probably had money with him. It seems incredible that a young man of 35, the Governor of the vast Territory of Louisiana, then on the way from his capital to that of the nation, where he knew he would be received with all the distinction and consideration due his office and reputation, should take his own life. His whole character is a denial of this theory. He was too brave and conscientious in the discharge of every duty, public and private; too conspicuous a person in the eyes of the country, and crowned with too many laurels, to cowardly sneak out of the world by the back way, a self-murderer. This idea was doubtless invented to cover up the double crime of robbery and murder and seems to have been the only version of his death that reached Mr. Jefferson and other friends in Virginia.

Mr. Park's version does not accord very well with Wilson's account in some important particulars, which is by no means any reflection on the former.

In 1899, hoping to obtain additional matter from Mr. Park, I wrote to him at Franklin, and received in reply a letter from his father, Dr. J. S. Park, announcing his son's death in 1897. I quote a sentence: "The further my son investigated the matter the more certain he believed that Lewis was murdered."

The *Army Magazine,* in 1894, reprinted from the *Southern Magazine* an article on the death of Captain Lewis, by Verne S. Pease. It is opposed to the idea of suicide, but whether based upon original investigation or upon Mr. Park's paper does not appear. It is an extremely readable paper, but quite variant, in many ways, from any other discussion of the event which I have seen, and gives as facts many details not found elsewhere.

He gives old man Grinder and his family a very hard name; states that he was practically under the surveillance of the whole neighborhood; that "a white servant girl, famous for her fine cooking [presumably Polly Spencer], was kept on the place, and the fame of the stand for dinners soon reached from one end of the trace to the other"; that "the sudden mysterious disappearance of several rich planters" travelling along the trace in that locality was ascribed to Grinder and his accomplices. He also stated that Grinder burned his house and fled the very night of Lewis's death, and that a coroner's inquest rendered a verdict of guilty of "murder at the hands of Joshua Grinder," after listening to the testimony of Polly Spencer and others.

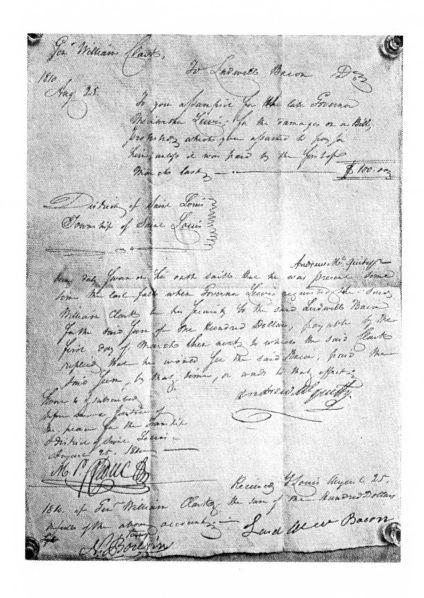

Receipt Showing Payment of a Protested Bill of Govenor Lewis's by General Wm. Clark, after the Death of Lewis.

It is now, undoubtedly, too late definitely and absolutely to decide this question. The evidence on both sides, so far as we have it, is circumstantial, contradictory, and indeterminate. Certainly the preponderance of testimony is hardly in favor of suicide. It seems a little odd, if Governor Lewis really suffered seriously from a recurrence of his old malady, that his family descendants know or, at least, say nothing of it and do not offer that as an excuse — a sufficient one truly — for the supposed act of suicide.

It seems strange too, that after passing through such discouragements and obstacles as beset him on his exploration, when there were periods during which one said to be so afflicted might well have become disheartened and done a rash act, Lewis succumbed to a supposed reappearance of a distressing malady when scarcely yet in the prime of life and when life held so much for him. It does not seem probable, but it may have been possible.

I cannot, however, but believe that time and the name of Jefferson have given a fictitious weight to the theory of suicide, and that now, considering the uncertain nature of the evidence, the time has come to give Governor Lewis the full and unreserved benefit of the doubt and relieve his name and fame of the imputation heretofore resting upon it.

The Lewis monument is made of Tennessee marble, is twenty and one half feet in height, and the broken column is two and one half feet in diameter at the base.

There are four different and appropriate inscriptions on the plinth, one on each side, which I reproduce exactly as given in Mr. Park's article, as shown by the galley proof:

(West Face)
MERIWETHER LEWIS
Born near Charlottesville, Va., Aug. 18,
1774, died Oct. 11, 1809, aged 35 years.

(South Face)

An officer of the Regular Army. Commander of the expedition to the Oregon
in 1803-1806. Governor of the Territory of Louisiana. His melancholy death occurred where
this monument now
stands, and under
which rest his mor-
tal remains.

(East Face)

In the language of Jefferson: "His courage was undaunted. His firmness and
perseverance yielded to nothing but
impossibilities. A rigid disciplinar-
ian, yet tender as a father to those
committed to his charge; honest,
disinterested, liberal, with a
sound understanding, and a
scrupulous fidelity to truth."

(North Face)

Immaturus obi: sed tu felicior annos
Vive meos, Bona Respublica! vive tuos.
Erected by the Legislature of Tennessee,
A.D. 1848

Mr. Park stated that at the time of his examination, the
monument was much the worse for time and wear. During
the Civil War, when iron had become a scarce commodity
in the South, it is asserted that the iron about the monument
was taken away for the purpose of making horseshoes.

Mrs. Octavia Zollicoffer Bond, in an article on "Lewis's
Tomb" in the *Land of Sunshine* for May, 1900, draws this
striking picture of the lone, time-worn shaft and locality:

Its stately column of limestone looming unexpectedly in the
heart of a monotonous woodland produces an effect which is
thrilling. The tall, sculptured shaft, surmounting a square
pyramidal base of rough hewn steps, is in striking contrast to the

*Monument over the Grave of Captain Lewis, Lewis County, Tennessee.
Erected by order of the Legislature of Tennessee.*

76

absence of man's art elsewhere in the dense forest in which it is hidden. Towering amid the gloom of primeval trees, its lofty, broken column awakens sensations of awe. Visitors rarely disturb the solemn silence of the place. The old road conducting to it is in many places so dim as to be almost obliterated.

Mr. Park concluded his contribution to the literature of this subject in these words:

Far out in the native forest, on the highlands, with no human dwelling near, it is, indeed, a lonely spot, where the wild deer and the fox are still pursued by the hunter's hounds. The existence of such a grave and monument is scarcely known outside of the State and to but few anywhere of the present generation. Tennessee would be 10th to give up the honored dust which has slept in her bosom for more than eighty years; but would it not be a graceful, if too long neglected act, should Congress authorize the erection of an appropriate monument of bronze at the national capital to the memory of the accomplished soldier and scientist who led the first expedition through the unknown gateways of the mountains of the Pacific and the mystery of whose untimely end will perhaps never be solved?

In these days of prolific monument building Mr. Park's suggestion may well be carried out by Congress, except that a monument should be erected to commemorate the achievements of both Lewis and Clark and their men. To the large number of military chieftains whose statues decorate the avenues and parks of the Capital of the nation, let those of two more military heroes be added, the two who antedate nearly all the rest and who were the real "Pathfinders" of our Western trans-Missouri domain.

It has been my privilege to peruse the original codices, or note-books of Lewis and Clark, and I have been much impressed with the manner in which they seem to serve as exponents of the characters of the two men. Those written by Lewis are in a fine, regular, symmetric handwriting, almost as clear and legible as engraving, and evince the conscientiousness of the man in his work.

After inspecting these books it is easy to understand how Lewis came by the appellation of the "sublime dandy," for he must have been excruciatingly particular and precise.

CAPTAIN CLARK

William Clark, whose surname has until recently been usually but incorrectly spelled with a final "e," was born in Virginia in 1770, and was therefore four years older than Captain Lewis. Clark too was one of a distinguished family, and was the ninth of a family of ten children. While William was yet a youth his parents removed from Virginia to the Falls of the Ohio, as Louisville, Ky., was then called.

Clark became an Ensign, U. S A., in 1788, was commissioned a Lieutenant of Infantry in 1791, and resigned from military service because of continued ill health, in 1796. He then went on a farm, where he remained, still in poor health, for several years. During his military service Lewis was, for a time, a subordinate under him.

For the purposes of the Lewis and Clark exploration Clark was made a Second Lieutenant of Artillery, which commission he resigned immediately upon the return to St. Louis in 1806. In 1807, Jefferson appointed him Brigadier-General of Militia of Louisiana, and also Indian Agent for Louisiana. He was made Governor of Missouri Territory – the same position under another title that Lewis held at the time of his death – in 1813, and he held this position until 1820, the year Missouri was admitted to statehood. He continued to hold other and important Federal positions, among them an appointment by President Monroe as Superintendent of Indian affairs, which position he held until his death. Captain Clark was twice married, was the father of seven children, and died in 1838, at St. Louis, aged sixty-eight years.

Supposed to be from an Old Portrait by Harding. Made when Clark was
Governor of Missouri Territory
Courtesy of John O'Fallon Clark, St. Louis, a grandson of Wm. Clark.

All the accounts we have of Captain Clark's career after he became a General of Militia and Indian Agent, and the records are far from meagre, prove that the fine qualities that blazed so conspicuously in the progress of the great exploration were not *ignes fatui* as it were. They were the exponents of a true, a manly man, and his subsequent record is one of unswerving fidelity, devotion to duty, honesty, and a braininess and discriminating common sense in his conduct of public and business affairs, worthy of study and to be patterned after in these latter days of feverish speculation and life.

Captain, or General, or Governor, as he was usually called in his later years, Clark's methods and success in dealing with the great mass of Indians, of diverse tribes, during the many years of his superintendency, were almost phenomenal. They were characterized by truthfulness, sympathy, fair dealing, and honesty, firmness, and diplomacy, and covered critical periods in our dealings with the hordes of red men who then, with the bison, jointly roamed the plains and prairies of the West and Northwest. Clark was known to the Indians as the "Red-head," and they trusted and loved him as a father and brother.

Had the Government, in its subsequent dealings with the Indians, taken several leaves from Clark's experience and copied them, the vast amount of treasure expended, the lives sacrificed, and trouble of all sorts endured in the recurring Indian wars, might have been saved.

There was nothing strange or occult in Clark's methods. He simply recognized the Indian as a man and human being entitled to the usual courtesies, decencies, and honorable treatment, including justice in all its aspects, that humanity in general in all its varying forms and nationalities is entitled to and expects to receive. This kindly spirit is shown in the following extract from a letter to Jefferson:

In my present situation of Superintendent of Indian affairs, it would afford me pleasure to be enabled to meliorate the condition of those unfortunate people placed under my charge, knowing as I do their retchedness, and their rapid decline. It is to be lamented that the deplorable situation of the Indians do not receive more of the humain feelings of the nation.

The return of the Lewis and Clark expedition with its stories of the vast and unknown regions explored, and its great wealth of fur-bearing animals, acted as a tremendous stimulus to the fur trade[1] among Americans. This trade, although assuming large proportions in 1800, had been mainly monopolized by foreigners whose headquarters were in Canada. St. Louis, an outgrowth of this American trade, had, in 1800, a population of less than 1000, but because of its location it now became the chief seat of the American efforts in this direction.

In 1808, the St. Louis Missouri Fur Company, commonly known as the Missouri Fur Company, was organized and Captain Clark was one of its members and the agent of the Company in St. Louis.

The Clark papers in the Draper manuscripts in the Wisconsin State Historical Library at Madison show how well Clark was trained and prepared for his future great work. The home of his father and brother, near Louisville, was the

centre[2] of hospitality and sociability for all the region round about. It was not only frequented by the sturdy pioneers of the Kentucky movement, with their tales of Indian warfare, and other perils and hardships of the early settlements: but the second generation of Kentucky emigrants also found here a welcome, the gentlemen and lawyers of the new settlement, the

---

[1] For a full and interesting account of the story of the fur trade in early days, consult *The American Fur Trade of the Far West*, by Capt. H. M. Chittenden, published by Francis P. Harper, New York 1902.

[2] Miss Louise Phelps Kellogg in *Proceedings of Wisconsin Historical Society for 1902*, pp. 37-40.

Revolutionary soldiers seeking new homes in the growing West, men of enterprise, culture, and promise, permanent founders of a new civilization.

Among them all, young "Billy" was a marked favorite. "Your brother William," writes one in 1791, "is gone out as a cadet with Genl Scott on the Expedition. He is a youth of solid and promising parts, and as brave as Cesar." His four

House of John Clark, Father of Captain Clark, near Louisville, Ky. Captain Clark Lived there in his Boyhood Days.
Photograph taken from an oil painting when the house was one hundred years old.

years' service in the Western army, concluded by acting as officer in Gen. Wayne's campaign, and taking part in the battle of Falling Timbers not only gave him an acquaintance with military discipline, the courage and resource needed to deal with savage foes, but put him in touch with the prominent men of his time, and gave him a knowledge of men and how to handle them, that was of great advantage to him thereafter. Twice he was intrusted by Gen. Wayne with important commissions to the Spaniards: an account of which is to be found in the Spanish papers of the Draper manuscripts. It is said that no officer impressed the Spaniards with a more wholesome respect than young Lieut. William Clark.

After his resignation from the army in 1796, he lived quietly at home with his family, chiefly occupied in attempting to adjust the tangled affairs of his brother, George Rogers Clark, in whose behalf he made several journeys to Virginia, Vincennes, etc., in the attempt to settle the suits entered against the latter for supplies for his Illinois campaigns. He not only gave his time and effort to accomplish this, but sacrificed for the purpose of settlement the small estate he had himself accumulated.

But after all the real story of William Clark is best told in the pages of the Lewis and Clark report. The man shines through his deeds, and it is a pleasure to turn the pages of the original note-books and read the painstaking, unembellished narrative set down in bold, manly chirography, even though the spelling and punctuation are of the eccentric order.

SERGEANT FLOYD

Sergeant Charles Floyd was one of the "young men from Kentucky" who joined Lewis and Clark. Floyd was of a pioneer family that suffered its full share of hardships and Indian-fighting in the days of Daniel Boone, when Kentucky was a "dark and bloody ground." The Floyds, led by Colonel John Floyd, figure prominently in Kentucky border history, in the days when George Rogers Clark, an elder brother of Captain William Clark, was the animating genius of the West. Charles Floyd was also the name of the Sergeant's father, but details of his life and death are meagre. He was a surveyor who emigrated from Virginia to Kentucky with Boone. Governor John Floyd of Virginia – 1829 – and the father of John B. Floyd, the noted Secretary of War under President Buchanan at the beginning of the Civil War, was a first cousin of the Sergeant.

Distinction attaches to Sergeant Floyd for four reasons. His was the only death that occurred among Lewis and Clark's men during the exploration; he was, so far as is known, the first citizen soldier of the United States to die in the great territory of the Louisiana Purchase west of the Mississippi River; his memory has been honored by the

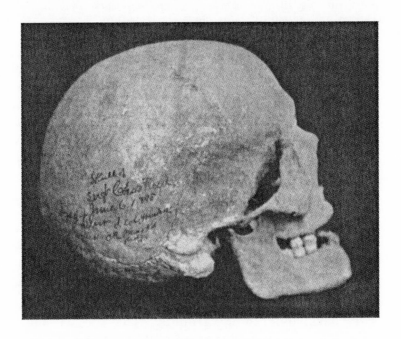

The Skull of Sergeant Charles Floyd.

recent erection of a splendid obelisk over his remains on the very bluff where his comrades interred him that August day in 1804; Floyd kept a journal and it was one of two, aside from that of Lewis and Clark, which saw the light of publication.

The circumstances surrounding Floyd's death, burial, reburial, the erection of the monument, and the finding of his journal justify some extended reference to them. The immediate events of the death and burial are given in the regular course of this narrative.

The explorers named the bluff where they interred the body "Floyd's Bluff," and carefully marked the grave, and from that day to this the bluff has been one of the landmarks of the river. It is now a park within the corporate limits of Sioux City, Iowa. Many of the travellers of succeeding years visited the bluff and grave, in passing up and down the river, and thus assisted in preserving the identity of the spot, and even more particularly, in keeping the grave itself marked.

John Bradbury – 1811 – in his journal, merely mentions passing the spot, but Henry Brackenridge – 1811 – describes the spot thus:

About a mile below our encampment we passed Floyd's Bluff and River, fourteen miles from the Maha village. . . . The place of his interment is marked by a wooden cross, which may be seen by navigators at a considerable distance. The grave occupies a beautiful rising ground, now covered with grass and wild flowers. The pretty little river, which bears his name, is neatly fringed with willow and shrubbery. Involuntary tribute was paid to the spot, by the feelings even of the most thoughtless, as we passed by. It is several years since he was buried here; no one has disturbed the cross which marks the grave; even the Indians who pass, venerate the place, and often leave a present or offering near it. Brave, adventurous youth! thou art not forgotten – for although thy bones are deposited far from thy native home, in the desert-waste; yet the eternal silence of the plain shall mourn thee, and memory will dwell upon thy grave!

Brackenridge did not, apparently, climb the bluff and probably imagined the cedar post at the grave to be a cross, as there is no record of a cross ever having been placed there.

George Catlin, who was evidently surcharged with sentiment, was greatly impressed by the lone grave on the hill and wrote this gushing apostrophe to its silent tenant:

Oh, sad and tear-starting contemplation! Sole tenant of this stately mound, how solitary thy habitation! Here heaven wrested from thee thy ambition, and made thee sleeping monarch of this land of silence. Stranger! Oh, how the mystic web of sympathy links my soul to thee and thy afflictions! I knew thee not, but it was enough; thy tale was told, and I, a solitary wanderer through thy land, have stopped to drop familiar tears upon thy grave. Stranger! Adieu. With streaming eyes I leave thee again, and thy fairy land, to peaceful solitude. My pencil has faithfully traced thy beautiful habitation; and long shall live in the world, and familiar, the name of Floyd's Grave.

Catlin states that the cedar post bore only "the initials of his name." If this be true, it was not the post placed there by Lewis and Clark, but the explanation may be found in the statement of Maximilian, who saw it a year later than Catlin, as follows:

On the following day (the 8th of May) we came to Floyd's Grave. . . . A short stick marks the place where he is laid, and has often been renewed by travelers when the fires in the prairie have destroyed it. A little further up is Floyd's River, and on Floyd's Hills there were a few fir trees, over which the kite hovered in the air.

In 1839, Joseph N. Nicollet, passing the bluff, recorded:

We stopped for the night at the foot of the bluff on which is Floyd's Grave; my men replaced the signal, blown down by the winds, which marks the spot and hallows the memory of the brave Sergeant, who died there during Lewis and Clark's expedition.

Mention is frequently made in the narrative part of this volume of the tremendously erosive character of the Missouri

---

[1] *Travels in the Interior of North America,* by Maximilian, Prince of Wied.

River. In the spring of 1857 a great freshet, supplementing the corrasion of fifty years, so washed away the water side of the bluff that the grave was eaten into and the skeleton exposed.

The following substance of a letter from M. L. Jones, a gentleman of advanced age living at Smithland, Iowa, at

The Site of Sergeant Floyd's Grave before the Re-interment.

the date of writing, December 28, 1895, is taken from the first *Report of the Floyd Memorial Association,* Sioux City, Iowa (p. 15), and tells an interesting story:

I first saw the grave in May, 1854. The cedar post was almost intact then, though pieces had been cut off by relic hunters. I passed the place frequently in 1854-55. The post stood in sight of a foot trail that ran along near the river, that the wagon road had to go round. It was some 100 feet or more from the edge of the bluff overlooking the river. Late in the fall of 1856 I passed that way, and not seeing the post in its accustomed place, I went to examine it, and found that it had been cut away till only a few inches remained above the ground. Late in April, 1857, as I was going that way from Sioux City, I was seized with chill and fever; but noticed that the river, then very high, was cutting into the bank. I walked as close to the edge of the bluff as I could; the ground had caved in, the post was gone, and it looked as if the grave had gone, too. I was quite dizzy from my sickness, but laid down and crawled to the edge, where, looking over, I saw some bones projecting from the ground. I continued on my way to the house of a friend, Mr. Traversier, a Frenchman, with whom Dr. F. Wixon was stopping. We sent word to the Sioux City post-office, and Floyd's remains were secured next day. I was not present at the rescue, nor at the reburial, as I was sick for some time.

The rescue of the remains was attended with danger, as the following excerpt from the same report – p. 16 – will show:

A strong cable was prepared to attach to the box, and Dr. Sloane, father of our fellow townsman, editor of the *Citizen,* being light of weight, volunteered to accept the post of danger. With a rope tied around his waist, securely held by strong hands, he was let down over the brink of the precipice until the box was reached and the cable adjusted. The remains were then brought to a place of safety.

As a matter of fact some of the bones had fallen from the coffin and were lost.

On May 28, 1857, a re-interment with appropriate cere-monies took place in the presence of a large assemblage from Sioux City, the coffin being made from black walnut trees growing near the spot. The new grave was on the same bluff, about "two hundred yards farther back from the river." The site of the original interment is now in the air one hundred feet above the surface of the water. Along the foot of the bluff on the bank of the river the tracks of the Sioux City and Pacific Railroad are now laid, which fact is almost an absolute guarantee that the further eating away of the bluff by the stream is at an end.

On June 6, 1895, the Floyd Memorial Association was organized at the place of re-interment, the object being to erect a suitable monument over the remains, which should also be commemorative of the important events which occurred in 1803-06. This association was composed of men and women from all parts of the country, many of whom were persons of prominence.

The project was not allowed to sleep. The United States Government appropriated $5000; the State of Iowa, $5000; Woodbury County, Iowa, $800; and the city of Sioux City, Iowa, $1500 for the prosecution of the work. Private contributions, the donations of railway companies in services rendered, the services of the local force of the United States Engineer Office at Sioux City, under whose direction the work was placed, added to the amounts named, aggregated a total sum of nearly $20,000 available for the accomplishment of the work.

On August 20, 1895, the ninety-first anniversary of his death, imposing ceremonies were held about Floyd's grave in the presence of five hundred or more people. All that remained of Sergeant Charles Floyd was placed in two earthenware jars; these were lowered into their last resting-place, and the place of interment was permanently marked by a large stone slab upon which was this inscription:

Sergeant
CHARLES FLOYD
DIED
Aug. 20, 1804.
Remains removed from 600
Feet West and Reburied at
This Place May 28, 1857.
This Stone Placed
Aug. 20, 1895.

The form of monument decided upon was a solid masonry

obelisk, after Egyptian models, and the matter of design and
construction was placed in the hands of Captain H. M.
Chittenden of the Engineer Corps, U. S. A. The material
used in construction was Kettle River, Minnesota, sandstone, a stone of warm, pink color, and very durable.

The shaft rises 100 feet above its base, which is 125 feet

*The Stone Slab Placed August 20, 1805, Marking Final Resting-Place of
Sergeant Floyd, on Floyd's Bluff.*

above the Missouri River. The foundation is a solid mono-
lith of the best concrete, and weighs 278 tons. Its bearing
surface upon the ground beneath is 484 square feet, and
the pressure upon this bed is 844 tons, or one and three
fourths tons per square foot. The foundation was laid May
29, 1900; the corner-stone August 20, 1900; the capstone
April 22, 1901, and the shaft was dedicated on Memorial
Day, 1901.

Captain Lewis, in sending back to St. Louis from Fort

Mandan the boat and collection of curios for the President, states in his letter that, "I have sent a journal kept by one of the Sergeants, to Captain Stoddard, my Agent at St. Louis in order, as much as possible, to multiply the chances of saving something." It is a fair inference that this journal was Floyd's, and that Captain Stoddard sent it to Floyd's family.

Dr. Lyman C. Draper, for long years the Secretary of the Wisconsin Historical Society, some forty years ago made collections of important historical papers in Kentucky, which were placed among the archives of the Society and – at least in some cases – forgotten. In February, 1893, quite by accident, Reuben G. Thwaites, the present Secretary of the Society, unearthed Floyd's manuscript journal in the Draper collection. The journal was read before the American Antiquarian Society at Boston, April 25, 1894, and by them printed, and one more account was thus added, as far as it went, to the chronicles of the Lewis and Clark exploration. As will be seen in the narrative, this journal was a valuable check on those of Lewis and Clark and Gass, notwithstanding its absurdities of composition. Floyd was highly thought of by the Captains, ans Lewis, in his report to the war Department at the close of the expedition, refers to him as "a young man of much merit," and suggests that his father should receive a gratuity in consideration of his loss.

Among all the men of the expedition, exclusive of the leaders, Floyd, I think, must stand as second, historically, Colter being the first.

SERGEANT ORDWAY

Sergeant John Ordway was one of the members of the expedition against whose name Dr. Coues wrote, "No more known of him."

Ordway was one of ten children and the home-tree seems to have been in New Hampshire. He came of a good family and some of his brothers and sisters emigrated to Ohio and Kentucky. He was a lineal descendant of James Ordway, who came from England or Wales to Newbury, Mass., between 1635 and 1640. James Ordway and his wife, Anne Emory, were persons of repute, and they accumulated much property.

After his return from the Lewis and Clark exploration, John Ordway travelled by boat and on horseback to New Hampshire. Later, returning to Missouri, he settled at or near New Madrid, married, and made some extensive land purchases. He is not known to have served in either the War of 1812 or the Mexican War. Both he and his wife died in Missouri, leaving no children.

Ordway kept a journal of the expedition, which was in possession of Biddle and Allen when they were preparing the original report of Lewis and Clark, — that of 1814, — but what became of it thereafter is not known.

Mrs. Martha Ordway Kibbler of San Francisco writes me as follows regarding Ordway and his journal:

Of all the men who enlisted or volunteered for the expedition he was the best educated. In an old letter which he wrote just after he returned from the expedition, and which I read in 1862, he distinctly stated that the diary he kept and which he wore beneath his shirt, was bought by the commanders of the expedition to be used by them in their report to the Government, and he thought the ten dollars they paid him for the diary was a good price. Probably the diary was copied and the original lost. This letter with several others, giving details of their journey, sufferings and eventual success was lost in a fire about 1865.

SERGEANT PRYOR

Of Nathaniel Pryor, one of the four Sergeants, but little is known. He was from Kentucky, performed his part well, and was often placed in independent and responsible situations.

After the expedition returned, Pryor was commissioned an ensign in the army and eventually became a captain. He remained a soldier until 1815.

It will be noted in the narrative that when the expedition reached the Mandan villages, on the return, in 1806, Shahaka, the Mandan Chief, accepted the invitation of Lewis and Clark and journeyed with them to St. Louis and Washington, to see the Great Father and the white man's country, under the distinct pledge that the Government would safely escort him back to his native heath. This return of the chieftain turned out to be a serious and expensive matter.

At St. Louis, in 1807, Pryor, then an ensign, was placed in charge of the party of escort, which consisted of forty-eight men and which was consolidated with another party convoying some Sioux Indians as far as the Sioux country. The total number in both parties, escort and Indians, upon leaving St. Louis, was ninety-four, among whom were a few Indian women and children and two fur-trading parties, one of the latter being in charge of Pierre Chouteau, and the other under "young Dorion," son of the older, or William Dorion, who was also with the Sioux Indians and their escort.

Late in May, 1807, the combined outfit left St. Louis, and they arrived at the Arikara Indian villages on September 9th. The Arikara, who, in 1803, had been so friendly with Lewis and Clark, were now at war with the Mandans and in the mood to fight everybody.

They fired on Pryor's boats, greatly to his astonishment, and compelled him to stop and land. A captive Mandan woman boarded the boat and managed to impart to the Mandan Chief and Pryor a true knowledge of affairs, so that they were put on their guard, and thus able to arrange for emergencies. After a fruitless series of councils, the Indians, among whom were also some hostile Sioux, forbade the party to continue the journey and demanded that they stop and trade with them. This being refused, although Chouteau did make them a fair trading offer, they attempted to capture the boats, and a battle resulted. There were hundreds of Indians opposed to Pryor's small force — for the friendly Sioux and their escort had now been dropped — and after the fight had raged until sunset it was determined to retreat and return to St. Louis. There were several killed and many wounded on both sides, and among the killed was a prominent Sioux Indian chief. It was in this scrimmage that George Shannon, a former member of the Lewis and Clark party, and who was one of Pryor's escort, was so severely wounded that he eventually lost his leg.

Pryor was undaunted. When he perceived that the boats could not get to the Mandan towns, he proposed to Shahaka that they go by land, — a three days' march, — making a wide detour in the plains to avoid the hostiles, but the chief, who was not a warrior, had no stomach for the adventure, alleging that the women and children would prove too much of an incumbrance. So they returned to St. Louis.

Now for the sequel, as given by Chittenden!

During the winter of 1808-09 the Missouri Fur Company was organized. Captain Lewis was now Governor Lewis, and he resided at St. Louis. He made a contract with the Fur Company to transport Shahaka to his village, the company to receive therefor $7000. The company bound itself to protect to its utmost power the chief and his party and to report at once the safe arrival at the Indian villages.

The party left St. Louis the latter part of May or early in June, 1809, under command of the same Pierre Chouteau who figured in the 1807 expedition. It consisted of one hundred and twenty-five men, forty of them expert American riflemen, and it delivered the chief to his people on September 24th, without difficulty.

The Sioux were now disposed to be hostile, but the formidable appearance of Chouteau's party caused them to think twice and not molest them. The Arikara were lamblike and hospitable.

SERGEANT GASS

Of all the men who accompanied Lewis and Clark none was, probably, a more striking character than Patrick Gass.

Gass was born of Irish parents near Chambersburg, Pennsylvania, in June, 1771, and he died near Wellsburg, West Virginia, April 33, 1870, having enjoyed, therefore, almost ninety-nine years of life, filled with varied experiences. His boyhood was that of the frontier boy in those early backwoods days. His father moved across the Allegheny Mountains to the vicinity of Pittsburg, Patrick and his sister making the journey in creels, or crates, lashed to the sides of a pack horse. The lad's days of schooling numbered just nineteen. Gass naturally became, even from boyhood, a woodsman and explorer, self-reliant in frontier matters, and accustomed to the hardships and vicissitudes of a rough, outdoor life.

In 1792, he saw his first military service, against Indians, and he then knew or saw Lewis Wetzel, the renowned Indian-killer and scout of the Ohio region. In 1793, he began his travels by making a trading trip down the Ohio and Mississippi rivers to New Orleans, returning home by way of Cuba and Philadelphia.

In 1794, Gass bound himself out in the carpenter's trade, and, as a carpenter, helped to build a house for President

James Buchanan's father when James, junior, was known as "little Jimmy."

In 1799, when war with France loomed on the horizon, Gass again enlisted as a soldier. He was in the army and stationed at Kaskaskia, Ill., when Captain Lewis appeared there searching for volunteer soldiers for the coming expedition. Gass volunteered, but his own captain objected to his going, his services as carpenter being too badly needed at Kaskaskia, but Gass got the ear of Lewis and the arrangement was effected.

After his return from the expedition, Gass had his journal published, and soon after returned to Kaskaskia, where he remained for several years, part of the time engaged in the lead business. When the War of 1812 broke out he again enlisted as a regular soldier. After serving in the West he finally joined the army in the vicinity of Niagara and took part in the battle of Lundy's Lane, where he was wounded.

He was discharged in 1815, being then forty-four years of age. His life had been an eventful, stirring, adventurous one, largely devoted to his country, but his days of soldiering and exploring were now over.

The remainder of his life was passed near Wellsburg, in various occupations. It is recorded that he became greatly addicted to liquor, and that for many years his condition was pitiable. In 1831, at sixty years of age, having at last fallen in love, he married, and for fifteen years – 1831-46 – lived a happy married life and had seven children born to him. His sole means of subsistence in his later life was a meagre pension from the Government of $96 per year. In consideration of his services to his country, he had received, in 1816, 160 acres of land, but this he allowed to be sold for taxes.

In politics Gass was a Democrat of Democrats, and in the days before the Civil War, a great admirer of Stephen

A. Douglas. Although his Democracy was of the rock-ribbed sort, when the Civil War broke upon the land he was an ardent Unionist and felt that his duty required him again to shoulder a rifle in defence of his country, although then ninety years old. This was clearly impossible, but it shows the stuff of which the man was made. After giving the best years of his life to his country, and then being allowed a beggarly pension of $8 per month, when red war again flamed, he, though verging well on to a century, felt the battle-glow and the call to the ranks. That was patriotism!

J. G. Jacob, in his *Life and Times of Patrick Gass,* from which these details are taken, pays a warm tribute to the modesty and integrity of Gass. Despite his relapse at one time into intemperance, he was respected for his rugged honesty and manliness, and his fellow-citizens were glad to do such honor to the old veteran as they could.

Gass, when about ninety years of age, became converted to the so-called Campbellite faith and joined that church. The aged sergeant, a national character, was immersed in the Ohio River on a beautiful Sunday afternoon, the whole town of Wellsburg turning out to see the hero of a journey across the continent more than a half-century before, and of numerous wars, signalize his last enlistment as a soldier, this time under the banner of the Cross. The old man was immersed to the music of *Shall We Gather at the River,* and we can conceive that the scene in all its setting was not the least dramatic of the many that filled up the measure of his long life.

He was, undoubtedly, the last survivor of the Lewis and Clark expedition, and he rests now in the little cemetery at Wellsburg, with nothing particular in connection with his grave to note the fact that he was one of a band of immortals whom their country now delights to honor.

It would be a most fitting tribute to the memories of

these men for the Government to ascertain, as far as possible, where each lies buried and to erect, where necessary, a suitable monument over the remains of each, reciting thereon the fact that he was a member of the Lewis and Clark expedition.

JOHN COLTER

It will, I think, be generally conceded among historians that, next to Lewis and Clark themselves, the member of the expedition who became the most important figure historically was John Colter. This was not because Colter was any better or abler than many of his fellows, but it was owing entirely to those accidents which so often occur in some men's lives whereby they become honored and exalted, while others of equal ability and merit, through the freaks of fortune go to the grave "unwept, unhonored, and unsung." There have been born into the world, perhaps, many "village Hampdens" and "mute inglorious Miltons," but the world knows of but one of each name. The achievements upon which Colter's fame rests were entirely aside from his connection with this expedition except as they may be said to have sprung, incidentally, from that connection. Colter was an innate, natural rover of the wilds; civilization had few charms for him, but the vast, illimitable plains and the snow-whitened mountains that bounded their horizons and on and among which dangers lurked, – these were the places where he loved to roam.

It will be seen, in the regular progress of the expedition, that Colter asked for and received his discharge when the explorers reached the Mandan villages on their return in 1806, and that he was commended as having "always performed his duty."

For much of the time subsequent to that period, Colter's movements are known only inferentially, but two events which occurred have given him an historical reputation, in conjunction with the fact that he was a member of the Lewis and Clark expedition.

On August 14, 1806, the expedition, returning, reached the Mandan villages and on the 15th or 16th, Colter, with two trappers whom they had met on the 11th and who had made him an alluring offer, once more turned his face west and again plunged into the wilderness. The Lewis and Clark journal refers to this willingness to inflict self-banishment upon himself as follows:

> The example of this man shows how easily men may be weaned from the habits of civilized life to the ruder but scarcely less fascinating manners of the woods. This hunter has been now absent for many years from the frontiers, and might naturally be presumed to have some anxiety, or some curiosity at least, to return to his friends and his country; yet, just at the moment when he is approaching the frontiers, he is tempted by a hunting scheme to give up those delightful prospects, and go back without the least reluctance to the solitude of the woods.

In the spring of 1807, as Manuel Lisa and his party of trappers and traders were ascending the Missouri to establish a trading post at the mouth of the Grosse Corne, or Big Horn River, they met, at the mouth of the Platte River, a man entirely alone, descending the Missouri. It was Colter. It evidently required little persuasion to induce him again – for the third time – to abandon the allurements of civilization before having even tasted them, and to embark with the outfit for the trapping grounds on the headwaters of the Yellowstone. He was indeed a valuable man for Lisa, and one cannot wonder that the latter was anxious to obtain his services.

On joining Lisa he found, also, one of his old comrades of the Lewis and Clark days, Drouillard, who was Lisa's right-hand man. It is not improbable that another one –

Potts — may also have been in the party, to judge from subsequent events.

Our knowledge of Colter comes to us in fragmentary shape. On Clark's map, published with the Lewis and Clark report of 1814, there is shown a long, winding, circular trail, and at one place are the words, "Colter's route in 1807," which would indicate that after Lisa arrived in the Big Horn country, Colter was sent on a mission to the Crows and other Indians, with the gratifying announcement that furs could be exchanged at a near-by post, for the white man's luxuries, including fire-water.

This trip was one of the two "accidents" which was destined, all unknown to the lone hero, to bring historical renown to Colter. Chittenden[1] rehearses the story of Colter in full, and is the best authority on the subject.

On this trip to the tribes in 1807, besides accomplishing something for Lisa, Colter, through no fault of his own, became embroiled in a battle between the Crows and the Blackfeet, so called, in which he was shot in the leg, and this fact, in connection with Captain Lewis's troubles with the Blackfeet in 1806, resulted in a bitter feud between them and the whites. His important work, however, of great moment to those coming after him, consisted in the geographical discoveries he made. Without going into fascinating detail, Colter was the first known white explorer to penetrate the mountain fastnesses about the sources of the Big Horn, Yellowstone, Wind, Green, and Snake rivers; he was the discoverer of important features of what is now the Yellowstone National Park, he first gazed upon the Pilot Knobs, or Three Tetons, which subsequently became such landmarks. Just how much of Yellowstone Park Colter

---

[1] *The Yellowstone National Park*, The Robert Clarke Company, Cincinnati; *The History of the American Fur Trade, etc.*, Francis P. Harper, New York.

saw is uncertain, but that he discovered Yellowstone Lake and the hot springs and geysers which abound along its shores is clear. He may have seen the Grand Cañon and the falls there, and possibly also the Mammoth Hot Springs. He saw too the boiling tar spring on the Stinking-water River, and this spot – not one in Yellowstone Park – became known as Colter's Hell.

The world was quite skeptical at that time about such natural curiosities as this region contains, and Colter may have been very discreet as to what he related about it or his friends have been even more cautious as to what was published.

Colter was also the principal figure in one of the most remarkable adventures that ever befell any man. It is one of those cases where truth surpasses fiction and the episode deserves recounting here in full. It is a picture of a time now gone and that can never be duplicated in this country. The tale was originally told by Bradbury, to whom Colter himself related it, and is given in his *Trawls in the Interior of America,* 2d edition, London, 1819, a volume rare in more senses than one:

This man came to St. Louis in May, 1810, in a small canoe, from the head waters of the Missouri, a distance of three thousand miles, which he traversed in thirty days. I saw him on his arrival, and received from him an account of his adventures after he had separated from Lewis and Clarke's party: one of these, from its singularity, I shall relate. On the arrival of the party on the head waters of the Missouri, Colter, observing an appearance of abundance of beaver being there, he got permission to remain and hunt for some time, which he did in company with a man of the name of Dixon, who had traversed the immense tract of country from St. Louis to the head waters of the Missouri alone. Soon after he separated from Dixon, and *trapped* in company with a hunter named Potts; and aware of the hostility of the Blackfeet Indians, one of whom had been killed by Lewis, they set their traps at night, and took them up early in the morning, remaining concealed during the day. They were examining their traps early one morning, in a creek about six miles from that branch of the Missouri called Jefferson's Fork, and were ascending in a canoe, when they suddenly heard a great noise, resembling the trampling of animals; but they could not ascertain the fact, as the high perpendicular banks on each side of the river impeded their view. Colter immediately pronounced it to be occasioned by Indians, and advised an instant retreat; but was accused of cowardice by Potts, who insisted that the noise was caused by buffaloes, and they proceeded on.

In a few minutes afterwards their doubts were removed, by a party of Indians making their appearance on both sides of the creek, to the amount of five or six hundred, who beckoned them to come ashore. As retreat was now impossible, Colter turned the head of the canoe to the shore; and at the moment of its touching, an Indian seized the rifle belonging to Potts; but Colter, who is a remarkably strong man, immediately retook it, and handed it to Potts, who remained in the canoe, and on receiving it pushed off into the river. He had scarcely quitted the shore when an arrow was shot at him, and he cried out, *"Colter, I am wounded."* Colter remonstrated with him on the folly of attempting to escape, and urged him to come ashore. Instead of complying, he instantly levelled his rifle at an Indian, and shot him dead on the spot. This conduct, situated as he was, may appear to have been an act of madness; but it was doubtless the effect of sudden, but sound reasoning; for if taken alive, he must have expected to be tortured to death, according to their custom. He was instantly pierced with arrows so numerous, that, to use the language of Colter, *"he was made a riddle of."*

They now seized Colter, stripped him entirely naked, and began to consult on the manner in which he should be put to death. They were first inclined to set him up as a mark to shoot at; but the chief interfered, and seizing him by the shoulder, asked him if he could run fast. Colter, who had been some time amongst the Kee-kat-sa, or Crow Indians, had in a considerable degree acquired the Blackfoot language, and was also well acquainted with Indian customs. He knew that he had now to run for his life, with the dreadful odds of five or six hundred against him, and those armed Indians; therefore cunningly replied that he was a very bad runner, although he was considered by the hunters as remarkably swift. The chief now commanded the party to remain stationary, and led Colter out on the prairie three or four hundred yards, and released him, bidding him to *save himself if he could.* At that instant the horrid war whoop sounded in the ears of poor Colter, who, urged with the hope of preserving life, ran with a speed at which he was himself surprised. He proceeded towards the Jefferson Fork, having to traverse a plain six miles in breadth, abounding with the prickly pear, on which he was every instant treading with his naked feet. He ran nearly half way across the plain before he ventured to look over his shoulder, when he perceived that the Indians were very much scattered, and that he had gained ground to a considerable distance from the main body; but one Indian, who carried a spear, was much before all the rest, and not more than a hundred yards from him. A faint gleam of hope now cheered the heart of Colter: he derived confidence from the belief that escape was within the bounds of possibility; but that confidence was nearly being fatal to him, for he exerted himself to such a degree, that the blood gushed from his nostrils, and soon almost covered the fore part of his body.

He had now arrived within a mile of the river, when he distinctly heard the appalling sound of footsteps behind him, and every instant expected to feel the spear of his pursuer. Again he turned his head, and saw the savage not twenty yards from him. Determined if possible to avoid the expected blow, he suddenly stopped, turned round, and spread out his arms. The Indian, surprised by the suddenness of the action, and perhaps at the bloody appearance of Colter, also attempted to stop; but exhausted with running, he fell whilst endeavoring to throw his spear, which stuck in the ground, and broke in his hand. Colter instantly snatched up the pointed part, with which he pinned him to the earth, and then continued his flight. The foremost of the Indians, on arriving at the place, stopped till others came up to join them, when they set up a hideous yell. Every moment of this time was improved by Colter, who, although fainting and exhausted, succeeded in gaining the skirting of the cotton wood trees, on the borders of the fork, through which he ran, and plunged into the river. Fortunately for him, a little below this place there was an island, against the upper point of which a raft of drift timber had lodged. He dived under the raft, and after several efforts, got his head above water amongst the trunks of trees, covered over with smaller wood to the depth of several feet. Scarcely had he secured himself, when the Indians arrived on the river, screeching and yelling, as Colter expressed it, "like so many devils." They were frequently on the raft during the day, and were seen through the chinks by Colter, who was congratulating himself on his escape, until the idea arose that they might set the raft on fire.

In horrible suspense he remained until night, when hearing no more of the Indians, he dived from under the raft, and swam silently down the river to a considerable distance, when he landed and travelled all night. Although happy in having escaped from the Indians, his situation was still dreadful: he was completely naked, under a burning sun, the soles of his feet were entirely filled with the thorns of the prickly pear; he was hungry, and had no means of killing game, although he saw abundance around

On the Jefferson River, near where Colter Escaped from the Blackfeet.
The Beaver's-head at the left.

him, and was at least seven days journey from Lisa's Fort, on the Bighorn branch of the Roche Jaune River. These were circumstances under which almost any man but an American hunter would have despaired. He arrived at the fort in seven days, having subsisted on a root much esteemed by the Indians of the Missouri, now known by naturalists as *psoralea esculenta*.

It may easily be imagined that such an experience might cool one's desire for life in a wild region, break one's constitution, and cause one to long for the flesh pots and comforts of even frontier civilization, but the victim and hero of this exploit seems to have remained in the Yellowstone country until the spring of 1810, when, as related by Bradbury, he descended the rivers, making three thousand miles in thirty days.

In the spring of 1811, Bradbury, in ascending the Missouri with Hunt's Astorian party, again saw Colter near La Charette. Notwithstanding his experiences, when he saw this large outfit pushing forth into the wilderness, along the precise route followed by Lewis and Clark, as was then intended, the old feeling asserted itself and, as Bradbury puts it, "he seemed to have a great inclination to accompany the expedition; but having been lately married, he reluctantly took leave of us."

Nothing further is positively known of Colter. Between this time and 1813 one "John Coulter" is known to have died in that region and it may have been Colter, the member of the Lewis and Clark expedition, the discoverer of the Yellowstone, the runner of the gauntlet, who nevertheless had little idea when alive that he had done anything that was to immortalize him in American history and hand down his name to successive generations as one who had served his country well.

GEORGE DREWYER

George Drewyer, or Drouillard, which is the correct form of the name, was beyond question one of the two or three most valuable men of the expedition. Where so many were deserving it is rather difficult to discriminate, but in this case it is a safe proposition.

Drewyer was the "interpreter and hunter" of the party, and as a hunter was invaluable. Lewis said of him: "A man of much merit; . . . peculiarly useful from his knowledge of the language of gesticulation, and his uncommon skill as a hunter and woodsman." Again, at Fort Clatsop, when game and meat became scarce they remarked:

Two hunters had been despatched in the morning, and one of them, Drewyer, had before evening killed seven elk. We should scarcely be able to subsist were it not for the exertions of this most excellent hunter. The game is scarce, and nothing is now even to be seen except elk, which for almost all the men are very difficult to be procured; but Drewyer, who is the offspring of a Canadian Frenchman and an Indian woman, has passed his life in the woods, and unites in a wonderful degree the dexterous aim of the frontier huntsman with the intuitive sagacity of the Indian, in pursuing the faintest tracks through the forest. All our men, however, have indeed become so expert with the rifle that we are never under apprehensions as to food; since, whenever there is game of any kind, we are almost certain of procuring it.

As will be seen in the course of the narrative, Drewyer was a right-hand man to the Captains and was with one or the other of them in most emergencies and situations of danger where skill, nerve, endurance, and judgment were needed.

After the disbandment of the expedition, Drewyer remained in the vicinity of St. Louis. Manuel Lisa, the astute Spanish trader, appreciated the value of the man and Drewyer became associated with him in his fur-trading expedition up the Yellowstone in 1807. It was popularly known as the expedition of Lisa and Drouillard. On this trip the latter became involved in a serious difficulty which is thus stated by Chittenden:

At the mouth of the Osage River, Antoine Bissonette, one of the engages, deserted. Lisa ordered a search for him and commanded that he be brought back dead or alive. Drouillard overtook and shot him, wounding him severely. Lisa put the wounded man in a boat and sent him back to St. Charles, doing all that was possible for his comfort; but he died on the way.

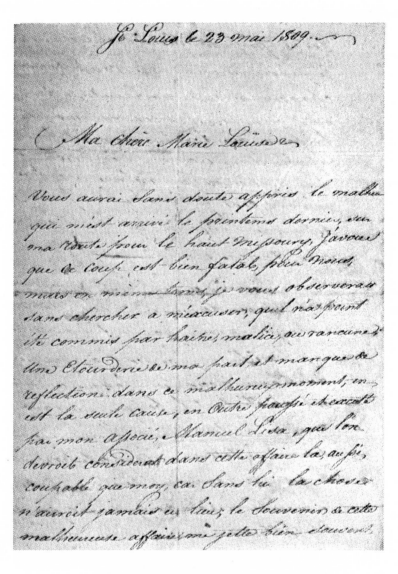

Facsimilie of the Drouillard Letter. Page 1

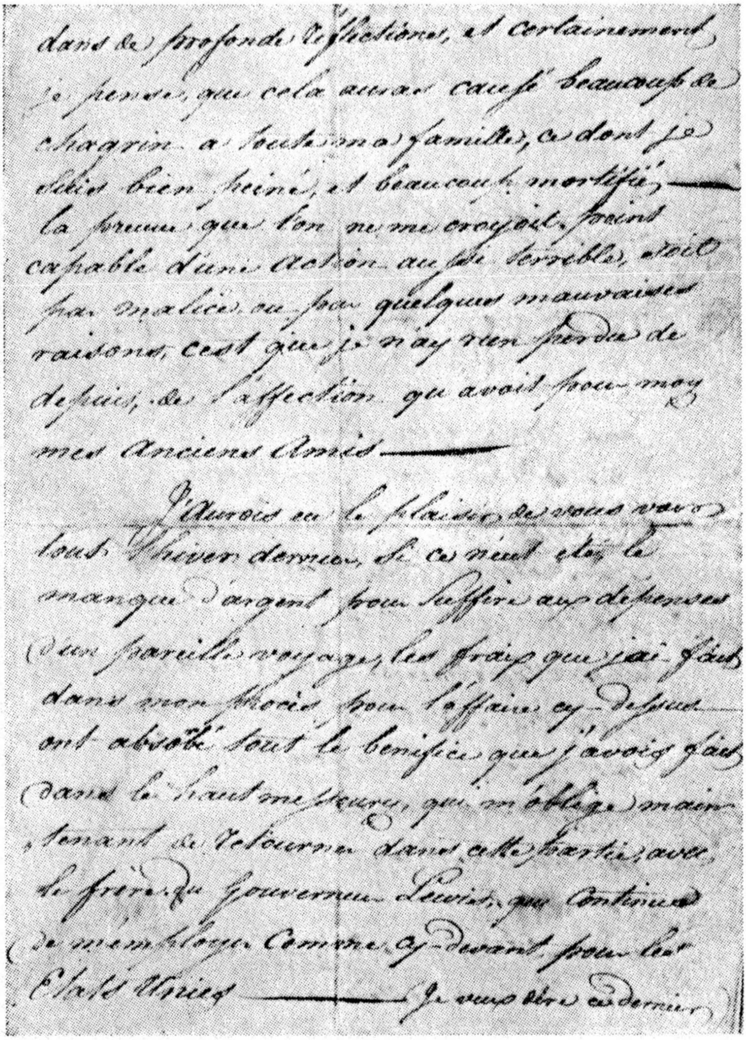
dans de profonde reflections, et certainement
je pense, que cela aurai causé beaucoup de
chagrin a toute ma famille, ce dont je
étois bien peiné, et beaucoup mortifié, —
la preuve que l'on ne me croyoit point
capable d'une action aussi terrible, étoit
par malice ou par quelques mauvaises
raisons, c'est que je n'ay rien perdu de
depuis, de l'affection qu'avoit pour moy
mes Anciens Amis —

J'aurois eu le plaisir de vous voir
tout l'hiver dernier, si ce n'eut été le
manque d'argent pour suffire aux depenses
d'un pareille voyage, les frais que j'ai fait
dans mon procès pour l'affaire cy-dessus
ont absorbé tout le benifice que j'avois fait
dans le haut missouri, qui m'oblige main-
tenant de retourner dans cette partie, avec
le frère du gouverneur Lewis, qui continue
de m'employer comme cy-devant pour les
Etats Unies ———— Je vous dirai en dernier

Facsimile of the Drouillard Letter. Page 2.

Je ne crois pas pouvoir revenir ou haut
missouri avant trois ans et aussitôt Je
me feray un devoir d'aller vous voir tous
Si quelques un de ma famille veulent me
faire l'amitié de m'écrire, ils adresseront leurs
lettres a Monsr Pascal Cerré a St Louis.

Ce dernier et son Epouse, quoique point connus
de ma famille au Détroit, se joignent à
moy et vous prie d'agréer leurs civilités,
ce sont les meilleurs Amis que je possède
. . . _____ Mes respects à notre
Maman que j'embrasse bien, ainsi que
tous mes freres et soeurs que je désire
beaucoup de voir _____

Votre très affectionné,

frère

yve Drouillard

NB. Ne m'oubliez point s'il vous plaît auprès de
made Raisonville, et sa famille

Made Jane Parrent, Détroit Sandwich

Facsimilie of the Drouillard Letter. Page 3

When Lisa and Drouillard returned the following year, 1808, Drouillard was tried for murder before J. B. Lucas, presiding judge, and Auguste Chouteau, associate. The jury found him not guilty.

The letter here reproduced, translated from the original French, and written by Drouillard in 1809, to his sister, evidently refers to the killing of Bissonette:

ST. LOUIS, May 23, 1809.

MY DEAR MARIE LOUISE:

You have without doubt learned of the misfortune which happened to me last spring on my way to the Upper Missouri. I admit that this misfortune was very fatal to us but at the same time, I would have you observe without trying to excuse myself, that this has not been done through malice, hatred or any evil intent. Thoughtlessness on my part and lack of reflection in this unhappy moment is the only cause of it, and moreover encouraged and urged by my partner, Manuel Lisa, who we ought to consider in this affair as guilty as myself for without him the thing would never have taken place. The recollection of this unhappy affair throws me very often in the most profound reflections, and certainly I think it has caused a great deal of grief to my family for which I am very sorry and very much mortified. That I have not lost the affection of my old friends proves that they did not believe me capable of an action so terrible through malice and bad intent.

I would have had the pleasure of seeing you all last winter if it had not been for the lack of money to cover the expenses of such a voyage. The expenses which I had through my lawsuit for the affair above mentioned have absorbed all my savings that I had made in the upper Missouri; this obliges me now to return to this part of the country with the brother of Governor Lewis who continues to employ me as before for the United States – (I mean the last one). [*I. e.,* Governor Lewis still employs him.]

I do not think I can return from the Upper Missouri before three years and just as soon as I return I shall be delighted to see you all. If some of my family will be kind enough to write to me they will address their letters to Monsieur Pascal Cerré at St. Louis. He and his wife although not known to my family in Detroit join with me and beg you to accept their civilities. They are the best friends that I possess in this country. My respects

to our Mother who I embrace well, also all my brothers and
sisters who I would like very much to see.

Your very affectionate brother,

(Signed)   GEORGE DROUILLARD.

P. S. Remember please to Madam Maisonville and her family.

Madam JAQUE PARRENT, Detroit, Sandwich.

This letter is inconsistent in its dates. "Last spring"
should undoubtedly be "spring before last," for the Lisa-
Drouillard expedition could not have left St. Louis in the
spring of 1808, reached the Big Horn River and built a fort,
trapped and returned so that Drouillard could think of
"seeing you all last winter" (1808-09) except for the expense
attendant upon his trial for shooting Bissonette. If the
expedition left St. Louis in the spring of 1807, the date given
by Chittenden, and "last spring" is changed to read as here
indicated, the letter is then consistent with itself.

Whether Drouillard returned "with a brother of Governor Lewis," I do not know, but when the first expedition of
the newly formed Missouri Fur Company, which left St.
Louis in the spring of 1809, arrived at the Three Forks of
the Missouri, Drouillard was one of them. Reuben Lewis, a
brother of Captain Lewis, is mentioned by Bradbury as
being in charge of the Missouri Fur Company's fort at the
Mandan towns in 1811, and Drouillard may have joined the
Three Forks expedition at that point as they came up the
river. If so, he never saw his family again. A fort was
built in the spring of 1810 at the Three Forks and Drouillard
was stationed there. But little trapping was done, however,
for the Blackfeet Indians hovered about and attacked the
trapping parties upon every occasion. I quote from Chittenden[1]:

Early in May, Drouillard with several Delaware Indians in
the employ of the company went out to hunt, contrary to the

[1] *The American Fur Trade, etc.*

advice of the rest of the party, who believed that Indians were prowling in the neighborhood. Their fears were quickly realized. Drouillard had not gone two miles when his party were ambushed by the Blackfeet and himself and two of his companions killed. From the appearance of the scene of this attack it was apparent that Drouillard made a desperate defense. He seems to have used his horse as a breastwork, turning him so as to shield himself constantly from the enemy. It was but a short time until the horse was killed and he himself was the next victim. A most painful feature of this affair was that it took place within ordinary hearing distance of relief, but owing to a high wind prevailing at the time, the firing was not heard.

Thus died a brave, valuable man who had rendered good service to his country, in that beautiful region which, five years before, he had first seen as an explorer.

WILLIAM BRATTON

Soon after the publication of *Wonderland 1900,* by the Northern Pacific Railway, its Passenger Department received a letter from Mrs. Fields, a daughter of William Bratton, who died in November, 1903, the receipt of which resulted in a correspondence between the writer and Mrs. Fields and her son, which developed facts of interest in connection with William Bratton, one of the members of the Lewis and Clark expedition.

Dr. Coues, in his complete work on Lewis and Clark, gave a roster of the expedition and, so far as known, brief statements concerning the individuals. Under the heading "Privates (23)," on page 254 (a foot-note), the first name and notation is, "William Bratton, Bratten, Brattin. No more known of him." The different spellings given refer to the varied manner in which the name Bratton was spelled in the journals of Lewis and Clark.

Of Bratton's earlier life, his descendants know little. He was born in 1778, in Augusta County, Va., of Irish parents. He was bound out at an early age to a gunsmith,

*The Discharge of Wm. Bratton from the Lewis and Clark Expedition
Signed by Captain Lewis.*

with whom he remained until he attained his majority. He became expert in the use of tools and made the best of the school facilities of the period, particularly after he became of age and was his own master.

After his return from the Lewis and Clark exploration he lived for a time in Kentucky, and he was near New Madrid, MO., at the time of the great earthquake in 1811. He was a soldier in the War of 1812, serving under Gen. Wm. Henry Harrison, was in the battle of Tippecanoe, saw Tecumseh after he was slain, and was one of those surrendered by General Winchester at Frenchtown, – now Monroe, – Mich., in 1813. For several years before marriage he followed the milling business and then devoted himself to farming. He was married in 1819, lived for a time at Bowling Green, Ky., then moved, first to the vicinity of Terre Haute, and then to the neighborhood of Waynetown, Ind. He was the father of eight sons and two daughters, and he died in 1841, and is buried at Waynetown, Montgomery County, Ind.

Upon Sergeant Floyd's death, Bratton was one of the three men voted for as his successor by the members of the expedition, Gass being the successful candidate. Bratton recounted to his family many of his adventures during the exploration and they tally with the published records. It is not improbable that Bratton was one of the "blacksmiths" that were so useful at Fort Mandan, his trade being that of a gunsmith, and an extended reference to this is made in dealing with the life of Shields.

As Sergeant Floyd is noted as the only one of this expedition who died, so Bratton, one of the candidates for Floyd's position, stands out prominently as the only man who was seriously ill for a long time. This experience he seems not to have related to his family, and as it was rather a remarkable one, I have picked it out from the records of the party. When the expedition reached the Pacific coast,

Bratton was one of the five men sent to the seaside to evaporate the sea water in order to obtain a supply of salt.

The men left Fort Clatsop on December 28, 1805. On February 10, 1806, Bratton and Gibson were reported as quite sick, and on February 15th, the two men returned to Clatsop. Gibson had fever and Bratton was suffering from lumbago, apparently. The journal of February 15th states: "Bratton is still weak and complains of lumbago, which pains him to move. We gave him barks," evidently, from what follows, a decoction made from the bark of some tree or trees, and tonic in its nature. Then follow "Dr. Scott's pills," and, on March 7th, a good rubbing from a prepared liniment of alcohol, camphor, castile soap, and laudanum. The latter benefited the patient considerably for a time, but he again grew weaker, so that on March 21st, two days before the return journey was begun, his recovery was doubtful. However, while unable to walk, he made the trip successfully to Camp Chopunnish, on the Clearwater River.

Bratton regained his flesh but not his strength, and finally heroic treatment was decided upon, and, as it was a terrible ordeal, one borrowed from the medical practice of the Indians and remarkable, in this case, for its results, I transcribe an account of it from the journal:

Besides administering medical relief to the Indians we are obliged to devote much of our time to the care of our own invalids. The child of Sacajaweah is very unwell; and with one of the men [Bratton] we have ventured an experiment of a very robust nature. He has been for some time sick, but has now recovered his flesh, eats heartily and digests well, but has so great a weakness in the loins that he cannot walk or even sit upright without extreme pain. After we had, in vain, exhausted the resources of our art, one of the hunters [Shields] mentioned that he had known persons in similar situations to be restored by violent sweats, and at the request of the patient, we permitted the remedy to be applied. For this purpose a hole about four feet deep and three in diameter was dug in the earth, and heated well by a large fire in the bottom of it. The fire was then taken out and an arch formed over the hole by means of willow poles, and covered with several blankets so as to make a perfect awning. The patient being stripped naked, was seated under this on a bench, with a piece of board for his feet, and with a jug of water sprinkled the bottom and sides of the hole, so as to keep up as hot a steam as he could bear. After remaining twenty minutes in this situation he was taken out, immediately plunged twice in cold water, and brought back to the hole, where he resumed the vapor bath. During all this time he drank copiously a strong infusion of horse-mint, which was used as a substitute for Seneca root, which our informant said he had seen employed on these occasions. . . . At the end of three-quarters of an hour he was again withdrawn from the hole, carefully wrapped, and suffered to cool gradually. This operation was performed yesterday; this morning he walked about and is nearly free from pain.

This kill-or-cure process seems to have cured effectually, for Bratton rapidly recovered and was soon able to perform his regular duties. His illness extended over a period of about four months, the first mention of it being February 10, 1806, and the last, June 5, 1806, but no permanent ill effects seem to have resulted.

No portrait of Bratton is extant. His connection with Lewis and Clark's expedition is recounted on his monument. The initial "E." there shown in his name was added by him in his later life,

It will at once be admitted that Bratton gave a full quota of service to his country, and future historians will not find it necessary now to place after Bratton's name the words, "No more known of him."

JOHN SHIELDS

John Shields was another Kentuckian – all fine fellows, those men from Kentucky! – and he was "an artist in repairing our guns and accoutrements," Lewis says. He is again highly mentioned in the same connection when the expedition was encamped at Maria's River.

This man has been supposed to be the Tubal Cain, the blacksmith, weapon repairer, and battle-ax maker at Fort Mandan, whose operations were so productive in procuring corn and meat during the long winter. From the foregoing excerpt and other references it seems hard to dispute that conclusion. But Bratton also was a gunsmith, although he did not follow his trade after his term of apprenticeship expired, and Willard was a gunsmith and blacksmith.

Many times does the Lewis and Clark report make mention of the blacksmith, and in the codices the word is used in the plural several times. On March 13, 1805, for example, we read: "Mr. McKenzie came to see us, as did also many Indians, who are so anxious for battle-axes that our smiths have not a moment's leisure, and procure us an abundance of corn." This would surely indicate that there were more than one. But there is, I find, some outside evidence relating to the blacksmith.

Larocque, a trader of the Northwest Fur Company, who was resident among these Indians a part of the same winter, in his[1] *The Missouri Journal,* under date of January 20, 1805, records:

My landlord went down to the Americans [Lewis and Clark] to get his gun mended; they have a very expert smith who is always employed making different things and working for the Indians, who are grown very fond of them, although they disliked them at first.

Charles MacKenzie, a member of Larocque's party, in his journal,[2] *The Mississouri Indians,* after referring to the fact that the Grosventres Indians did not feel very kindly toward the Americans, continues:

"Had these Whites come amongst us," said the chiefs, "with

[1] In Masson, I – 1889 *The Missouri Journal,* 1804-05, by Fr. Antoine Larocque
[2] In Masson, I – 1889.

charitable views they would have loaded their Great Boat with necessaries. It is true they have ammunition, but they prefer throwing it away idly than sparing a shot of it to a poor Mandane."

The Indians admired the air gun, as it could discharge forty shots out of one load, but they dreaded the magic of the owners. "Had I these white warriors in the upper plains" said the Gros Ventres chief, "my young men on horseback would soon do for them, as they would for so many wolves, for," continued he, "there are only two sensible men among them, the worker of iron and the mender of guns."

This rodomontadian address may or may not have been exaggerated, but it seems to indicate that there were two metal workers among the Lewis and Clark men that winter.

In examining the chronology of this matter a possible explanation would seem to be that, at the beginning, there was one iron worker, and later, when the value of the work was apparent, a second one was discovered and set to work. Under the circumstances it is hardly a violent assumption that Shields was the first, and Bratton or Willard the second one, of the "workers of iron and menders of guns."

Shields did considerable hunting while at Fort Mandan, and even though he may have been the original blacksmith, he by no means confined himself to that work.

GEORGE SHANSON

Dr. Coues in his reference to George Shannon says that he was "perhaps the one man on the expedition whom either of the Captains would have been most likely to meet at home on terms of social equality."

Shannon was of a good Protestant Irish family. The father had fought in the Revolution and he died in 1803, frozen while out hunting, near his home in St. Clair County, Ohio, leaving a widow and nine childlen. George was the eldest, and Wilson Shannon, afterward Governor of Ohio,

Housewife and needles used by George Shannon on the Lewis and Clark expedition, and now owned by Mrs. Rev. F. P. Farmer, Shannon's granddaughter, of Portland Ore. This housewife was of read leather, was provided with pockets, and measured, when open, 7-1/2 by 15-3/8 inches.

was the youngest. George was born in Pennsylvania in 1785, and at fourteen years of age he was sent back to that State to his mother's people to go to school. When about seventeen he met Captain Lewis, who was on his way to St. Louis, and he ran away to join him. He is described as being a handsome man, with blue eyes, black hair, always smooth faced, very graceful, and a fine conversationalist.

He graduated from Transylvania University at Lexington, Kentucky, studied law in Philadelphia, and graduated in the same law class with Sam. Houston. He married Miss Ruth Snowden Price, at Lexington, Ky., in 1813, and he was Judge of the Circuit Court at Lexington for many years, removed to St. Louis in 1828, and then to St. Charles, MO., where he again became Judge. He died suddenly at Palmyra, MO., while holding court, in 1836.[1] Shannon was a prominent Mason and was buried with Masonic ceremonies at Palmyra. His wife died about the same time, and the family soon after being broken up, the remains were never removed to St. Charles, as was contemplated, and all traces of the grave have since been lost.

So slow were the means of communication in those days, that Judge Shannon was dead and buried before his family even knew he had been ill.

It was almost a marvel that Shannon ever returned alive from the great exploration. Twice, at least, he got lost. One is, at first, inclined to feel that he must have lacked one important requisite for such work – a good head for topography, – or, as a topographer would say, that he did not possess the faculty of orientation. But as one studies the situation and reflects upon it, I think this view will hardly hold and that the reverse was true. Neither time that he

[1] This is as his descendants understand it I find no public record of his second judgeship, but instead, that he was United States Attorney for Missouri.

was lost does Shannon seem to have been much, if at all, at fault in the matter, and he certainly exhibited excellent judgment in finding the party again, entirely unaided by them. As the expedition progressed he appears to have improved in mountaineering and woodcraft, for time and again he was sent way alone, or with only one companion, to hunt and explore.

The traditions of his family tell of one of the times when he was lost and wandered into an Indian encampment. An old squaw prepared a cake for him and just before giving it to him to eat she spit upon it. This act, Shannon always thought, proceeded from kindness on the squaw's part and was intended to prevent him from too rapid and over indulgence, which in his famished condition might have had a disastrous effect. The woman afterwards carefully nursed him back to strength.

I find no incident related by Lewis and Clark that this episode seems to fit. It may have occurred, however, during the winter at Fort Mandan.

That Shannon was a man of ability, even in his earlier years, is proved by the fact that he was the one man of the entire party sent on to Philadelphia to assist Biddle in the preparation of the report of the expedition, in 1810, and Clark's letter of introduction is highly commendatory.

Shannon was one of the party of Ensign Nathaniel Pryor-Sergeant Pryor of the Lewis and Clark expedition – that, in 1807, escorted the Mandan Chief Shahaka, or Big White, on his return to his village. The attempt failed, the party being attacked by the Arikara Indians near Bismarck, N. D., and compelled to relinquish the effort. In this fight Shannon was shot in the leg and he was unable to receive proper surgical attention until they had retraced their entire course down the river to St. Louis. He was eighteen months in an army hospital at Fort Bellefontaine, and he suffered the amputation of his leg near the knee. He used a wooden leg the remainder of his life and it is stated was known as Peg-leg Shannon, because of that fact.

ALEXANDER H. WILLARD

It is but recently that those specially interested in Lewis and Clark have come into possession of facts relating to Alexander H. Willard.

Through Mrs. Eva Emery Dye, I have been privileged to examine some correspondence between her and some of Willard's descendants, and to extract therefrom the facts here recorded.

Willard was born in New Hampshire in 1777, and ran away from home when very young.

He was another of the "young men from Kentucky" who joined Lewis and Clark, and in later years he enjoyed telling how his fine physique enabled him to pass the inspection for enlistment in the expedition. Willard said there were more than one hundred who failed to pass the examination.

Like Bratton, Willard was at all times alert to serve his country. In 1798, when a bitter war with France seemed imminent, Willard enlisted; he was engaged in the campaign against Tecumseh in 1811, and he, with four sons, also served in the Black Hawk War in 1832.

After the return of the Lewis and Clark expedition, Willard settled near St. Louis. He removed for a time to Illinois, but soon returned to Missouri. Willard maintained his connection with Captain (General) Clark, and was a personal friend and neighbor of his at St. Louis for several years. Clark at one time sent him on an important mission as bearer of dispatches to Prairie du Chien, which he accomplished successfully.

Willard married Miss Eleanor McDonald, in 1807, it is
said, and had a large family, being the father of seven sons
and five daughters. One son was named after Lewis and
another after Clark. Lewis Willard and a sister are still

Alexander H. Willard and Wife.

living at Cottonwood, Ariz.; another sister, eighty-nine
years of age, resides at Ball's Ferry, Cal.

In 1823 Willard settled near Platteville, Wis., and remained there until 1852, when he followed some of his
family who had gone to California in 1839. He crossed the
plains with ox teams in the good old-fashioned way, and

located in the Sacramento Valley. He died on March 6,
1865, aged almost eighty-eight years, and is buried at
Franklin, near Sacramento, Cal.

Willard and his progeny have literally done their part
to fulfil the scriptural injunction to replenish the earth, for
at the time of his death Willard counted twelve children,
fifty grandchildren, and thirty great-grandchildren.

Willard is said to have been both a skilful gunsmith and
blacksmith, and he may have been the unknown blacksmith,
at Fort Mandan, or one of two or three blacksmiths whose
knowledge of that trade was there utilized.

Willard is said to have kept a journal of the exploration,
which was accidentally destroyed. If this is so, it may settle the question as to who was the seventh individual who
kept a journal, mentioned in the Lewis and Clark narrative.

SACÁGAWEA

There were many heroes, there was but one heroine in
this band of immortals. And at the start I wish to take off
my hat to the modest, womanly, unselfish, patient, enduring
little Shoshone squaw, the Bird-woman of the Minnetarees,
or Hidatsa, who uncomplainingly canoed, trudged, climbed,
starved, with the best men of the party, and that too with
a helpless papoose strapped to her back. All honor to her!
Her skin was of the color of copper, her heart beat as true
as steel. Through all the long, dreary, racking months of
toil, she bore her part like a Spartan. While among the
women of nearly every tribe the expedition encountered,
conduct, to our minds, of a questionable, unchaste sort was
a common experience, not a breath of suspicion was whis-
pered against this unpretentious slave-wife of a frontier
Frenchman. Instead of being a drag on the progress of the
party, she proved time and again the inspiration, the genius
of the occasion. Although only a squaw of the Shoshone

tribe, captured when a child and carried as a slave to the
Mandan country and purchased by Chaboneau for a wife,
she interpreted when her husband could not, and at critical
points gave suggestions and advice which the chivalrous
Captains weighed at their true value. They were not afraid,
either, frankly to acknowledge their debt to her, and they
speak most highly of her in referring to their parting at the
Mandan towns in 1806.

This woman should, long ago, have had a granite shaft,
taken from her native hills, erected in her memory on that
limestone rock at the Three Forks of the Missouri, where
every traveller on the Northern Pacific railway trains can
see it and be reminded of what we owe to a poor Snake
Indian squaw, who never received a cent from a civilized
nation for all that she underwent in five thousand miles of
wanderings.

I think I am not hypercritical in saying that, unless there
were prohibitive reasons unknown to us, it reflects no credit
on Lewis or Clark that this woman was not paid a sum of
money or made the recipient of suitable presents commensurate with the services she rendered them. Worded appreciation is all very well in its way, but it does not fill the
measure of indebtedness due in cases like this, and the
President and Congress were not blameless, in that, when
substantial rewards were made to many of the men, this
woman received no recognition whatever at the hands of a
great nation.

The State of Montana should erect a monument to her
at the Three Forks of the Missouri, and it now appears
probable that this may be done. I am glad to state that,
at the suggestion of my friend, Dr. F. W. Traphagen,
late of Bozeman, Mont., the United States Geological
Survey has recently made belated acknowledgment of
Sacágawea's services and has named one of the finest

peaks in the Bridger Range in Montana, Sacágawea Peak.[1] It overlooks the valleys of the Gallatin, Jefferson, and Madison rivers, including the Fort Rock; the spot where this woman was captured, when a child, by the Minnetarees; the place where she stood and pointed out to her Captain the pass – Bozeman – he should take to cross the mountains to the Yellowstone; and it looked down upon the little band of heroes, guided by her as they trailed their way up the Gallatin River Valley to that same pass, which should have been called Sacágawea Pass long before Bozeman ever saw it.

The orthography of the Bird-woman's name, as given by the Captains, Sacajaweah, is wrong. The word is a Hidatsa, not a Shoshone word, and is formed from two Indian words. In a letter to me Dr. Washington Matthews of Washington, D. C., an army surgeon and author of a Hidatsa Dictionary, says:

> In my dictionary I give the Hidatsa word for bird as *"Tsakáka."* *Ts* is often changed to *S* and *K* to *G* in this and other Indian languages, so "Sacága" would not be a bad spelling and thus Charbonneau may have pronounced his wife's name; but never "Sacaja" [the Hidatsa language contains no j]. I fancy that all this confusion may have arisen from an editorial mistake and that Captain Lewis [or Clark?] did not form his *G* well. *Wea* [or Wia or mia] means woman.

There are then four simple forms in which the word may be correctly used: Tsakákawea, Sakákawea, Sakágawea, Sacágawea. The last more nearly approaches the form used by Lewis and Clark and is, perhaps, the preferable one to use.

Sacágawea was of the royal family of the Shoshoni, her brother, Cameahwait, being their chief. This fact proved a most fortunate circumstance for the explorers at a time

---

[1] It now seems probable that a bronze statue of Sacágawea will be seen at the Lewis and Clark Centennial in Portland, Ore., in 1905, erected by contributions from the patriotic women of the Northwest.

Sacágawea, the Bird-woman, from a Drawing by E. S. Paxson.

127

when success and failure were balancing themselves in the
scales of chance.

The little Bird-woman became greatly attached to the
Captains and their men, met all the hardships of that long
journey like the splendid heroine and good mother that
she was, and with her husband, left the party upon arrival
at the Mandan villages, on the return, in 1806.

That she was something more than a common squaw, one
of some little ambition to lift herself above the lot to which
nature and her husband held her, is evidenced by the following quotation from Brackenridge, who saw her in 1811:

We had on board a Frenchman named Charboneau, with his
wife, an Indian woman of the Snake nation, both of whom had
accompanied Lewis and Clark to the Pacific, and were of great
service. The woman, a good creature, of a mild and gentle
disposition, [is] greatly attached to the whites, whose manners
and dress she tries to imitate, but she had become sickly, and
longed to revisit her native country; her husband, also, who
had spent many years among the Indians, had become weary of
a civilized life.

It was hard to transform herself and live after the
manner of her white sisters, undoubtedly, and it was not
necessary to do so to establish her place in history. As Dr.
J. K. Hosmer, the well-known historical writer, says:

Her doing was of such a character as to make it quite right
to claim for her a high place among heroines; in the whole line
of Indian heroines indeed from Pocahontas to Ramona, not one
can be named whose title to honored remembrance is any better
than hers.

And what of that sturdy infant explorer, who, while yet
at his mother's breast, voyaged across the continent? What
became of him after the return to the villages on the
Missouri?

A few years ago it befell the writer to rescue from

obscurity the writings of Warren Angus Ferris,[1] an employee, from 1830 to 1835, of the American Fur Company, and afterwards a land surveyor by profession. Ferris's story was a valuable one of the fur days, and covers much of the territory previously explored by Lewis and Clark. The chronology of his narrative was, however, badly mixed by the compositors or editors, or both, and therefore it requires careful scrutiny in its interpretation.

The only reference to Sacágawea's infant known to me, after Lewis and Clark, occurs in Ferris's narrative. While at Ogden's Hole, in the latter part of 1830, Ferris heard from another frontiersman, J. H. Stevens, of the adventures of a party under the well-known trapper Robidoux, or Roubidoux, that same year, which he incorporates in his story. The party were en route from the falls of Snake River — Shoshone Falls — to the "Malade" River, in southern Idaho, and after narrowly escaping death on the desert from thirst, finally found the river and thus saved their lives. The narrative then runs as follows:

We spent the night and following morning in the charitable office of conveying water to our enfeebled companions who lingered behind, and the poor beasts that had also been left by the way, and succeeded in getting them all to camp, except the person and animals of Charbineau, one of our men, who could no where be found, and was supposed to have wandered from the trail and perished.

Then, in a foot-note, is added:

This was the infant, who together with his mother, was saved from a sudden flood near the Falls of the Missouri, by Capt. Lewis, — *vide* Lewis in Lewis and Clark's Expedition. [It was Clark, however, not Lewis, who saved his life.]

---

[1] For the story of this discovery see *Wonderland 1901*, published by Northern Pacific Railway Company, St. Paul, Minn.

Ferris's narrative then continues:

We trapped the Maladi to its source, then crossed to the head of Gordiaz River, and trapped it down to the plains of Snake River, from whence we returned to Cache Valley by way of Porteneuf, where we found Dripps and Fontenelle, together with our lost companion Charbineaux. He [Charbineau] states that he lost our trail but reached the river Maladi after dark, where he discovered a village of Indians. Fearing they were unfriendly, he resolved to retrace his steps and find the main company. In pursuance of this plan he filled a beaver skin with water, and set off on his lonely way. After eleven days wandering, during which he suffered a good deal from hunger, he attained his object and reached the company at Porteneuf. The village he saw was the lodges of the Hudson Bay Company, and had he passed a short distance below, he would have found our camp. But his unlucky star was in the ascendant and it caused him eleven days toil, danger, and privation to find his friends.

If this account is to be relied upon, it would appear that the boy retained the habits of travel acquired in earliest infancy, and in the great competitive period of the fur-trading days, drifted far from his old geographical moorings. At the time alluded to he was twenty-five years of age.

George F. Ruxton, in *Life in the Far West* – 1849 – mentions a Chabonard, but gives no clue as to who he may have been. Other early writers also mention, in the same way, an individual, or individuals, of this name.

TOUSSAINT CHABONEAU

Perhaps the most picturesque and unique character of the expedition was Toussaint Chaboneau, the French-Canadian interpreter, whom the explorers found at Fort Mandan. Chaboneau was living at Metaharta, the middle one of the Grosventre or Minnetaree villages on Knife River, where he acted as an interpreter when opportunity offered. After Lewis and Clark the next mention we find of Chaboneau, or Charbonneau, as he becomes with later writers, is by Brackenridge, in 1811, as noted in the remarks regarding Sacágawea. He was a familiar character on the Missouri River for years and is mentioned by some of the early writers, notably by Maximilian, whose book is full of "Charbonneau." Neither Maximilian nor any other of the explorers, traders, and scientific men who visited the upper Missouri after Lewis and Clark, with the exception of Brackenridge, so far as I have observed, refers to Chaboneau's wife, the Bird-woman, or to the infant.

Chaboneau – to adhere to the name as Lewis and Clark rendered it – seems to have been connected with the Northwest Fur Company in 1793, and he went to live at the Mandan towns in 1796.

The three Minnetaree or Hidatsa villages on the Knife River then "stood precisely as they do now," Maximilian says in 1833, but the Mandan towns were several miles farther down the Missouri. The trade relations with St. Louis which later became so important had not been established in 1796, and Chaboneau, the only white man in the locality, procured his supplies from the English traders to the north.

Chaboneau related to Maximilian the "circumstances which took place" during the thirty-seven years of his residence there.

Chaboneau served as interpreter for the American Fur Company and also for Sublette and Campbell. The last mention of the Frenchman that I have found was by Larpenteur in 1838, when "old Mr. Charbonneau," as he had then become, served the latter a good turn at an opportune time.

It has been rather the fashion of latter-day writers and

critics to sneer at and decry the old interpreter. That the man was not a bright and shining light, that he had his faults and frailties, that he easily lost his head in emergencies, is all true enough, but this is just as true of many a man higher in the social and intellectual scale than was Chaboneau. He was not a sailor or steersman, a soldier or blacksmith; "he was useful as an interpreter only, in which capacity he discharged his duties with good faith," Lewis says. That he attempted a bit of sharp practice with the Captains at Fort Mandan and tried to make a better bargain for number one was likely enough owing to certain evil influences rather than to an innate sense of knavery, and he soon repented his action, was manly enough to apologize for it, and performed his duty thereafter in the main satisfactorily. Larocque, the Northwest Company trader, in his journal for 1804-05, at the Mandan towns, refers to "Charbonneau" in a way entirely creditable to him: "Spoke to Charbonneau about helping as interpreter in the trade to the Big-Bellies; he told me that, being engaged to the Americans, he could not come without leave from Captain Lewis, and desired me to speak to him, which I did," with the result that Lewis gave consent. This certainly was as honorable an action on "Charbonneau's" part as one could ask.

That the man struck his wife, the patient little Bird-woman, at least once, was certainly an inexcusable, reprehensible act; but he was a volatile French-Canadian, and thus to chastise an Indian woman was not an uncommon thing among the Indians themselves. I have been informed more than once that unless this was done once in a while the woman herself had little or no respect for her liege lord, particularly if he was a white man, as was Chaboneau, but how true this may really have been or is now I know not. Certainly it is repugnant enough to our sense of conjugal reciprocity, but it may serve to mitigate the man's action in a degree, and better white men than Chaboneau have done the same thing to white wives. That the man had sense enough to marry the slave, after buying her, is something to his credit.

No one, I think, can read Maximilian without feeling that Chaboneau was, after all, a man of fairly commendable traits considering his environment, notwithstanding that he struck his wife, in comparison with whom he was, as Coues states, "a minus function."

Chaboneau probably lived among the Hidatsa until his death. He found their language a hard one to master, and to Maximilian "he candidly confessed, he could never learn to pronounce it correctly," at which Dr. Matthews "marvels not," for it seems to be a language of intricacies.

I have made considerable effort to ascertain definitely what became of Chaboneau and the Bird-woman, and when they died, but without pronounced success.

The old men among the Hidatsa Indians really know nothing of them. Lean, or Poor Wolf, an admirable man, but now eighty-three years of age, blind, infirm, and of treacherous memory, thinks he has a dim recollection of the name Charbonneau and of a girl who died in 1837 who was his daughter or granddaughter. Her name was Hopatówiash, Cornstalk woman. This, however, even if reliable, adds little or nothing to our knowledge of Chaboneau, Sacágawea, or the younger Chaboneau.

F. F. Gerard, an old interpreter among these people at Fort Berthold, says that he was told that both Chaboneau and his wife were carried off in the epidemic of smallpox that raged in 1837, but this conflicts with Larpenteur, who saw the former in 1838. They may have died during a subsequent epidemic of smallpox. One, "Tonsart Chabono," undoubtedly the Lewis and Clark Chaboneau, was made interpreter at the "U. S. MO. Sub-Agency," July 1, 1837, at a salary of $300.

THE OTHER MEN

Of the other men who made the round trip to Fort Clatsop and return to St. Louis, no extended mention can be made. Of Collins, M'Neal, and Wiser, absolutely nothing seems to be known; Potts may have been the man killed on the tributary of the Jefferson River in the adventure noted in recounting Colter's life; Cruzatte and Labiche were French "watermen" or boatmen; Lepage was enlisted at Fort Mandan to replace Newman, discharged; Warner and Whitehouse were two of the "nine young men from Kentucky"; Gibson was from Mercer County, Penn.; Frazier of Vermont; Goodrich, Hall, Howard, of Massachusetts; Thompson of Indiana, and Windsor were taken from various forts after inspection by either Lewis or Clark.

The two Fields brothers, of whom little seems to be known, were Kentuckians and were "two of the most active and enterprising young men" who joined the exploration, and "it was their peculiar fate to have been engaged in all the most dangerous and difficult scenes of the voyage," a statement that is entirely true, and it may well be added that they justified every responsibility and trust placed upon them.

York, it is easily imagined, was the observed of all observers, the curiosity of all the party, to the red men. He was a negro slave servant to Captain Clark, and the one individual who extracted from the exploration the largest amount of purely physical and superficial enjoyment. His color, kinky hair, size, and prodigious strength were a revelation to the Indians, and he was looked upon as a very god. He was the greatest kind of "great medicine," and the tribes from the mouth of the Missouri to the mouth of the Columbia took particular pains to propitiate his sable majesty, and he was overwhelmed with feminine attentions. The Lewis and Clark exploration was the golden age of existence to York, the Virginian negro.

NOTE TO PAGE 126

A curious coincidence has recently come to my notice regarding the name "Sacágawea."

K. E. Wadsworth, United States Indian Agent at the Shoshone Indian Agency, Wyoming, writes me that the agency interpreters insist that the form of the word as given by Lewis and Clark, "Sacajaweah," comes from two Shoshone words, "Saca," boat, or canoe, and "Jawea," to launch, or push off, the meaning of "Sacajaweah," therefore, being boat launcher.

The fact that Lewis and Clark rendered "Sacajaweah" as "Bird-woman," however, disposes of the contention that the word, as they used it, is of Shoshone origin; it was beyond doubt a Hidatsa word, but the coincidence is an interesting one.

The Bureau of Ethnology, Washington, D. C., inform me that it is not at all probable that the word is a Shoshone word.

CHAPTER IV

WOOD RIVER TO FORT MANDAN

THE long winter was ended and spring, with its melting snows, streams running full-banked to the gulf, trees putting forth their leaves, and birds carolling their lays, had burst in full tide. We can imagine that after the long delay and the winter of inaction, our forerunners of empire were impatient to be off and away, to launch their boats upon the swirling flood and pull away into the heart of the unknown region which lay before them. The Louisiana Purchase had changed greatly the aspect of matters. They were to explore now their own country – and their own country – men behind them were looking forward with more and more interest to the results of their exploration.

We have already discussed the composition of the expedition. A most important feature was its means of transportation. The first stage of its journeyings was to be by water, up the swift, muddy current of the Missouri, and the navigation of this stream was no child's play, with its snags and "sawyers," sandbars and caving banks, high winds and dangers from hostile Indians.

The means of transport were three boats; a keel-boat or batteau, fifty-five feet long, drawing three feet of water, having "one large square sail and twenty-two oars" for motive power; and two open boats, "periogues," one propelled by six and the other by seven oars. The large boat was quite an affair, having a forecastle and cabin, and so arranged that in case of attack those on board might fight under cover. Two horses were also "to be led along the banks of the river, for the purpose of bringing home game, or hunting in case of scarcity."

Before the day of the steamboat on the Missouri – 1819 – the keel-boat was the most pretentious and important means of water transportation. The methods of operating this craft, especially on an upstream journey, were novel and interesting, and I quote a portion of Chittenden's description:

> The means of propulsion were various, and were intended to utilize all the forces which man and nature rendered available. The cordelle was the main reliance – a long line attached to the top of a high mast, which stood a little forward of the center of the boat. It passed through a ring, which was fastened by a short line to the bow to help guide the boat, and was drawn by from twenty to forty men strung along the shore. The reason for attaching it to the mast was that it might swing clear of the brush on the bank.
>
> It often happened at river crossings and elsewhere that the cordelle could not be used, and in such cases poles had to be resorted to. These were of various lengths suited to convenient handling, and were equipped with balls or knobs at the upper ends to rest in the hollow of the shoulder. To propel the boat by means of these poles the voyageurs were ranged in single file on each side of the deck near the bow, facing aft. Planting their poles on the river bottom, pointing down stream, they pushed steadily against them, at the same time walking towards the stern along the *passe avant,* a narrow walk some fifteen inches wide on each side of the cargo box, while the boat, yielding to their pressure, moved ahead.

The oars were used only in deep water and the sail was a very effective adjunct oftentimes, as the winds on the river frequently blow with great violence. The average rate of progress of these boats was from twelve to fifteen miles per day.

The "periogue" or pirogue seems to have been what was afterwards known among watermen as the Mackinaw.

It was flat-bottomed, forty or fifty feet long, twelve feet wide, and had three or four feet depth of hold. It appears to have been made after one of two patterns, one short or tapering at both ends, the other having a pointed bow but square stern. They were commodious, of light draft, yet carried heavy loads.

The quantity of supplies, camp equipment, arms, and ammunition, etc., necessary for the comfort and subsistence of such a body of men as constituted this expedition was of course large. In addition, there were sundry articles of barter suitable for trade with the Indians, whose good-will they were to propitiate, and from whom they must necessarily obtain much that was needed to support life, it being impossible to transport enough food supplies for this purpose. They carried along flour, pork, meal, etc., with whiskey, but no mention appears of tea or coffee. Fresh meat was to be supplied by the fish and wild game found.

The necessary stores were subdivided into seven bales, and one box containing a small portion of each article in case of accident. They consisted of a great variety of clothing, working utensils, locks, flints, powder, ball, and articles of the greatest use. To these were added fourteen bales and one box of Indian presents, distributed in the same manner, and composed of richly laced coats and other articles of dress, medals, flags, knives, and tomahawks for the chiefs, ornaments of different kinds, particularly beads, looking-glasses, handkerchiefs, paints, and generally such articles as were deemed best calculated for the taste of the Indians.

The rifles, tomahawks, and knives for the expedition were made at Harper's Ferry. There, too, was made the steel frame of a canoe which was the apple of Lewis's eye and which it was hoped would prove, as the Indians would say, "great medicine." It weighed ninety-nine, and its "burthen" was 1770 pounds, and we shall learn more of it at the Great Falls of the Missouri.

Of the medals taken along and of which much use was made by the explorers, there were three sizes or grades, one, the largest and the preferred one, "a medal with the likeness

Route of Lewis and Clark – Wood River to Heart River.

of the President of the United States"; the second, "a medal representing some domestic animals"; the third, "medals with the impression of a farmer sowing grain." A description and illustrations of the first are given farther along, the medal itself having been, as will be explained, taken from the grave of an Indian chieftain on the banks of the Clearwater River in Idaho. I have found in *The Northwest Coast,* by James G. Swan, a cut of a medal of the third class, but I have seen no representation of the one of the second class. The third class medal was made of pewter, Swan states. These medals were given to chiefs only. At the present time the U. S. Mint seems to strike off a new medal at the incoming of each new administration, but the Mint authorities appear to know nothing of the medals used by Lewis and Clark.

At length the ice in the Missouri had passed out and, everything being ready, at from three to four o'clock P.M., May 14, 1804, the *voyageurs,* leaving their winter's cantonment, pushed out into the stream, and the great exploration had begun. Floyd states the hour of leaving as three o'clock; Gass makes no mention of the hour, and Clark, as per the literal excerpt from the codex here given, makes the hour four o'clock. "I Set out at 4 o,clock P.M, in the presence of many of the neighbouring inhabitants, and proceeded on under a Jentle brease up the Missourie."

Captain Lewis was detained by business at St. Louis and thus was prevented from actually making the start with his comrades.

On the 15th and 16th the party went leisurely on, reaching St. Charles at two o'clock P.M. of the 16th, where they remained until May 21st.

The matter of having a careful and complete daily record kept of the progress, incidents, and results of the expedition had been carefully considered by Mr. Jefferson and Captain Lewis. In pursuance of this object the two Captains kept an elaborate itinerary, notes were made of scientific and all other matters of importance, maps and sketches were drawn, and particular care was taken to provide against loss or danger to these papers by keeping them in sealed tin receptacles.

In addition, as we know from Lewis's letter of April 7, 1805, to Jefferson, from Fort Mandan, "we have encouraged our men to keep journals, and seven of them do." Five of these men were Sergeants Floyd, Ordway, and Gass, and Robert Frazer, or Frazier, and Joseph Whitehouse. Sergeant Pryor is supposed to have kept a journal and Shannon would have been a seventh man likely to do so, but if he did, his descendants know nothing of it.

Of these journals, those of Gass and Floyd are the only ones that have ever been published, and no knowledge exists as to what became of the others except Whitehouse's, which has recently been purchased from his descendants and will be published by Dodd, Mead & Co., in connection with the Thwaites edition of the Lewis and Clark journals. The descendants of the men who kept these unpublished journals – or any others who could do so – would confer a benefit upon the public if they could aid in unearthing those manuscripts if, perchance, they have not been lost or destroyed.

Now that the explorers are fairly off, and while waiting a day or so at St. Charles for Captain Lewis, it will be interesting, for several reasons, to read what each journal says of the start and the reflections, if any, induced thereby.

The Lewis and Clark report thus chronicles their departure:

All the preparations being completed, we left our encampment on Monday, May 14, 1804. This spot is at the mouth of Wood [Du Bois] River, a small stream which empties itself into the Mississippi, opposite the entrance of the Missouri. . . . We found that our boat was too heavily laden in the stern, in consequence of which she ran on logs three times to-day. It became necessary to throw the greatest weight on the bow of the boat, a precaution very necessary in ascending both the Missouri and Mississippi rivers, in the beds of which lie great quantities of concealed timber.

Gass, in his journal, indulges in some serious reflections anent the enterprise upon which they have embarked. Whether these were genuine, or were an afterthought suggested by David McKeehan, his Irish-American pedagogue editor, has been a subject for discussion.

Patrick Gass, although an illiterate man, was a remarkable and shrewd Irishman. And he was a warrior. If he and Fluellen could only have met, what a discussion about "wars" would have ensued! That he was weak on grammatical construction signified little then, and Floyd and Gass were, in this respect, in a class with Lewis and Clark themselves. If Gass did not indulge in the reflections credited to him, he and the others might with perfect propriety have done so, the time and occasion being worthy of them:

The corps consisted of forty-three men (including [excluding] Captain Lewis and Captain Clarke, who were to command the expedition) part of the regular troops of the United States, and part engaged for this particular enterprise. The expedition was embarked on board a batteau and two periogues. . . . Here we had leisure to reflect on our situation, and the nature of our engagements: and, as we had all entered this service as volunteers, to consider how far we stood pledged for the success of an expedition, which the government had projected; and which had been undertaken for the benefit and at the expense of the Union; of course of much interest and high expectation.

The best authenticated accounts informed us, that we were to pass through a country possessed by numerous, powerful and warlike nations of savages, of gigantic stature, fierce, treacherous and cruel; and particularly hostile to white men. And fame had united with tradition in opposing mountains to our course, which human enterprise and exertion would attempt in vain to pass. The determined and resolute character, however, of the corps, and the confidence which pervaded all ranks, dispelled every emotion of fear, and anxiety for the present; while a sense of duty, and of the honour which would attend the completion of the object of the expedition; a wish to gratify the expectations of the government, and of our fellow citizens, with the feelings which novelty and discovery invariably inspire, seemed to insure to us ample support in our future toils, sufferings and dangers.

Floyd, apparently, knew nothing of commas, periods, and the like, as the following exact quotation from his journal shows:

A Journal commenced at River Dubois – monday may 14th 1804 Showery day Capt Clark Set out at 3 oclock P m for the western expidition the party consisted of 3 Serguntes and 38 working hands which maned the Batteow and two Perogues . . . Saturday may 19 1804 a Rainey day Capt Lewis joined us Sunday may 20th 1804 nothing worth Relating to day Monday 21th 1804 Left St Charles at 4 oclk P m Showerey encamped on the N side of the River

It will be noticed that, as is natural, each journal refers to matters not mentioned by the others. Herein was the value to be derived from many diaries. Each was a check upon the others, and was often explanatory of some obscurity in them. This will be seen as we progress with the narrative, where Gass makes plain some ambiguous or uncertain statement of the main chronicle. There was no "hifalutin" and little of the imaginative in Gass's narrative. It was plain, straightforward, blue-pencilled fact – indeed, too much so. A little more detail and amplification would now be appreciated.

On Sunday, May 20th, Captain Lewis joined his companions; this fact is not mentioned in the published journals of Lewis and Clark, or of Gass, but Floyd notes it. The original note-books of the Captains, however, *do* state that Captain Lewis left St. Louis at 10 A.M. on that day, accompanied by Captain Stoddard, A. Chouteau, C. Gratiot, and others, and reached Captain Clark at 6.30 P.M. On the 20th, Clark pens the following: "I gave the party leave to go and hear a Sermon to day delivered by Mr. [blank space in MS.] a roman Carthlick Priest."

On the 22d they exchanged two quarts of whiskey for four deer with the Kickapoos, a tribe now little known and of whom but a handful still exist. It will thus be seen that even Lewis and Clark added their mite to the infernal trade in the white man's fire-water which has cursed us as a nation in our dealings with the red men. If a picture showing the horrible effects of this traffic among the Indians in the early years be desired, Father De Smet's *History of Western Missions,* page 322, will give it.

On the 24th after successfully passing a bad rapid known as the Devil's Race-ground, they came to a second one where "the bank fell in so fast as to oblige us to cross the river instantly, between the northern side and a sand bar which is constantly moving and banking with the violence of the current. The boat struck on it, and would have upset immediately if the men had not jumped into the water and held her until the sand washed from under her."

This experience was one of the first of a large number that harassed them as long as they were on this river. The character of the Missouri River for the continual and rapid cutting away of its banks is well known. Maximilian, a world-wide traveller, writes[1]:

"Some parts of its banks were rent in a remarkable manner by the rapid stream, when the water was high." He also describes the sand-banks with their masses of driftwood, and the snags and bars which rendered navigation next to impossible. Audubon, in 1843, writes:

The banks are falling in and taking thousands of trees, and the current is bearing them away from the places where they have stood and grown for ages. It is an awful exemplification of the course of Nature, where all is conflict between life and death.

---

[1] *Travels* in *the Interior* of *North America,* by Maximilian, Prince of Wied, 1832-34.

Chittenden – U. S. Engineer Corps – dwells at length upon these characteristics of this remarkable stream, but I quote one sentence only: "At certain seasons this action [the erosion of its banks] is rapid and destructive and hundreds

"Burlington" Railroad Bridge across Missouri River, near the Point from which Lewis and Clark Began their Exploration.

of acres in a single locality are frequently washed away in the course of a few days." The bearing of all this will appear more particularly as the narrative progresses.

On May 25th, they reached the small French village, La Charette. Near here, at that time, lived the noted frontiersman and woodsman, Daniel Boone, the hero of every American boy. Crowded out of his beloved Kentucky, he had made his way across the Mississippi and was spending the sunset of his days near this little hamlet on the edge of the Great Plains, and here he died, on September 26, 1820, more than ninety years old.

When the overland party of Astorians under Wilson Price Hunt reached La Charette, in 1811, they found Boone still there, and Irving, in *Astoria,* thus describes the meeting:

> Here they met with Daniel Boone, the renowned patriarch of Kentucky, who had kept in the advance of civilization, and on the borders of the wilderness, still leading a hunter's life, though now in his eighty-fifth year. He had but recently returned from a hunting and trapping expedition, and had brought nearly sixty beaver skins as trophies of his skill. The old man was still erect in form, strong in limb, and unflinching in spirit; and as he stood on the river bank, watching the departure of an expedition destined to traverse the wilderness to the very shores of the Pacific, very probably felt a throb of his old pioneer spirit, impelling him to shoulder his rifle and join the adventurous band.

Their experiences along the river were much the same from day to day. Rain, untoward winds with now and then a favorable one, much hunting and killing of deer, — for it required many to feed forty-five men,-rapids or "hard" or "strong water" to navigate, sandbars and snags to dodge, pestilent mosquitoes, these were the daily events, with an occasional accident like the breaking of a mast to vary the usual routine.

Quite frequently they met rafts or boats loaded with peltries and furs and tallow en route from various parts of the up-river country to St. Louis; the beginnings of the large fur trade to come.

The islands, rapids, bluffs of prominence, and all points to which interest in any form attached which they passed were noted and described and almost invariably with such detail and precision that many of them even now, after the lapse of a hundred years, can be identified from their descriptions.

June 1, 1804, the explorers were at the mouth of the Osage River:

> The Osage River gives or owes its name to a nation inhabiting its banks at a considerable distance from this place. Their present name, however, seems to have originated from the French traders, for both among themselves and their neighbours they are called the Wasbashas.

The Osages are of the Siouan family, a considerable number of whom still live on a reservation in Indian Territory.

June 5th:

> Two miles farther we reached on the south Little Manitou creek, which takes its name from a strange figure resembling the bust of a man with the horns of a stag, painted on a projecting rock, which may represent some spirit or deity. . . . The rapidity of the current, added to our having broken our mast, prevented our going more than twelve and a half miles.

On June 7th they passed a pictograph "limestone rock," and their first bear was killed this day, which fact Floyd thus states:

> one mile past a rock on the N Side whare the pictures of the Devil and other things we kild 3 Rattel Snakes at that Rock 5 miles to Creek on the N Side Called Good woman Creek Strong water past severall Isd. George Druer [Drewyer] Kild one Bar.

The regular narrative says there were three bears brought in. These minor discrepancies among the journals are often to be noted.

A good example of the varied way in which the three diaries recounted current happenings is seen in the chronicles for June 12th, on which day an event of some importance occurred – the engagement of an interpreter.

The Lewis and Clark narrative recites:

At one o'clock we met two rafts loaded, the one with furs, the other with the tallow of buffaloe; they were from the Sioux nation, and on their way to St. Louis; but we were fortunate enough to engage one of them, a Mr. Durion, who had lived with that nation more than twenty years and was high in their confidence, to accompany us thither.

Gass recounts the day's experiences thus:

TUESDAY 12th. We set out early, and proceeded until five o'clock in the afternoon, when we met five periogues loaded with fur and peltry from the Sioux nation of Indians. We remained with the people to whom these periogues belonged all night; and got from them an old Frenchman, who could speak the languages of the different nations of Indians up the Missouri, and who agreed to go with us as an interpreter.

Floyd says:

we met 5 Cannoes from the Soux nations Loaded with peltry and Greece [Greece is a small state, but it is rather hard to imagine it being transported about in 5 "cannoes"] they have been 13 mounthes up the missorea River . . , one Frenchman hiard to go with us up the missorea who Can Speak the Difernt   . .

The Durion here mentioned was the father of Pierre Dorion, the Sioux interpreter who accompanied Mr. Astor's overland expedition to Astoria in 1810 *et seq.* The old man was one of the peculiar products of the time and frontier, and is graphically described by Irving in *Astoria.*

Captain Lewis, in accordance with his understanding with Mr. Jefferson, was particular to counsel with and win over the Indian tribes and to endeavor to impress them with the power of their new masters, the United States, and of the importance of cultivating trade relations with them. He devoted much time to obtaining their history, vocabularies of their language, and statistics of them, and embodied this miscellaneous knowledge in *A Statistical View of the*

Indian Nation Inhabiting the Territory of Louisiana and the Countries Adjacent to Its Northern and Western Boundaries.

In their running chronicle the Captains usually referred to the various tribes and their experiences with them at some length, all of which form interesting and valuable linguistic etchings of the tribes of that time. Marvellous changes have taken place since those days. Many of the tribes or their subdivisions enumerated by the explorers have completely vanished from the earth and are known to-day only through Lewis and Clark. Others have all but disappeared and the remainder, instead of wandering unchecked over the plains and among the mountain valleys or hugging the river banks, ofttimes to pester and annoy parties of adventurous white men, are now on reservations and surrounded on all sides by these same palefaces who followed the trails of Lewis and Clark and the fur traders. All this serves to heighten the pictures which these harbingers of civilization draw from time to time of these aboriginal people and their country. Some of these now depleted tribes that once were lords of the plains and whose lands embraced the Missouri River Valley were the Otoes, Missouris, Pawnees, Omahas, and Poncas.

They had a remarkable sunset the evening of June 21st, if Clark's orthography is any criterion: "at Sunset the atmespier presented every appearance of wind, Blue & White Streeks centiring at the Sun as She disappeared and the Clouds situated to the S. W. Guilded in the most butifull manner."

On the 24th, Captain Lewis and Sergeant Floyd went hunting, during a two hours' halt, and returned with a deer and a turkey. Both Floyd and Gass give the reason for this stop, which was from twelve o'clock to two o'clock. In the words of Gass, it was, "to jirk [jerk] our meat," and he tersely and correctly explains this as "Jirk is meat cut into

small pieces and dried in the sun or by a fire. The Indians
cure and preserve their meat in this way without salt."

There are few men who have mountaineered it in the
West who are not familiar with this very satisfactory process
of meat preservation. The beef, whether wild or domestic,

The Indian Process of "Jerking" Meat on Scaffolds.

was cut into strips of moderate length, — dipped in a salt
brine in later years where possible, — and hung upon a
scaffolding of poles in the sun until well dried, a small fire
often being used to hasten the process. If the meat itself
was sweet and good, the jerked beef or "jerky," as it was
usually called, was a most palatable morsel. In their old
days of mountain life the writer and his companions always
carried in their pockets or saddle-bags a supply of "jerky."

Besides providing a handy bit to munch between meals, in crossing the hot sandy plains of southern Utah and Arizona, where water was scarce, it performed a useful office in promoting the flow of saliva.

The origin of the word "jerked" is ascribed to the Chilian word "charqui," sun-dried meat.

On this date the codex has this snake story, from Captain Clark:

> I joined the boat this morng at 8 oClock (I will only remark that dureing the time I lay on the sand waiting for the boat, a large Snake Swam to the bank immediately under the Deer which was hanging over the water, and no great distance from it, I threw chunks and drove this snake off Several times. I found that he was so determined on getting to the meet, I was compelld. to kill him, the part of the Deer which attracted this Snake I think was the Milk from the bag of the Doe).

On the 26th, the expedition reached the junction of the Missouri and Kansas rivers, where Kansas City now stands. On this day they saw "a number of paroquets." That parrots and paroquets were ever known in that part of the country will probably surprise most people, but such is the fact, and one of Maximilian's plates shows a species of parrot which he saw on the Wabash River in Indiana.

In proceeding up the Missouri, Lewis and Clark, finding the river flowing eastward, applied the words "north" and "south" to the right and left banks of the stream respectively, and this nomenclature they consistently used throughout all the windings and changes of direction of the river.

In reading Lewis and Clark this point should be well understood, for between the mouths of the Missouri and the Kansas the "north bank" was on their north; from the Kansas River to Fort Mandan the "north" bank was to the east of them; from Fort Mandan to the mouth of the Marias River, the "north" bank was again to their north; and from the Marias to the Three Forks and Shoshone Cove, the "north" was to their west. In the customary way and beginning at the source of that branch of the stream which the explorers followed, Lewis and Clark's north would have been the left, and their south the right, bank.

The narrative mentions that "on the banks of the Kanzas reside the Indians of the same name, consisting of two villages, one at about twenty, the other forty leagues from its mouth, and amounting to about three hundred men."

Lewis, in his *Statistical View,* paints the Kansas or Kaw Indians in very black colors, calls them "dissolute, lawless banditte." They too are of the large Siouan family, and a remnant still exists in Indian Territory.

My friend, J. V. Brower of St. Paul, known for his archaeologic researches, informs me that a persistent effort to obtain the meaning of the words "Kaw," or "Kansas," has availed naught. The Indians know not the meaning of their tribal name.

On June 30th the party passed the Little Platte River, near which the city of Leavenworth, Kansas, now stands. The weather was extremely hot and the men suffered "very much from the heat."

July 4th was ushered in "by the discharge of our gun." It was further celebrated, we learn from Floyd, by Joseph Fields being bitten by a snake, though not seriously; by naming one creek Fourth of July Creek, and another one Independence Creek; the latter, near which is now Atchison, Kansas, is still so called – and they wound up the day, "after 15 miles' sail," by "an evening gun and an additional gill of whisky to the men."

Floyd had an eye for fine scenery and expressed his feelings through his journal as best he could. He remarks on this same day:

Sunday July 15th 1804 Set out at Six oclock
A.M. passed a Creek on the South Side called Plum
Run water verry Strong passed a Creek on the South Side
Called Memahow Creek the it is about 30 yards wide
the Land is high and good timant on the South Side

Monday July 16th we Set out verry early and
profsed on the Side of a Prarie the wind from the South
Sailed over Beat Run on a Sawyer boiled all day made 10
miles pased Sevrall psd Camt on the North Side

Tuesday July 17th 1804 Lay by all this day
for to kill some fresh meat Capt Lewis & Ge Druyer
went out hunting Druyher Killed 3 Deer the Land is

A Page from the Journal of Sergeant Charles Floyd.

Back of these wood is an extensive Praria open and High whigh may be Seen Six or Seven [miles?] below / saw Grat nomber of Goslins today nearley Grown / the Last mentioned prairie I Call Jo. Fieldes Snake prarie / Capt. Lewis walked on Shore / we camped at one of the Butifules Praries I ever Saw / open and butifulley Divided with Hills and vallies all presenting themselves.

On July 7th, one of the men "had a stroke of the sun," but "he was bled, and took a preparation of nitre, which relieved him considerably." On this day they "saw a large rat," of which Gass remarks: "The principle difference between it and the common rat is, its having hair on its tail." Coues states that this wood rat was unknown to science until Lewis and Clark thus discovered it.

On July 14th they had a serious time for an hour, in a terrific storm that threatened the demolition of all their boats, but they came through it safely and camped on an island a short distance above the mouth of the Nishnabatona River. This day they saw their first elk.

In their journey up the river they often camped on islands, probably because they were thus rendered more secure from prowling Indians, and the posting of sentinels at night was made less necessary, and the islands probably provided better camping grounds:

Under date of July 20th the journal records:

For a month past the party have been troubled with boils, and occasionally with the dysentery. These were large tumors, which broke out under the arms, on the legs, and generally in the parts most exposed to action, which sometimes became too painful to permit the men to work. After remaining some days, they disappeared without any assistance, except a poultice of the bark of the elm, or of Indian meal. This disorder, which we ascribe to the muddiness of the river-water, has not affected the general health of the party, which is quite as good as, if not better than, that of the same number of men in any other situation.

On July 21st, they reached the Platte River and camped just above its mouth, and on the following day they encamped at a point ten miles farther up the stream, and from there Drewyer and Cruzatte were sent to the Otoe, or Pawnee Indian towns, some forty-five miles inland, to gather the Indians together for a council. But the Indians were hunting the buffalo, or bison, in the plains. The party therefore proceeded up the river, passing the present sites of Omaha, Nebraska, and Council Bluffs, Iowa.

The regular narrative is somewhat deficient and inconsistent here as, for example, under date of July 22d it is stated that one object for the halt at this point was to prepare "dispatches and maps of the country we had passed, for the President of the United States, to whom we intend to send them by a periogue from this place." No further reference is made to this and no periogue with maps and dispatches was sent to the President until the spring of 1805, from Fort Mandan. The journal here gives a long statement of what the Captains had learned regarding the Otoe, Pawnee, and other Indian tribes.

On July 28th, some of their hunters stumbled upon some Missouri Indians who lived with the Otoes. One of them, evidently a trusting sort of fellow, accompanied the hunter or hunters — the regular narrative says one hunter, Gass and Floyd say two or more — to the boats, where he remained that night. On the 29th, the Captains sent the Indian, accompanied by one of their Frenchmen, — Liberté as a messenger to the Otoes, inviting the latter to meet them at a point on the river above for a council. This point was reached on the morning of July 30th; it has become one of the milestones in our dealings with the Indians and it was, as well, a very important moment in the annals of the Lewis and Clark exploration.

For nearly seven hundred miles they had been slowly

ascending the turbid stream, penetrating farther and farther into the wild land of the red men. And now they were to have their first talk, hold their first formal council with them. What would be the result? Would their presents be received, would their talk be acceptable, would their diplomacy be successful, would it be war or peace? No wonder they were anxious as to the result, for the Indians, true to their nature, were in no hurry and did not appear until the evening of August 2d. The varied renderings by the journals of the "doings" of those waiting days form interesting passages and give us a good picture also of the way in which the time was passed, the diversions and occupations of the camp, etc.

Floyd, as usual, ignoring all grammatical stops, as Gass probably did in his original manuscript, covers a good deal of ground in his unique narrative, which I partially quote and mark with slanting lines to render it more intelligible:

Tuesday July 31th 1804 / we Lay BY for to See the Indianes who we expect Hear to See the Captens. I am verry Sick and Has ben for Somtime but have Recoverd my helth again / the Indianes have not Come yet / this place is Called Council Bluff / 2 men went out on the 30th of July and Lost ouer horses / . .

Thursday august 2d / to day the Indianes Came whou we had expected / thay fired meney Guns when thay Came in Site of us and we ansered them withe the Cannon / thay Came in about 2 hundred Yardes of us Capt Lewis and Clark met them / at Shakeing Handes we fired another Cannon / thare wase 6 Chiefs and 7 men and one Frenchman with them who has Lived with them for som yeares and has a familey with them / Friday august 3dth the Council was held and all partes was agreed / the Captens Give them meney presentes.

The Lewis and Clark journal, beginning with August 1st and ending with the entry for August 2d, runs in part as follows:

AUGUST 1st and 2d. We waited with much anxiety the return of our messenger to the Ottoes. . . . Our apprehensions were at length relieved by the arrival of a party of about 14 Ottoe and Missouri Indians, who came at sunset, on the 2d of August, accompanied by a Frenchman who resided among them and interpreted for us. Captains Lewis and Clark went out to meet them, and told them that we would hold a council in the morning. In the meantime we sent them Some roasted meat, Pork flour and meal, in return they sent us Watermillions. every man on his Guard & ready for any thing. We learned that our man Liberte had set out from their camp a day before them.

The First Council with the Indians Held by Lewis and Clark.
From an old illustration "A Journal of the Voyages and Travels
of a Corps of Discovery," etc, by Patrick Gass, published by
Mathew Carey, Philadelphia, 1810.

We were in hopes that he had fatigued his horse, or lost himself in the woods, and would soon return, but we never saw him again.

AUGUST 3d. This morning the Indians, with their six chiefs, were all assembled under an awning formed with the mainsail, in presence of all our party, paraded for the occasion. A speech was then made announcing to them the change in the government, our promise of protection, and advice as to their future conduct. All the six chiefs replied to our speech, each in his turn, according to rank. They expressed their joy at the change in the government; their hopes that we would recommend them to their Great Father (the President), that they might obtain trade and necessaries; they wanted arms as well for hunting as for defense, and asked our mediation between them and the Mahas, with whom they are now at war. We promised to do so, and wished some of them to accompany us to that nation, which they declined, for fear of being killed by them. We then proceeded to distribute our presents. The grand chief of the nation not being of the party, we sent him a flag, a medal, and some ornaments for clothing. To the six chiefs who were present, we gave a medal of the second grade to one Ottoe chief, and one Missouri chief; a medal of the third grade to two inferior chiefs of each nation – the customary mode of recognizing a chief being to place a medal round his neck, which is considered among his tribe as a proof of his consideration abroad. Each of these medals was accompanied by a present of paint, garters, and cloth ornaments of dress; and to this we added a cannister of powder, a bottle of whiskey, and a few presents to the whole, which appeared to make them perfectly satisfied. The air-gun too was fired, and astonished them greatly. . . . The incident just related induced us to give to this place the name of the Council-Bluff; the situation of it is exceedingly favorable for a fort and trading-factory, as the soil is well calculated for bricks, there is an abundance of wood in the neighborhood, and the air is pure and healthy. . . .

As already mentioned, this place was named Council-bluff in honor of their first general council with the tribes. Lewis and Clark state that at that time the Otoes numbered about five hundred. Contrary to general supposition, however, this spot was not where the city of Council Bluffs, Iowa, now stands, nor was it even on the same side of the river. The true Council-bluff was some twenty miles, at least, above Omaha, and the error in location undoubtedly arose from the fact that on Lewis and Clark's map of 1814, the lettering "Council Bluffs" was, apparently for convenience, placed on the eastern side of the river, so that if the map alone was taken as a guide the natural inference was that the spot itself was on the Iowa side of the river.

Lewis and Clark's itinerary makes the distance of the

Union Pacific Railroad Bridge across the Missouri River, between Omaha, Neb., and Council Bluffs, Iowa

159

bluff from the mouth of the Platte River forty-nine miles. By the Missouri River Commission's maps, Omaha is twenty-five miles above the Platte River, and Fort Calhoun is forty-seven miles distant therefrom. Council-bluff would therefore be near the latter place.

On May 13, 1811, H. M. Brackenridge passed the Bluffs and records as follows:

The Council bluffs are not abrupt elevations, but a rising ground, covered with grass as perfectly smooth as if the work of art. They do not exceed in height thirty or forty feet above the plain below. On ascending, the land stretches out as far as the eye can reach, a perfect level. The short grass, with which the soil is covered, gives it the appearance of a sodded bank, which has a fine effect, the scene being shaded by a few slender trees or shrubs in the hollows.

Major Stephen H. Long's expedition to the Rocky Mountains, in 1819-20, established their winter cantonment, called Engineer Cantonment, near Council-bluff, and Long describes it as "a beautiful position," from which "is presented the view of a most extensive and beautiful landscape." This bluff, if not now entirely removed by the action of the river, must certainly have been greatly changed in configuration since 1804.

In 1839, Nicollet, on an exploration of the Missouri, located the spot and marked it on his map. Even then, only thirty-three years after Lewis and Clark had completed their exploration, Nicollet remarks that the changeable Missouri had already obliterated many of the bends described by those men:

Thus we could not recognize many of the bends described by Lewis and Clark; and, most probably, those determined by us in 1839, and laid down upon my map, will ere long have disappeared; such is the unsettled course of the river. Already have I been informed, in fact, that the great bend opposite Council Bluffs has disappeared since our visit; and that the

Missouri, which then flowed at the foot of the bluff, is now further removed, by several miles, to the east of it. It is, in this respect, curious to compare our journal of travelling distances with that of Lewis and Clark. They are found always to differ, and sometimes considerably. Yet, on arriving at any prominent station, as the confluence of a large river, the amount of partial distances computed agree as nearly as could be expected, from the methods employed to estimate them.

This statement of Nicollet regarding the distances of Lewis and Clark is curiously true, many times, in other cases.

In 1809-11 John Bradbury, an English naturalist, travelled in this country and he wrote an account of his travels that is a standard authority to-day. He ascended the Missouri, in 1811, as far as the Mandan villages and Knife River, accompanying Mr. Astor's overland Astorian party, under Wilson P. Hunt, as far as they proceeded up the Missouri — to the mouth of Grand River. Bradbury gives an instance of the fickle nature of the Missouri. At the mouth of the Platte it became necessary for him to wade the stream and the water reached to the arm-pits. The next day he recrossed the river at the same place and the water then did not reach to the waist, and yet the river had not fallen. Bradbury adds: "Such changes in the bottom of the river, Rogers [an interpreter to a French trader] told me were very frequent, as it is composed of a moving gravel, in which our feet sank to a considerable depth."

After Lewis and Clark had returned, and as the fur trade grew in importance and emigration increased, the country about the mouths of the Kansas and Platte rivers became strategic ground, and numerous trading and other posts were established there. Some of them were abandoned only to be replaced by others and the list of posts is quite an imposing one. Among the more important were Fort Osage, Chouteau's Post, Blacksnake Hills, where St. Joseph, Missouri, now stands, Fort Leavenworth, Bellevue Post,

Fort Lisa, Cabanne's Post, Fort Calhoun, etc. In the fifty years following 1804 Chittenden states, "there were probably not fewer than twenty posts established between this point [Council-bluff] and the mouth of the Platte, but all are now swallowed up in the great cities that have taken their places on both sides of the river," a most striking sequence, it will generally be admitted.

The desertion of the Frenchman, noted under August 1st and 2d, was followed on August 4th by another, as shown by the following entry in Floyd's journal:

Tuesday August 7th / Set out at 6 oclock A. m / prossed [proceed] on / day Clear / wind from the North west / on the 4th of this month one of ouer men by the name of Moses B. Reed went Back to ouer Camp whare we had Left in the morning, to Git his Knife which he had Left at the Camp / the Boat went on and He Did not Return, that night nor the next day nor Night, pon examining his nap-Sack we found that he had taken his Cloas and all His powder and Balles, and had hid them out that night and had made that an excuse to Desarte from us with out aney Jest Case.

A part of the regular narrative for August 7th reads:

We dispatched four men back to the Ottoe village in quest of our man Liberte, and to apprehend one of the soldiers [Reed], who left us on the 4th under pretense of recovering a knife which he had dropped a short distance behind, and who we fear has deserted. We also sent small presents to the Ottoes and Missouris, and requested that they would join us at the Maha village where a peace might be concluded between them.

The four men sent after the runaways were Drewyer, R. Fields, Bratton, and Labiche, and their orders were, "if he did not give up Peaceibly to put him to Death." Bratton related to his family, and the story was told to me in 1900, by his only surviving daughter, that, after capturing Reed and going with the deserter to a stream to allow him to wash his moccasins, the latter made tentative propositions to be allowed to escape, but gave it up when Bratton informed him that if it was attempted, he would certainly shoot him. Nothing was ever again seen of Liberté, the French deserter, by Lewis and Clark. Bradbury, however, in 1811, mentions a man of the same name who was a member of Hunt's Astorian party, and he may have been the Lewis and Clark deserter.

August 11th, the expedition reached what was and still is a prominent landmark on the Missouri River, the Blackbird Hill.

At nearly five miles, we halted on the south side for the purpose of examining a spot where one of the great chiefs of the Mahas [Omahas], named Blackbird, who died about four [in 1800] years ago of the smallpox, was buried. A hill of yellow soft sandstone rises from the river in bluffs of various heights, till it ends in a knoll about 300 feet above the water; on the top of this a mound, of twelve feet diameter at the base and six feet high, is raised over the body of the deceased king: a pole of about eight feet, high is fixed in the center, on which we placed a white flag, bordered with red, blue, and white. Blackbird seems to have been a personage of great consideration; for ever since his death he has been supplied with provisions, from time to time, by the superstitious regard of the Mahas.

Brackenridge and Bradbury, Irving, Long, De Smet, and others relate in some detail the story of this famous – also infamous – chief. The former says:

At seven arrived at Black-bird hill. . . . It takes its name from a celebrated chief of the Mahas, who caused himself to be interred on the top: a mound has been erected on the pinnacle, with a branch stuck in it, a flag was formerly attached to it. He was buried, sitting erect on horse back; the reason which he gave for choosing this spot, was that he might see the traders as they ascended. This chief was as famous in his lifetime amongst all nations in this part of the world, as Tamerlane or Bajazet were in the plains of Asia: a superstitious awe is still paid to his grave. Yet, the secret of his greatness was nothing more than a quantity of arsenic, which he had procured from some trader. He denounced death against any one who displeased him, or opposed his wishes: it is therefore not surprising, that he, who held at his disposal the lives of others, should possess unlimited power, and excite universal terror. The proud savage, whenever this terrible being appeared, rendered the homage of a slave.

Irving, in *Astoria,* devotes several pages to this remarkable man. It is stated that the large mound noted by Lewis and Clark over the remains of the once powerful chieftain is now scarcely noticeable. Catlin, in his trip up the Missouri in 1832, carried away the skull of Blackbird, and it is now in the National Museum at Washington.

As the expedition proceeded it met with striking evidence of the smallpox which had swept over this region in 1800, *et seq.,* with frightful effect. They made efforts to reach the Maha or Omaha Indians in order to hold a council with them, but met with failure, the Omahas probably being absent hunting the bison. Sergeant Ordway headed this embassy.

August 17th the party sent after Liberte and Reed returned with the latter and three more Otoe chiefs. Liberte had also been taken, but had craftily escaped. On August 18th and 19th there was more powwowing with the Indians and present-making, and "the council was ended with a dram to the Indians." In the evening, among other things exhibited to excite the curiosity of the natives and impress them, the wonderful "air gun" was fired. I have seen no description of this gun, and there is no mention of it in the published enumeration of supplies, etc., but whenever its occult powers were exhibited, its effect upon the "untutored mind" was instantaneous and lasting.

We have now to chronicle the only case of mortality that occurred during the exploration. During more than two years of wanderings, "of moving accidents by field and

20th August Monday 1804
Sergeant Floyd much weaker
and no better. Made Mr. Faufon
the interpeter a few presents, and
the Indeains a Canister of Whiskey
we Set out under a gentle braze
from the S.E. and proceeded on
verry well — Sergeant Floyd as
bad as he can be no pulse &
nothing will Stay amoment
on his Stomach or bowels —
Passed two Islands on the S.S.
and at the first Bluff on the
Sd. Side Sergt Floyd Died with a
great deel of Composure, before
his death he Said to me "I am
going away" I want you to write"
me a letter" — We buried him
on the top of the bluff ½ Mile
below a Small river to which we
gave his name, he was buried
with the Honors of war much

Page 14 from Codex "B," Clark, Regarding Sergeant Floyd's Illness and Death.

flood," of sickness, discomforts, dangers from wild beasts
and wild men, of facing death almost continuously and in
many forms, the one and only death came suddenly, quickly,
before the eight hundredth mile of their many thousands
had been covered. Our Kentucky friend, Sergeant Floyd,
was the victim. On August 19th he was attacked by
bilious colic, and despite all that could be done for him,
died on the afternoon of the 20th. Jacob, in his life of Gass,
states that this attack was brought on by Floyd having lain
down on a sandbar when in an overheated condition after
an evening of dancing. This is the only place in which I
have seen any reference to the cause of the attack. Gass's
account is as follows:

MONDAY 20th. Sergeant Floyd continued very ill. We embarked early, and proceeded, having a fair wind and fine weather,
until 2 o'clock, when we landed for dinner. Here sergeant
Floyd died, notwithstanding every possible effort was made by
the commanding officers, and other persons, to save his life. We
went on about a mile to high prairie hills on the north side of
the river, and there interred his remains in the most decent
manner our circumstances would admit; we then proceeded a
mile further to a small river on the same side and encamped.
Our commanding officers gave it the name of Floyd's river; to
perpetuate the memory of the first man who had fallen in this
important expedition.

Clark's original journal entry regarding Floyd's sickness
and death is both curious and interesting:

Serjeant Floyd is taken verry bad all at once with a Biliose
Chorlick we attempt to reliev him without success as yet, he
gets worse and we are much allarmed at his situation, all attention to him . . . Sergeant Floyd much weaker and no
better . . . as bad as he can be no pulse and nothing will
stay a moment on his stomach or bowels. . . . Died with a
great deel of composure, before his death he said to me "I am
going away I want you to write me a letter" – We buried him
on the top of the bluff ½ mile below a small river to which we

gave his name, he was buried with the Honors of War much lamented, a seeder post with the Name Sergt. C. Floyd died here 20th of August 1804 was fixed at the head of his grave – This man at all times gave us proofs of his firmness and Determined resolution to doe service to his countrey and honor to himself after paying all the honor to our Deceased brother we camped

Floyd Obelisk, Floyd's Bluff, Sioux City, Ia.

in the mouth of *floyds* river about 30 yards wide, a butifull evening.

Imagination easily pictures the events of the day. As it became certain that death had set its seal on the uncomplaining victim, all would endeavor to render to their comrade such physical comfort as was possible, and to ease his passage to

The undiscovered country from whose bourn
No traveller returns.

After death had claimed its own we can realize the gloom which settled o'er each brow as the rude coffin was fashioned; can see the little procession as it slowly, laboriously climbed the bluff, dug the narrow cell, Floyd's last earthly home; gently and with loving arms, – for death softens us all, rough though we may be – lowered all that was mortal of their friend into the tomb; filled the excavation, and sadly retraced their steps to the boats, leaving the body of their late companion alone in his last long sleep, his soul in "the bosom of his Father and his God." We can imagine, too, that as they once more turned their prows to breast the current, it was with muffled oar-stroke and softened speech, and that the solitary "seeder post" was the cynosure of all eyes as long as it was within vision.

The expedition proceeded but a short mile when they camped at the mouth of a small stream, now just below Sioux City, to which they appropriately gave the name, Floyd's River. This, with Floyd's Bluff, where the remains were interred, and Sergeant's Bluff, a short distance below the latter, have formed, and will continue to form, a perpetual remembrance of the first citizen soldier who gave up his life in his country's service and on his country's soil in the vast region comprised in the Louisiana Purchase.

Floyd's journal continued to within two days of his death, and it is here reproduced from August 15th to 18th inclusive:

Wendesday august 15th / Capt Clark and 10 of his men and myself went to the Mahas Creek a fishen and Caut 300 and 17 fish of Difernt Coindes / ouer men has not Returnd yet /
Thursday august 16th / Capt Lewis and 12 of his men went to the Creek a fishen Caut 709 fish Differnt Coindes /
Friday august 17th / Continued Hear for ouer men / thay did not Return Last night /
Satturday night augt 18th / ouer men Returnd and Brot with them the man and Brot with them the Grand Chief of the ottoes and 2 Loer ones and 6 youers of thare nattion.

Upon the dedication of the splendid obelisk to Floyd's memory, on May 30, 1901, the writer was an invited guest. The object was a most praiseworthy one, the day perfect, the multitude large, and the commemorative address worthy the time and occasion. The day – Memorial Day – and time were peculiarly appropriate for a dedication such as this. Floyd was one of a band engaged in exploration of the country covered by the first and greatest territorial expansion made by the United States, and the time of the dedication happened to fall upon a period almost a full century later, when we were engaged in a far-away struggle brought upon us by the latest phase in an evolution of expansion of which the Louisiana Purchase was the first, As for the day itself, it was the one when the graves of the soldiers of the Republic throughout the length and breadth of the land are sought out and garlanded with flowers, in commemoration of deeds done in the body "that government of the people by the people for the people shall not perish from the earth," a day most fitting for the exercises of such a dedication.

The principal address, by Hon. John A. Kasson, was stately, dignified, statesmanlike, and gave fitting expression to the thoughts which surged through the minds of the vast audience present.

The Floyd obelisk is a stately and beautiful one and in striking harmony with its surroundings. For miles, both up and down the Missouri River, its one hundred feet of tapering shaft can be seen telling "to the last syllable of recorded time" the great story of one hundred years ago. Upon the east and west faces of the monument are bronze tablets commemorative of the events it symbolizes.

Floyd's Bluff is now one of the parks of Sioux City, Iowa, and the view from the base of the obelisk is one which few parks in this country can equal for beauty and wide extent.

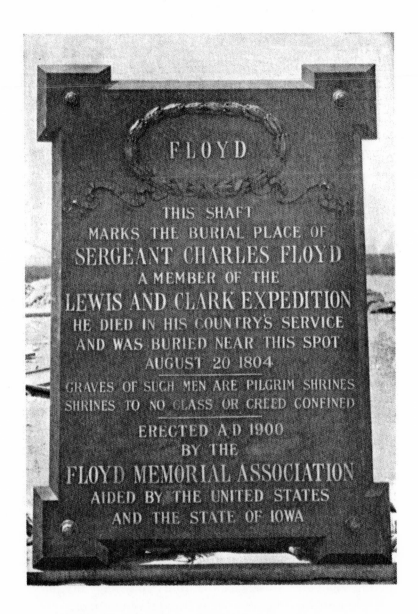

Bronze Plate Attached to Floyd Monument, Sioux City, Ia.

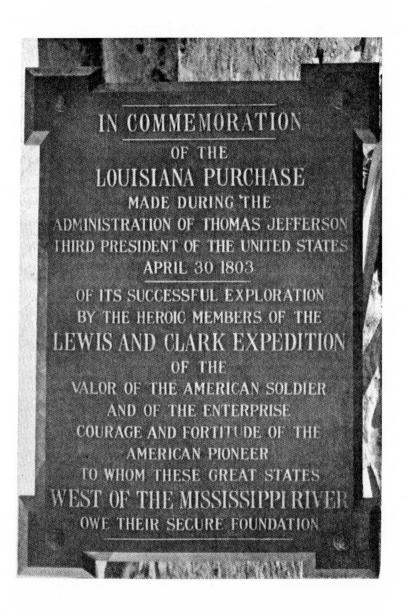

Bronze Plate Attached to Floyd Monument, Sioux City, Ia.

171

The glistening river winds in long, sweeping curves between timber-fringed bottoms, whose wide levels range back to hills and bluffs gracefully configured and verdured in varied tints of refreshing green, with the thriving city nestling among the hills. Could the lone occupant of that now historic grave have chosen his place of sepulture, he could not have found a more restful, beautiful spot for that last long sleep that knows no waking.

Here, on the bluffs of the great river are buried the remains of two men, exponents of antagonistic types of humanity – of savagery and civilization. Not many miles below the last reach of shining river visible from the spot where Floyd sleeps, the great Omaha chieftain, Blackbird, is buried on a western hill, erect on horseback, facing the river and the east, that he might continue to see the traders come up the river – the advancing wave of white civilization, as it swept onward to possess the land.

Following out the same idea, Floyd, from his resting-place, beheld the tide of barbarism, with its attendant herds of bison, recede in the track of the setting sun until it has almost utterly vanished, and the race of which he was a forerunner has usurped the place of the former and now occupies the wide domain over which the savage once ruled supreme.

On August 21st, the expedition passed the mouth of the Big Sioux River, four miles beyond Floyd's Bluff. This stream was a noted one among the Indian tribes because of the fact that on its headwaters were situated the red pipe-stone quarries which supplied the peculiar red stone from which most of their pipes were made. The "pipestone quarry" has been a noted locality since white men first entered the Northwest. Jonathan Carver – 1766-68 – evidently refers to it; Bradbury speaks of it and describes a pipe six feet in length; Catlin made a special journey to the spot in 1837, from New York, and carried away samples of the red pipestone and had it chemically analyzed. The chemist gave to the rock the name Catlinite, by which it is still, to some extent, known. The quarry is located near Pipestone City, in Pipestone County, western Minnesota.

Concerning the quarry,[1] Prof. N. H. Winchell says, in part:

> The *pipestone*, or *cathinite*, of the pipestone quarry, is a fine clay varying in color from blood-red to pale red or pinkish, or even to a pale yellowish red. The lighter colors fade into the darker, but sometimes the light appears in the red as round spots, on a polished surface, but the red is not thus distributed through the lighter shades. . . .
>
> Although this substance has usually a red color, like that which prevails in the formation to which it pertains, it should be added that this redness suffers all the variations that it does in the quartzyte. It passes nearly to white, through pink; it is intensified to a brown, and in small patches it is deepened to lilac or lavender-brown, becoming reddish purple. . . .
>
> The Indians of the Northwest have resorted to this place ever since their acquaintance with Europeans, for the purpose of getting this material for their pipes.

On a red quartzite wall near the quarry there are found many wide pictographic inscriptions of bears, turtles, birds' feet, elks, bison, etc., and this particular spot was sacred ground to the tribes. Catlin and also Nicollet – 1836-43 – state that "the Indians of all the surrounding nations" made regular pilgrimages annually to the quarry, "to renew their pipes," believing that it had been opened by the Great Spirit. These red pipestone pipes are to be found to this day among the tribes of the Northwest, far and near, passing by barter from tribe to tribe. The stone is easily worked and many of the pipes are wrought out very elaborately.

---

[1] For a detailed description of this locality and quarry, see *The Geological and Natural History Survey of Minnesota*, vol. i., published by the State of Minnesota, and the works of Catlin and Nicollet.

The Lewis and Clark journal, referring to the river, quarry, and Indians, remarks:

> This river comes in from the north, and is about 110 yards wide. Mr. Durion, our Sioux interpreter, . . . says that it is navigable upward of 200 miles to the falls, and . . . that its sources are near those of the St. Peter's [Minnesota River]. He also says that below the falls a creek falls in from the eastward, after passing through cliffs of red rock; of this the Indians make their pipes, and the necessity of procuring that article has introduced a sort of law of nations, by which the banks of the creek are sacred; even tribes at war meet without hostility at these quarries, which possess a right of asylum. Thus we find even among savages certain principles deemed sacred, by which the rigors of their merciless system of warfare are mitigated.

After leaving the Big Sioux River the men were afflicted with "disorders of the stomach," which was accounted for when they reached certain mineral bluffs on the 22d instant. These bluffs so impregnated the water of the river with cobalt, alum, and copperas as to cause the disorders mentioned. In testing the minerals, Captain Lewis was "considerably injured by the fumes and taste of the cobalt, and took some strong medicine to relieve him from its effects."

On this day a new sergeant was elected in place of Sergeant Floyd, deceased. Bratton, Gass, and Gibson were voted for, and Gass receiving nineteen votes, out of forty-two if all save Lewis and Clark were allowed to vote, was elected. This was a plurality not a majority, of all the votes, which indicates that the result may have been somewhat close.

On the 23d instant their first buffalo was killed by Joseph Fields, and they salted two barrels of the meat.

August 27th they passed the mouth of the Jacques, Yankton, or James River, near Yankton, S. D., and also met some Indians of the Yankton Sioux, whom they sent, together with Sergeant Pryor, "Durion," and another, as a delegation to the main body of Indians with a request that they assemble for a council.

August 28th, one of their priogues ran upon a snag and was much damaged, and one of the illustrations of Gass's volume gives a most remarkable representation of the catastrophe.

On this day Reed, the deserter, who, it will be remembered, had been brought in on the 18th, was tried, sentenced, and punished-leniently. He confessed that he "Deserted & Stold a public Rifle shot-pouch Powder & Ball," and his sentence and punishment was "to run the gantlet four times through the Party & that each man with 9 switchies should punish him and for him not to be considered in future as one of the Party."

The descendants of Bratton inform me that Bratton stated that there was no latitude allowed the men in this matter, but that each one was "compelled to hit him [Reed] a hard lick with his ram-rod under penalty of having to take his place for refusal to do so." The three principal chiefs who came in at the same time that Reed did petitioned for his pardon. What effect this had on the verdict is not stated.

The council with the Yanktons was held on August 30th, in the usual impressive manner.

Of this tribe the journal remarks:

What struck us most was an institution peculiar to them, and to the Kite Indians further to the westward, from whom it is said to have been copied. It is an association of the most active and brave young men, who are bound to each other by attachment, secured by a vow, never to retreat before any danger, or give way to their enemies. In war they go forward without sheltering themselves behind trees, or aiding their natural valor by any artifice. Their punctilious determination not to be turned from their course, became heroic, or ridiculous, a short time since, when the Yanktons were crossing the Missouri on the ice. A hole lay immediately in their course, which might easily have been avoided by going around. This the foremost of the band disdained to do, but went straight forward and was lost. The others would have followed his example, but were forcibly prevented by the rest of the tribe.

The chronicle continues with a long account of the Sioux, as they ascertained the facts through their interpreters.

The word "Sioux," according to Major John W. Powell and the early explorers and historians, means the "snake-like ones," or, "the enemies," and is to be used in a family, a comprehensive linguistic sense, and the word is of Ojibwa or Algonquian origin. Charlevoix said, in 1721, "The name of Sioux . . . is entirely of our own making . . . it is the last two syllables of the name of Nadouessioux." Catlin says that the word was pronounced as if spelled See-ooo. The word "Dakota," meaning "friend," is a word of restricted use and is applicable only to those of the Siouan family living in the Dakotan region. The two words "Sioux" and "Dakota" are often, but incorrectly, used synonymously. Neill says that the word "Dakota" is equivalent to our *E pluribus unum*. These people were formerly known as "Gens du Lac," "People of the Lake." The Siouan family was a very large one – including the Mandans, Kaws, Crows, Minnetarees, Omahas, Otoes, etc. – and on Powell's linguistic map their territory extends from well north of the International Boundary line, southeasterly to the northwestern corner of Louisiana, and east and west from Lake Michigan to the northwestern corner of Wyoming. The boundary line is an irregular one, but their territory comprised, in a general way, the greater part of all of North and South Dakota, Iowa, Nebraska, Kansas, and Missouri; about one half each of Montana, Minnesota, Wyoming, Indian Territory, and Arkansas, and parts of Wisconsin and Louisiana.

Formerly most of the Siouan tribes dwelt east of the Mississippi River, but they are now found, almost entirely, west of the Missouri. The Sioux whom Lewis and Clark met were of the Dakota tribes proper. There are now between 40,000 and 50,000 of the Sioux enumerated; Lewis and Clark gave their numbers as between 8000 and 9000, but that did not include the entire nation.

The Ojibwa, of the Algonquian family, were inveterate enemies of the Sioux and appear to have waged unceasing and successful war against them. The various tribes of the Sioux were also more or less continually at war among themselves.

On September 2d the party passed Bon Homme Island, of which they gave an elaborate description on the supposition that it was covered with aboriginal fortifications, a fact since disproved. The islands of the Missouri show many such earthworks, the work of the river and of the high winds which prevail.

September 5th they "saw some goats or antelopes, which the French call *cabres*," as Gass states it. The antelope was unknown to science until Lewis and Clark discovered it, but it was not scientifically named until 1815.

The mornings were now very cold, there was much wind, and progress was slow, but they were living luxuriously on buffalo humps, antelope and elk steaks, venison, beavers' tails, wild turkeys and geese, and fish.

September 7, 1804, is the date of an incident of interest and of value in natural history. Their journey this day was a short one, and they camped at a "dome" mountain, or what is now known as the Tower, a few miles below Fort Randall and Whiteswan, S. D. The narrative then continues:

As we descended from this dome we arrived at a spot, on the gradual descent of the hill, nearly four acres in extent, and covered with small holes. These are the residence of a little animal called by the French *petit chien* (little dog), which sit erect near the mouth and make a whistling noise, but when alarmed take refuge in their holes. In order to bring them out we poured into one of the holes five barrels of water without filling it, but we dislodged and caught the owner. After digging down another of the holes for six feet, we found on running a pole into it that we had not yet dug halfway to the bottom. We discovered, however, two frogs in the hole, and near it we killed a dark rattlesnake, which had swallowed a small prairie dog; we were also informed, though we never witnessed the fact, that a sort of lizard and a snake live habitually with these animals. The *petit chiens* are justly named, as they resemble a small dog in some particulars, though they have also some points of similarity to the squirrel. The head resembles the squirrel in every respect, except that the ear is shorter; the tail is like that of the ground-squirrel; the toe-nails are long, the fur is fine, and the long hair is gray.

Gass also refers briefly to this episode, which relates to the now well-known prairie dog of the West, a most interesting little animal. Dr. Coues says that the earliest notice he had seen of a prairie dog was in a letter of Captain Clark to Governor Harrison, "dated Fort Mandan, April 2, 1805, and, I think, published in 1806."

He also states that Lieutenant Z. M. Pike, who in 1805-7 made extensive explorations up the valley of the Mississippi to its headwaters, and also into the interior of the country west from St. Louis, mentions the animal in his manuscripts, under date of August 24, 1806, but these were not published until 1810. The record of discovery of this little animal would appear to be:

First – Letter of Captain Clark, Fort Mandan, April 2, 1805, published in 1806.

Second – Gass's account of the incident of September 7, 1804, published in his journal, in 1807.

Third – Pike's publication of 1810, of what he observed in 1806.

Point of Observation N° 49

Wednesday October 17th 1804.

On the Star'd. shore, opposite to a high projecting Bluff; which from the great number of rattlesnakes found near it, we called the rattlesnake Bluff.

Observed meridian altd. of ☉'ll. L. with Sextant by the fore observatio — } 69. 17. ~

Latitude deduced from this observation N. 46. 23.57'

Point of Observation N° 50.

Monday October 29th 1804.

On the star'd. shore at council camp, about half a mile above the upper Mandan Village.

Observed meridian altd. of ☉ ll. L. with Sextant by the fore observation — } 58. 55. 15"

Latitude deduced from this observation N. 47° 22'.56."7

℞. The Chronometer run down today. I was so much engaged with the Indians, that I omited winding her up. —

At the same place.

Tuesday October 30th 1804.

Wound up the Chronometer, and observed equal Altitudes of the ☉ with Sextant. —

A. M. 8. 4. 44. — P. M. } last in consequence
" 7. 31. — — { of the sun's being ob-
" 10. 31. — — { scured by clouds.

Altitude given by Sextant at the time of altd. 44. 53. 15"

Wednesday October 31st 1804.

A Page of "Celestial Observations" for Codex "O" – Lewis.

179

Fourth – Lewis and Clark's own report of their exploration covering the event of September 7, 1804, first published in 1814.

The animal was first technically and scientifically recognized by George Ord in 1815, who gave it the specific name, *Arctomys ludoviciana.* Prof. Spencer F. Baird, in 1857, gave it its present and more appropriate designation of *Cynomys ludovicianus. Cynomys* means dog-mouse, from two Greek words – *Kuown,* dog, and *mus,* mouse. *Ludovicianus,* from the Latin word *ludovicus,* indicates that the species was first found or studied in the vicinity of St. Louis.

The prairie dog belongs to the family of *Sciurda* – squirrels – which includes ground hogs or marmots on the one hand, and flying squirrels, on the other; it is, strictly speaking, a marmot, and not a dog, although its general appearance is much like that of a fat puppy. The animals run impulsively from hole to hole with a sort of amble, stopping suddenly and sitting upright on their haunches. Then they place their fore-paws together and near their noses, and take on an attitude of prayer or supplication, or even appear as if about to indulge in a little preaching. This is all done quicker than it can be told, and with an air of the utmost soberness and dignity. They flirt their little tails continually, jerk their heads about, give utterance at quick intervals to a sharp, saucy little bark, and will, in a twinkling, throw themselves head first into their holes, the stub tails giving a farewell flirt as they disappear. The dogs range from thirteen to sixteen or seventeen inches in length, with tails from two and a half to four inches long.

The prairie dogs live in underground colonies, some of them of large extent, and it is ordinarily deemed impossible to dig down to them or drown them out, as related by Lewis and Clark.

These animals seek sandy, sterile soil in which to burrow, far from water, of which they seem to be practically independent. The little creatures have small cheek pouches, doubtless for carrying food, and their fore-paws are admirably adapted for their burrowing operations. Their bodies are quite heavily and compactly formed for their size, and they are of a pale chestnut brown, or rather tawny color.

The fact mentioned by Lewis and Clark and others, of finding snakes, owls, frogs, etc., in the holes of these animals, gave rise to a theory that these apparently antagonistic creatures lived in peace and harmony together. Scientific men assert that this is untrue; that burrows that have, for any reason, been deserted by the dogs may be, and are, pre-empted by the owls— who also burrow – and snakes, but that they are all at enmity with each other, and this was also affirmed by Maximilian in 1833. Prairie dogs, or prairie marmots, are common to nearly all parts of the great Western plains, and are familiar objects to most Western people.

On September 11th a lost man reappeared; –Shannon, who, on August 28th, had been sent to find their two horses which had strayed.

Clark describes Shannon's adventure in his characteristic way:

Here the Man who left us with the horses 22 days ago and has been ahead ever since joined us nearly Starved to death, he had been twelve days without any thing to eate but Grapes & one Rabit, which he Killed by shooting a piece of hard Stick in place of a ball. This Man Supposeing the boat to be a head pushed on as long as he could, when he became weak and feable deturmined to lay by and Waite for a tradeing boat, which is expected, Keeping one horse for the last resorse, thus a man had like to have Starved to death in a land of Plenty for the want of Rullitts or Something to kill his meat.

On September 16th, an important decision was made. It had been the intention to send back to St. Louis, during the fall, a periogue, with progress reports, the natural history collections made, etc., but this intention was now abandoned, and in accordance with it the boats were reloaded, the loads being more equally distributed and navigation thus made much easier.

The journal now has much to say about the wild game seen. Herds of antelope and buffalo, deer of several varieties, elk, wolves, barking squirrels, or prairie dogs, were numerous. Of smaller game, grouse, plover, larks, and brant were found. Large quantities of fine plums were also observable.

Lewis and Clark usually speak of antelopes as *goats.* In this they were not wrong, as one not a naturalist would imagine them to be. Some years since I had occasion to write to Mr. F. W. True of the National Museum, Washington, D. C., concerning the white or wild goat – *Oreamnos montanus* – of the Rockies. His reply is pertinent to this matter and I give it here:

The goats belong to the *bovide* or ox family. The antelopes also belong to this family, and, as often happens, the different sections of the family grade into each other, so that it is difficult to point out, characters which will include all the members of one section and exclude all the members of the next most closely-related section. This is especially true in the ox family. Nevertheless, the so-called "white goat," in the form, structure and color of its horns, is more like the typical antelope than the typical goats. Furthermore, there are other antelopes, such as the "goat antelopes" of Asia, which are closer to our "white goat" than the latter is to the true goats.

September 20th, the expedition reached the Great or Big Bend of the Missouri, where the river forms a great loop, or bend. Lewis and Clark give the distance around by water as thirty miles, and the width of the neck of land at its narrowest point as two thousand yards, it having been stepped off by one of their men. Later estimates were somewhat less than this.

The night of the 20th the party narrowly escaped a catastrophe. The journal for September 21st reads:

> Between one and two o'clock the sergeant on guard alarmed us, by crying that the sand-bar on which we lay was sinking. We Jumped up, and found that both above and below our camp the sand was undermined and falling in very fast. We had scarcely got into the boats and pushed off, when the bank under which they had been lying fell in, and would certainly have sunk the two periogues if they had remained there. By the time we reached the opposite shore the ground of our camp sunk also.

The Expedition went into camp September 24th at the mouth of Teton, or Bad River, where they remained during the 25th, and held a council with the Teton Sioux. Here, for a time, the fate of the expedition hung on a very fine thread and the story is best told in the words of the journal:

> We invited the chiefs on board and showed them the boat, the air-gun, and such curiosities as we thought might amuse them. In this we succeeded too well; for after giving them a quarter of a glass of whisky, which they seemed to like very much, and sucked the bottle, it was with much difficulty that we could get rid of them. They at last accompanied Captain Clark on shore in a periogue with five men; but it seems they had formed a design to stop us; for no sooner had the party landed than three of the Indians seized the cable of the periogue, and one of the soldiers of the chief put his arms round the mast. The second chief, who affected intoxication, then said that we should not go on, that they had not received presents enough from us. Captain Clark told them that we would not be prevented from going on; that we were not squaws, but warriors; that we were sent by our great father, who could in a moment exterminate them. The chief replied that he too had warriors, and was proceeding to offer personal violence to Captain Clark, who immediately drew his sword, and made a signal to the boat to prepare for action. The Indians who surrounded him drew their arrows from their quivers and were bending their bows, when the swivel in the boat was instantly pointed toward them, and

twelve of our most determined men jumped into the periogue to join Captain Clark. This movement made an impression on them, for the grand chief ordered the young men away from the periogue; they withdrew and held a short council with the warriors. Being unwilling to irritate them, Captain Clark went forward and offered his hand to the first and second chiefs, who refused to take it. He turned from them and got into the periogue, but had not gone more than ten paces when both the chiefs and two of the warriors waded in after him, and he brought them on board. We then proceeded for a mile and anchored off a willow-island, which from the circumstances which had just occurred we called. Bad-humored island.

The situation was in reality more serious than the narrative gives it, as appears from Clark's note-books.

For the first time a real danger confronted the explorers, and had a bow twanged or a gun been fired, intentionally or accidentally, no one can tell what the result might have been. Likely enough part of the Indians' conduct was of the nature of a bluff, but nevertheless, the firm and unflinching attitude of the party, well led by both the Captains, was what saved the day and determined the progress and success of the expedition. As will be seen, notwithstanding that the temper of the Indians changed and they provided a feast and dance, the explorers underwent a touch of this hostility once again before they were done with these rascally Tetons, and these experiences were really the only serious ones of the sort that the explorers encountered in the entire course of the expedition.

Gass evidently did not take quite so serious a view of the "ruction" of the 25th as Clark did; he says of the second difficulty, on the 28th:

At nine o'clock we made preparations to sail; some of the chiefs were on board, and concluded to go some distance with us. When we went to shove off, some of the Indians took hold of the rope and would not let it go. This conduct had like to be attended with bad consequences, as Captain Lewis was near giving orders to cut the rope and to fire on them. The chiefs, however, went out and talked with them: they said they wanted a carrot of tobacco, and that if we gave that we might go. The tobacco was given them, and we went off under a gentle breeze of wind.

October 1st, the explorers reached the Cheyenne River, so named from the Cheyenne Indians, – of Algonquian stock, – who formerly roamed the country to the northeast, on the Cheyenne River, a tributary of the Red River of the North, whence they removed to the sources of the Cheyenne River west of the Missouri River. The Cheyennes are now established at the Tongue River Agency, Montana, the Pine Ridge Agency, South Dakota, and the Cheyenne and Arapaho Agency, Indian Territory.

October 8th, the expedition reached Grand River, and near there they first met the "Ricara" Indians, among whom they remained until October 12th.

Here York, Captain Clark's negro servant, appears in a conspicuous role.

The original note book says:

Those Indians were much astonished at my Servant, they never Saw a black man before, all flocked around him & examined him from top to toe, he Carried on the joke and made himself more turribal than we wished him to doe.

Of the "Ricaras" the journal records:

We then made or acknowledged three chiefs, one for each of the three villages; giving to each a flag, a medal, a red coat, a cocked hat and feather, also some goods, paint and tobacco, which they divided among themselves. . . . On our side we were equally gratified at discovering that these Ricaras made use of no spirituous liquors of any kind, the example of the traders who bring it to them, so far from tempting, having in fact disgusted them. Supposing that it was as agreeable to them as to the other Indians, we had at first offered them whiskey; but they refused it with this sensible remark, that they were surprised that their father should present to them a liquor which would make them fools. On another occasion they observed to Mr. Tabeau that no man could be their friend who tried to lead them into such follies. . . .

Of Pawnee stock, the Arikara originally settled at the mouth of the Cheyenne River, subsequently joined the Mandans, and later, in consequence of a quarrel, left them and removed down the Missouri.

These women are handsomer than the Sioux; both of them are, however, disposed to be amorous, and our men found no difficulty in procuring companions for the night by means of the interpreters. These interviews were chiefly clandestine and were of course to be kept a secret from the husband or relations. . . . The black man York participated largely in these favors; for, instead of inspiring any prejudice, his color seemed to procure him additional advantages from the Indians, who desired to preserve among them some memorial of this wonderful stranger. Among other instances of attention, a Ricara invited him into his house, and, presenting his wife to him, retired to the outside of the door; while there one of York's comrades who was looking for him came to the door, but the gallant husband would permit no interruption until a reasonable time had elapsed. . . .
They cultivate maize, or Indian corn, beans, pumpkins, watermelons, squashes, and a species of tobacco peculiar to themselves. Their commerce is chiefly with the traders, who supply them with goods in return for peltries, which they procure not only by their own hunting, but in exchange for corn from their less civilized neighbors. . . .

At this time the "Ricaras" numbered two thousand, the explorers state.

On the 13th and 14th they summarily disposed of the one case of mutiny that occurred on the exploration. Private John Newman, who had conducted himself properly theretofore, in a moment of depression or thoughtlessness gave expression to mutinous sentiments for which he was "confined." He was evidently tried on the evening of the 13th by "9 of his Peers" and — "they did centence him [to]

75 lashes & [be] Disbanded [from] the party." On the 14th, after dinner, they halted on a sand-bar and executed "centence." Newman tarried with them, made himself very useful thereafter, and was virtually forgiven, but although he exposed himself so greatly, while on a winter

Northern Pacific Railway Bridge across Missouri River at Bismarck and Mandan. N. D. This point is an old bison and Indian ford.

hunting expedition from Fort Mandan, that he was badly frozen, and suffered for weeks, "and beged that I [Lewis] would permit him to continue with me through the voyage," he was not permitted to go beyond Fort Mandan.

Lewis thought it not wise to remit the remainder of the sentence, although he evidently desired to do so, and in a letter to the War Department in 1807, he virtually asked that the man be given extra compensation for the service he did render, which request Congress granted. The "Ricara" Chief Ahketahnasha was much affected upon witnessing "Newmon's" punishment and "cried aloud," but upon explanation being made he admitted the justice of the sentence and the necessity for the punishment.

As the expedition now proceeded they found game in abundance; bison, antelopes, elk, and deer, and they met numerous bands of "Ricara" Indians hunting, and saw several of their villages, some of them abandoned ones.

The Indians, in hunting the antelope, would drive the graceful creatures into the river and then, lining the banks, so as to prevent their escape, would shoot them down indiscriminately, and the boys would even go into the water and kill them with sticks.

October 18th, they reached the mouth of Le Boulet, or Cannon-ball River. The origin of this name is well stated by Maximilian:

This river has its name from the singular regular sand-stone balls which are found in its banks, and in those of the Missouri in its vicinity. They are of various sizes, from that of a musket ball to that of a large bomb, and lie irregularly on the bank, or in the strata, from which they often project to half their thickness when the river has washed away the earth; they then fall down and are found in great numbers on the bank. . . .

The rotundity of many of these stones is almost perfect, if some of them that I have seen, eighteen or twenty inches in diameter, are to be taken as criteria.

October 19th, they saw fifty-two herds of bison and three of elk "at a single view," and they camped opposite a cliff, in the water-worn holes of which the well-known calumet bird – golden eagle – built its nest, and a ruined village of the Mandans that had been fortified was close at hand. This was the first old Mandan village seen by them, those

Site of old Fort Abraham Lincoln, just below mouth of Heart River, North Dakota, from which General Custer started on his last campaign, May 17, 1876. Lewis and Clark camped at this spot October 20, 1804

previously met with having belonged to the "Ricaras," but being similar to those of the former in construction.

October 21st they passed the Heart River. Just above this point are now the towns of Bismarck and Mandan, N. D., on either side of the Missouri River, joined by the costly steel bridge of the Northern Pacific Railway. Just below Heart River are the remains of Fort Abraham Lincoln, Custer's old post and the one from which he and the Seventh United States Cavalry started on May 17, 1876, on their last and tragic campaign. Of all the buildings that were once to be found at old Fort Lincoln, there were, in the fall of 1902, but two left. Lewis and Clark's camp of October 20th was just above where Fort Lincoln was subsequently built. A new Fort Lincoln is now in course of construction on the opposite side of the river, just below Bismarck.

From Heart River to the Mandan towns, at and near Knife River, they found the ruins of many old Mandan villages. Between Heart River and the present town of Mandan, N. D., they found one on low grounds, and it is observable at the present day, usually, however, being spoken of as an Indian burial-place.

On the Bismarck side of the river they discovered another set of ruins, not far from where the railway bridge spans the stream. About ten miles north of Bismarck well-defined mounds that indicate an ancient village are plainly distinguishable on a bluff immediately overlooking the Missouri River, and I am informed that there are others within four or five miles of Bismarck.

Near the railway bridge, on a high bluff and in the vicinity of the reservoir of the water company that supplies Bismarck with water, I saw, some years ago, what was said to be an old Indian fortification and certainly the appearance of the spot sustained this assumption. As there never was any trading post or fort at that point, and as the

Indians did construct fortifications, it appears to be a reasonable conjecture that this is what it was claimed to be. It consisted of embankments surrounded by a ditch, with a central opening in the former, and it was decidedly "military" in appearance.

In inspecting Clark's codices, with their lack of punctuation and their orthographic peculiarities, one is tempted to believe at times that the Captain had in mind when writing, a vague idea of a system of short-longhand, to be elaborated later on. The following excerpt, under date of October 22, 1804, is a fair example:

> last night at 1 o'clock I was violently and Suddenly attacked with the Rhumetism in the neck which was So violent I could not move. Capt. [Lewis] applied a hot Stone raped in flannel, which gave me some temporey ease. We Set out early, the morning Cold at 7 oClock we came too at a camp of Teton Seaux on the L. S. [larboard (left) side] those people 12 in number were nackd. and had the appearance of war, we have every reason to believe that they are going or have been to Steel Horses from the Mandins, they tell two Stories, we gave them nothing after takeing brackfast proceeded on my Neck is yet very painfull at times Spasms.

The weather now grew very cold, snow fell, and the expedition pushed along to reach winter quarters, among the Mandan Indians. They met numerous parties of Mandans, and also some Teton Sioux who, notwithstanding the cold, were clad only in their royal dignity and breech-clouts; or, as the narrative runs, "having only a piece of skin or cloth round the middle, although we are suffering from cold."

Of the village ruins seen so frequently, the account says:

> These villages, which are nine in number, are scattered along each side of the river within a space of 20 miles; almost all that remains of them is the wall which surrounded them, the fallen heaps of earth which covered the houses, and occasionally human skulls and the teeth and bones of men and different animals, which are scattered on the surface of the ground.

On the 22d of October they passed Butte Carrée, or Square Butte, then, as now, a well-known landmark, and on the 23d they camped near the present town of Washburn, N. D. Here they reached the point where the Missouri, coming from the west, makes its final bend to the south.

Now, turning from a northerly to a northwesterly course, the expedition hurried onward past sand-bars, rocks, old villages, and "handsome plains" until, on the 26th of October, they reached the Mandan villages – the live towns, not the old, dead ones – "and camped for the night on the south side, about half a mile below the first village of the Mandans," and their travels for the year 1804 were virtually ended. It was not until November 2d, however, that, after much searching, the location of their winter's camp, Fort Mandan, was selected and they began the actual construction of their fort. The story, as told by Captain Clark, of the first meeting with these people, I transcribe literally from the codex account of October 26th:

Several Indians came to see us this evening, amongst others the Sun of the late Great Chief of the Mandins *(morning for his father)* this man has his two little fingers off; on inquireing the cause, was told it was customary for this nation to Show their greaf by some testimony of pain, and that it, was not uncommon for them to take off 2 Smaller fingers of the hand *(at the 2d joints)* and some times more with other marks of Savage effection.

The wind blew verry hard this evening from the S.W. verry cold R. Fields with the Rhumitism in his neck, P. Crusat with the Same complaint in his Legs – the party other wise is well, as to my self I feel but slight Simptoms of that disorder at this time.

We came too and camped on the L. S. [larboard side] about ½ a mile below the 1st Mandin Town on the L. S. soon after our arrival many man womin & children flocked down to See us, Capt. Lewis walked to the village with the principal Chiefs and our interpters, my Rhumatic complaint increasing I could not go. If I was well only one would left the Boat & party untill we niew [knew] the Disposition of the Inds.

I smoked with the Chiefs who came after. Those people ap^d. [appeared] much pleased with the Corn Mill which we were obliged to use, & was fixed in the boat.

On May 14th the expedition had started from Du Bois River, on October 26th the first stage of the journey was ended, – after five months and twelve days, or 165 days, of continuous travel, toil, hunting, and exploring. Even such

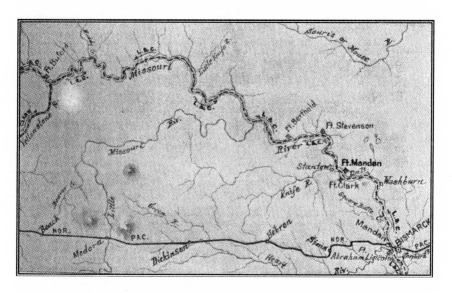

Route of Lewis and Clark. Mouth of Heart River – Bismarck – to Mouth of Yellowstone River – Fort Buford –.

rest as was in prospect must have seemed an agreeable change, and they arrived at their cantonment none too soon, for winter was upon them.

Great good fortune had attended them in their buffetings with fate – and the Missouri River; Providence had smiled on them, for, notwithstanding their struggles, dangers, and sickness, of all that chosen band that started from Wood River, but one had fallen by the way, – the silent form that lay entombed on Floyd's Bluff.

VOL. 1 .- 13.

CHAPTER V

THE WINTER AT FORT MANDAN, 1804-1805

A LONG and, as it turned out, a cold winter was ahead of the explorers. To select a site for their cantonment that would fit the necessities of the case required discrimination and judgment, and to this task Captain Clark vigorously applied himself, both Captains taking time, however, to cultivate the friendship of the Indians.

After carefully examining the country for several miles up and down and bordering on the river, Captain Clark found a suitable spot in the wooded bottom lands on the north, or east bank of the Missouri. Wood and water, the first requisites, were at hand; the Indians were not far away and the haunts of the game were reasonably near, and this, as far as possible, certified them an ample provision of food.

According to their reckoning, the party were now one thousand six hundred miles from their starting-point, or, in other words, their progress up-stream had been at an average rate of about ten miles a day. As we have seen, it was through an unsettled region in which the changes to take place during the next hundred years could hardly have been foreseen by even the most sanguine among them. The first steamboat seen at St. Louis was in 1817, and the first one to navigate the Missouri was in 1819, fifteen years after our party of adventurers passed up the river, and it was not until 1832 that the Mandans beheld a "big thunder canoe." There are now spanning this river, between St. Louis and Bismarck, twenty-two railway bridges, across which is transported a great interstate commerce which reaches out literally to the ends of the earth.

The system of trading posts, forts, etc., which, subsequent to Lewis and Clark's exploration, lined the lower river, and to which reference has heretofore been made, was continued to the northward as the fur trade gained strength, and between the White and Cheyenne rivers there was a thick cluster of these forts. It would seem that during the days of rivalry between the American Fur Company, Columbia Fur Company, Missouri Fur Company, etc., nearly every available site along the river in this immediate locality was seized upon as a trading mart, and these posts, together with those established in earlier days by individuals, left few strategic points unoccupied by the trader at one time or another.

The two most important forts between the mouth of the Missouri and the Mandan villages were Fort Pierre, near the mouth of the Teton, or Bad River, and Fort Clark, near the Mandan towns. Fort Pierre was begun in 1831 and was named after Pierre Chouteau, Jr., the well-known fur trader of St. Louis. This fort was the second post in point of importance on the entire river. Maximilian gives a lively description of Fort Pierre and its surroundings:

Fort Pierre is one of the most considerable settlements of the Fur Company on the Missouri, and forms a large quadrangle, surrounded by high pickets. . . . At the north-east and south-west corners there are block-houses, with embrasures, the fire of which commands the curtain; the upper story is adapted for small arms, and the lower for some cannon; each side of the quadrangle is 108 paces in length; the front and back, each 114 paces, the inner space eighty-seven paces in diameter. From the roof of the block-houses, which is surrounded with a gallery, there is a fine prospect over the prairie; and there is a flag-staff on the roof, on which the colors are hoisted. The timber for this fort was felled from forty to sixty miles up the river, and floated down, because none fit for the purpose was to be had in the neighborhood. . . . The fort has two large doors, opposite each other, which are shut in the evening. . . . Indians, on foot and on horseback, were scattered all over the plain, and their singular stages for the dead were in great numbers near the fort; immediately behind which, the leather tents of the Sioux Indians, of the branches of the Tetons and the Yanktons, stood, like a little village; among them the most distinguished was the tent of the old interpreter, Dorion, a half Sioux, who is mentioned by many travellers, and resides here with his Indian family. This tent was large, and painted red; at the top of the poles composing it some scalps fluttered in the wind.

The fort stood on the right – west – bank of the Missouri, opposite the present Pierre, S. D.

Fort Clark was situated almost directly opposite Lewis and Clark's Fort Mandan, – three quarters of a mile below it, Maximilian says – and was established in 1831 to control the Mandan trade. It was named for Captain, or, as he was then generally known, General Clark. It was not as large as Fort Pierre, although it was an important post, and I understand that remains of it were visible until recent years.

Maximilian spent a winter at Fort Clark, which was but a short distance below the first Mandan village, going northward.

The rapid development of the American fur trade, of which these various posts were the exponents, followed the purchase of Louisiana in 1803 and the return of Lewis and Clark in 1806. Manuel Lisa, a well-known Spaniard and trader of St. Louis, and a man of great ability, shrewdness, bravery, and diplomacy, headed an expedition to the Yellowstone country in the spring of 1807, thereby taking instant advantage of the opening made by those explorers and profiting by the knowledge spread abroad by them of the valuable fur grounds to be found in the Northwest. The Missouri Fur Company was organized in 1808-09, the

American Fur Company was chartered in 1808, the Pacific Fur Company in 1810, and the Rocky Mountain Fur Company in 1822; – and the widespread operations of these companies naturally resulted in the advertising of the West and the steadily increasing emigration to and settlement of its wide spaces, as the years rolled on.

Another important factor in this matter, too, was the

Fort Clark, 1831, opposite the Fort Mandan of Lewis and Clark. From "Maximilian's Travels," etc.

number of Government expeditions which, supplementing that greater one of Lewis and Clark, eventually covered the country in all directions. Prominent among them were the explorations of Pike, Long, Nicollet, Frémont, Stansbury, Stevens, and Warren, between 1805 and 1855. But with all the exploring and investigating, for there were scientific observers attached to some of these expeditions, real knowledge of this mighty land was gained but slowly. It was not until after the great Civil War, when a tremendous outburst of emigration surged across the Mississippi Valley, that any real, adequate conception dawned upon the public of what the Louisiana Purchase had brought to the country.

A statement of the popular idea regarding this region as late as 1857 will be interesting.

Lieut. G. K. Warren's report of an expedition in 1855 covers an irregular bit of territory in Nebraska of which Sioux City formed the eastern, Fort Pierre the northern, Fort Kearny, the Platte River, and Fort Laramie the southern and western limits. Nebraska then included the country between the Missouri and Platte rivers west to the main range of the Rocky Mountains and north to the northern boundary, or large parts of the Dakotas, Montana, and Wyoming, besides the present Nebraska. Warren's exploration included the *Mauvaises Terres,* or so-called "Bad Lands" of South Dakota, a region then and now unsuited to extensive agricultural uses. Dr. F. V. Hayden was the geologist of the survey and Warren and Hayden's report attracted much attention.

It was a general conclusion of Warren that west of the ninety-seventh meridian it was useless to look for "continuous settlements" and agricultural conquests of the soil. This obliterated nearly all of the Dakotas, Nebraska, and Oklahoma, and two thirds of Kansas as future agricultural communities, besides all of the Great Plains region and the mountain valleys to the westward.

There lies before me an editorial from *Harper's Weekly* of March 21, 1857, based upon Warren's report and entitled, "Are We as Great a Country as We Think We Are?" The following extracts from it will convey an idea of the agitation of the public mind at that time regarding the value of the territory under consideration:

Lawrence and Lecompton, in Kansas, lie on about the 96th parallel [*sic*] of longitude, so that if the 97th parallel [*sic*] is, according to Lieutenant Warren's opinion, to be the farthest western boundary of continuous agricultural settlements, the truth and fact is, that the population of the United States has, at all events on our parallel of latitude, where the tide has been most steady and active, substantially reached its utmost inland western limit. Minnesota, Washington, Oregon, and the eastern edge of Kansas are the only exceptions, and form the only remaining available portions of that vast domain which we are in the habit of talking of as stretching from the Atlantic to the Pacific Ocean.

If these facts be true, we shall have to pull in our horns and talk less mellifluously of the future. Where are the elements of the hundred States that, with Oriental magnificence of imagination, we speak of as the future number of the members of the Confederacy?

If all the western parts of Kansas and Nebraska are, in the picturesque language of the French, who have left in their original appellation a trace of the early rule of that great nation, *"Mauvaises Terres,"* or "Bad Lands," where are the materials that we had feared or hoped for to keep up an unextinguishable feud about the admission of new territories as Slave or Free?

If Utah is as hopeless as Kansas and Nebraska, will not the Mormon problem be settled by drought and grasshoppers before the intelligence and power of the Federal Government is compelled to consider the question?

If the lands west of the 97th meridian are valueless for agricultural purposes, what has become of our magnificent territorial domain? How much is left of this treasure once supposed to be inexhaustible?

Last and most important of all: If the eastern edge of Kansas is to be the western inland limit of the United States, what is to be the effect upon our institutions and our Government? Is the escape-valve so soon to be shut down? Is the refluent wave of population to be turned back thus early on the national heart?

These questions are more easily asked than answered. But the prominent fact seems to be that we are not so great a country as we thought we were.

In view of the phenomenal development of this region, both agriculturally and mineralogically, a development still continuing, these pessimistic utterances are now somewhat amusing, and yet they were not at all unnatural at the time. The problem of successful exploitation of this region was a peculiar one and was to be solved only after thought, study, experiment, success, and failure had, each and all combined, taught their lessons.

Even in 1874, Major-General W. B. Hazen, U. S. A., stationed at Fort Buford, Dakota, in a letter to the New York *Tribune,* reflected particularly and most unjustly upon the country through which it was proposed to construct the Northern Pacific Railway, and asserted that the whole country west of meridian 101° – which, curiously enough, passes almost through the very site of *Fort Mandan* – "will not produce the fruits and cereals of the East for want of moisture, and can in no way be artificially irrigated," a statement as wide of the facts as they exist to-day as it is possible to conceive.

No time was lost by the explorers in beginning the construction of Fort Mandan, the first trees being felled on November 2d. The work of preparation for winter was hastened and the men were divided into details, some to build huts, others to hunt, etc.

The story of those days will be best told, perhaps, in occasional extracts from the journals. Beginning with the narrative for October 27th, the day the party anchored off the Mandan towns, the record runs:

SATURDAY, OCTOBER 27th, 1804. At an early hour we proceeded and anchored off the village. Captain Clark went on shore, and after smoking a pipe with the chiefs, was desired to remain and eat with them. He declined on account of being unwell; but his refusal gave great offense to the Indians, who considered it disrespectful not to eat when invited, till the cause was explained to their satisfaction. We sent them some tobacco, and then proceeded to the second village on the north, passing by a bank containing coal, and the second village, and camped at four miles on the north, opposite a village of Ahnahaways. We here met with a Frenchman named Jesseaume, who lives among the Indians with his wife and children, and whom we take as an interpreter. The Indians had flocked to the bank

(Mandan) 64

27th of October Satturday 1804

We set out early Came too at the
Village on the LS. this Village is
Situated on an emenance of about
50 feet above the Water in a handsom
Plain it Contains houses in a
kind of Picket work, the houses are
round and verry large Containing
several families, as also their houses which is tiered on one Side of
the enterance, a Description of
those houses will be given here-
after, I walked up & Smoked a
pipe with the Chiefs of this Village
they were anxious that I would
Stay and eat with them, my
indisposition prevented my eating
which displeased them, untill a
full explenation took place, I
returned to the boat and Sent

Page 64 from Codex "C" – Clark – Noting Arrival at Mandan Villages.

201

to see us as we passed, and they visited in great numbers the camp, where some of them remained all night . . .

Sunday, October 28th, . . . we entertained our visitors by showing them what was new to them in the boat; all which, as well as our black servant, they called "great medicine," the meaning of which we afterwards learned. We also consulted the grand chief of the Mandans, Black Cat, and Mr. Jesseaume, as to the names, characters, etc., of the chiefs with whom we are to hold the council. In the course of the day we received several presents from the women, consisting of corn, boiled hominy, and garden stuffs.

Clark's original note-book says at this point, "I prosent [present] a jah [jar] to the chiefs wife who vewed it with much pleasure."

OCTOBER 29th. . . . At ten o'clock the chiefs were all assembled under an awning of our sails, stretched so as to exclude the wind, which had become high. That the impression might be more forcible, the men were all paraded, and the council was opened by a discharge from the swivel of the boat. We then delivered a speech which, like those we had already made, intermingled advice with assurances of friendship and trade. While we were speaking the old Ahnahaway chief grew very restless, and observed that he could not wait long, as his camp was exposed to the hostilities of the Shoshones. He was instantly rebuked with great dignity by one of the chiefs for this violation of decorum at such a moment, and remained quiet during the rest, of the council. . . . This being over, we proceeded to distribute the presents with great ceremony. One chief of each town was acknowledged by a gift of a flag, a medal with the likeness of the President of the United States, a uniform coat, hat and feather. To the second chiefs we gave a medal representing some domestic animals and a loom for weaving; to the third chiefs, medals with the impressions of a farmer sowing grain.

I reproduce from the codex an interesting account of a prairie fire which occurred on the night of the 29th:

a Iron or Steel Corn Mill which we gave to the Mandins, was verry thankfully receved. The Prarie was set on fire (or caught by accident) by a young man of the Mandins, the fire went, with such velocity that it burnt to death a man & woman, who Could not get to any place of Safety, one man a woman & Child much burnt and Several narrowly escaped the flame. a boy half white was saved unhurt in the midst of the flaim, Those ignerent people say this boy was Saved by the Great Medison Speret because he was white. The cause of his being Saved was a Green buffalow Skin was thrown over him by his mother who perhaps had more fore Sight for the pertection of her Son, and [l]ess for herself than those who escaped the flame, the Fire did not burn under the Skin leaveing the grass round the boy. This fire passed our Camp last [night] about 8 oClock P.M. it went with great rapitidity and looked Tremendious.

The event referred to in the last paragraph may have supplied the idea which Cooper so deftly utilizes in *The Prairie*. Hard Heart, the noble young Pawnee chieftain, by wrapping himself in a green buffalo hide, saves his life in a prairie fire set by these same Teton Sioux, whose deviltries Lewis and Clark had so recently circumvented, as related in the narrative.

The journal continues:

THURSDAY, NOVEMBER 1st. Mr. M'Cracken, the trader whom we found here, set out to-day on his return to the British fort and factory on the Assiniboin river, about 150 miles from this place. He took a letter from Captain[s] Lewis [and Clark] to [Charles Chaboilles of] the Northwest Company, inclosing a copy of the passport granted by the British minister in the United States.

NOVEMBER 2nd. . . . Captain Clark went down with the boats three miles, and having found a good position where there was plenty of timber [cottonwood, ash, and elm], camped and began to fell trees to build our huts. . . .

NOVEMBER 3rd. We now began the building of our cabins, and the Frenchmen who are to return to St. Louis are building a periogue for the purpose. We sent six men in a periogue to hunt [30 or 40 miles] down the river. We were also fortunate enough to engage in our service a Canadian Frenchman [Lepage] who had been with the Chayenne Indians on the Black mountains, and last summer descended thence by the Little Missouri. Mr. Jessaume, our interpreter, also came down with his squaw and children to live at our camp. . . .

NOVEMBER 5th. The Indians are all out on their hunting parties. A camp of Mandans caught within two days 100 goats [antelopes] a short distance below us. Their mode of hunting them is to form a large strong pen or fold, from which a fence made of bushes gradually widens on each side. The animals are surrounded by the hunters and gently driven toward this pen, in which they imperceptibly find themselves inclosed, and are then at the mercy of the hunters. . . .

The interpreter, Jesseaume, mentioned under date of October 27th, was a temporary acquisition only, and it may be was of questionable utility to Lewis and Clark. Henry, who mentions him several times in his journal, speaks of him in July, 1806, thus:

This man has resided among the Indians for upward of 15 years, speaks their language tolerably well, and has a wife and family who dress and live like the natives. He retains the outward appearance of a Christian, but his principles, as far as I could observe, are much worse than those of a Mandane; he is possessed of every superstition natural to those people, nor is he different in every mean, dirty trick they have acquired from intercourse with the set of scoundrels who visit these parts — some to trade and others to screen themselves from justice, as the laws of their own country would not fall to punish them for their numerous offenses.

And again, when leaving the Mandan towns, or more particularly, the Grosventres, or Minnetarees, he says:

At ten o'clock we were ready to bid adieu to the S. side of the Missourie, and glad to get away from such a set of hypocrites. At the head of the gang is that old sneaking cheat Mons. Jussaume, whose character is more despicable than the worst among the natives.

Maximilian more than once questions the correctness of many of the names given by Lewis and Clark and ascribes the errors to poor interpreting. He says:

These celebrated travellers passed the winter among the Mandans, and give many particulars respecting them, which, on the whole, are correct; but their proper names and words from the Mandan and Manitari languages are, in general, inaccurately understood and written. It is said, they derived their information from a person named Jessaume, who spoke the language very imperfectly, as we were assured everywhere on the Missouri. Of this kind are many of the names mentioned by those travellers, which neither the Indians nor the Whites were able to understand; for instance, Ahnahaways, a people who are said to have formerly dwelt between the Mandans and the Manitaries; likewise Mahawha, where the Arwacahwas lived; the fourth village is said to have been called Metaharta, and to have been inhabited by Manitaries; of all these names, except perhaps, Mahawha, which ought probably to be Machaha, nobody could give us the slightest information, not even Charbonneau, though he has lived here so many years. It is necessary to be much on your guard against bad interpreters, and I acted in this respect with much caution.

The Charbonneau mentioned is the same Chaboneau who acted as interpreter for Lewis and Clark on their long trip to the sea-coast and return to Fort Mandan. While at Fort Mandan both Jessáume and Chaboneau acted as interpreters for Lewis and Clark.

The iron corn mill which gave such satisfaction was welcome, apparently, not for its corn-grinding qualities, but because it afforded an excellent means of obtaining iron "to barb their arrows," as we learn from Henry, and "the largest piece of it, which they could not break or work up into any weapon, was fixed to a wooden handle, and used to pound marrow bones to make grease."

The construction of the huts was pushed as rapidly as possible. Gass's journal gives us more details regarding their house-building than does the Lewis and Clark journal. As before stated, they began felling trees on November 2d, and on November 19th and 20th, they moved into the huts, although they were not finished, but the weather was cold and canvas tents were thin. On November 21st they "despatched a periogue and collected stone for our Chimneys," and on the 24th, "we continued to cover our Huts with hewed Punchins." On November 25th Lewis and Clark state that the huts were "compleated," but Gass says the roofs were not finished until the 27th. They were then ready to cut pickets for the fortification, or stockaded part of the fort, but as it was very cold, the snow falling, and a northwest wind blowing, it was impossible to commence this work before December 1st. December 19th they began setting up the pickets, and on Christmas eve, December 24th, the entire work was finished. The narrative for Christmas Day reads thus:

TUESDAY, DECEMBER 25th [1804], we were awaked before day by a discharge of three platoons from the party. We had told the Indians not to visit us, as it was one of our great medicine days; so that the men remained at home and amused themselves in various ways, particularly with dancing, in which they take great pleasure. The American flag was hoisted for the first time in the fort; the best provisions we had were brought out, and this, with a little brandy, enabled them to pass the day in great festivity.

These huts are briefly described by Lewis and Clark under date of November 20th, but Gass's journal gives the better account of them and I transcribe his record.

The regular journal says:

NOVEMBER 20th. We this day moved into our huts, which are now completed. This place, which we call Fort Mandan, is situated in a point of low ground, on the north side of the Missouri, covered with tall and heavy cotton-wood.

Gass, under date of November 3d, records as follows:

The following is the manner in which our huts and fort were built. The huts were in two rows, containing four rooms each, and joined at one end forming an angle. When raised about 7 feet a floor of puncheons or split plank were laid, and covered with grass and clay; which made a warm loft. The upper part projected a foot over and the roofs were made shed-fashion, rising from the inner side, and making the outer wall about 18 feet high. The part not inclosed by the huts we intend to picket. In the angle formed by the two rows of huts we built two rooms, for holding our provisions and stores.

Larocque, the Northwest Company trader, describes Fort Mandan in his journal as —

"Captain Clark and His Men Building a Line of Huts" at Fort Mandan. 1804. From an old print from Gass's "A Journal of the Voyages and Travels," etc.

constructed in a triangular form, ranges of houses making two sides, and a range of amazing long pickets, the front. The whole is made so strong as to be almost cannon ball proof. The two ranges of houses do not join one another, but are joined by a piece of fortification made in the form of a demi circle that can defend two sides of the Fort, on the top of which they keep sentry all night; the lower parts of that building serve as a store. A sentinel is likewise kept all day walking in the Fort.

This word-picture of the historic fort states some facts not detailed elsewhere and gives perhaps the best idea of the structure that we have.

There were eight huts of one room and a loft each to house forty-five or more individuals. If we consider that one hut was allotted to the two Captains, as the note-books appear to indicate, there would then have been an average of six men in each of the other seven huts, besides the interpreters and their families.

The story of those wild, untutored people of the north-land among whom Lewis and Clark lived during the winter of 1804-5 is full of fascination, as, indeed, is that of most of the aboriginal tribes of this country, properly wrought out. From our point of view there was little in their existence, in those days, that would be termed happiness, pleasure, contentment. Life, to use a current, phrase, was of the most strenuous sort, and if now and then there seemed to be a period of inertness and laziness, it was more than counter-balanced by the hard struggle for food and raiment that was omnipresent. Their philosophy seems to have been of the practical sort and one suited to their needs and conditions, so that if, when food was plentiful, they sometimes ate with an apparent disregard of what the morrow might bring forth, when famine confronted them they starved with composure and fortitude.

The history and migrations of the Mandans, Minnetarees, and the Arikara, as learned by the explorers, is thus recounted in their journal:

NOVEMBER 21st. The villages near which we are established are five in number, and are the residence of three distinct nations: The Mandans, the Ahnahaways, and the Minnetarees. The history of the Mandans . . . illustrates more than that of any other nation the unsteady movements and the tottering fortunes of the American Indians. Within the recollection of living witnesses, the Mandans were settled 40 years ago in nine villages, the ruins of which we passed about 80 miles below, seven on the west and two on the east side of the Missouri. These two, finding themselves wasting away before the smallpox and the Sioux, united into one village, and moved up the river opposite the

Ricaras. The same causes reduced the remaining seven to five villages, till at length they emigrated in a body to the Ricara nation, where they formed themselves into two villages, and joined those of their countrymen who had gone before them. In their new residence they were still insecure, and at length the three villages ascended the Missouri to their present position.

. . . They are now two villages, one on the southeast of the Missouri, the other on the opposite side, at the distance of three miles across. The first, in an open plain, contains about 40 or 50 lodges, built in the same way as those of the Ricaras; the second, the same number; and both may raise about 350 men.

On the same side of the river, and at a distance of four miles from the lower Mandan village, is another called Mahaha. It is situated on a high plain at the mouth of Knife river, and is the residence of the Ahnahaways. This nation, whose name indicates that they were "people whose village is on a hill," formerly resided on the Missouri, about 30 miles below where they now live. . . . They are called by the French Soulier Noir or [Black] Shoe Indians; by the Mandans, Wattasoons; and their whole force is about 50 men.

On the south side of the same Knife river, half a mile above the Mahaha [village] and in the same open plain with it, is a village of Minnetarees surnamed Metaharta, who are about 150 men in number. On the opposite side of Knife river, and one and a half miles above this village, is a second [village] of Minnetarees, who may be considered as the proper Minnetaree nation. It is situated in a beautiful low plain, and contains 450 warriors.

The accounts which we received of the Minnetarees were contradictory. The Mandans say that this people came out of the water to the east and settled near them in their former establishment in nine villages; that they were very numerous, and fixed themselves in one village on the southern side of the Missouri. . . . The Minnetarees proper assert, on the contrary, that they grew where they now live and will never emigrate from the spot, the Great Spirit having declared that if they moved they would all die. . .

The French name of *Grosventres,* or Bigbellies, is given to the Minnetarees as well as to all the Fall Indians.

The inhabitants of these five villages, all of which are within the distance of six miles, live in harmony with one another. The Ahnahaways understand in part the language of the Minnetarees. The dialect of the Mandans differs widely from both; but their long residence together has insensibly blended their manners, and occasioned some approximation in language, particularly as to objects of daily occurrence and obvious to the senses.

Regarding the Mandan religion they thus discourse:

The whole religion of the Mandans consists in the belief of one Great Spirit presiding over their destinies. This Being must be in the nature of a good genius, since it is associated with the healing art, and "great spirit" is synonymous with "great medicine," a name applied to everything which they do not comprehend.

Their belief in a future state is connected with this tradition of their origin: The whole nation resided in one large village underground near a subterraneous lake; a grape-vine extended its roots down to their habitation and gave them a view of the light; some of the most adventurous climbed up the vine and were delighted with the sight of the earth, which they found

A Winter Village of the Minnetaree, or Grosventre, Indians. From Maximilian.

covered with buffalo and rich with every kind of fruits; returning with the grapes they had gathered, their countrymen were so pleased with the taste of them that the whole nation resolved to leave their dull residence for the charms of the upper region; men, women and children ascended by means of the vine; but when about half the nation had reached the surface of the earth a corpulent woman who was clambering up the vine broke it with her weight, and closed upon herself and the rest of the nation the light of the sun. Those who were left on earth made a village below, where we saw the nine villages; and when the Mandans die they expect to return to the original seats of their forefathers, the good reaching the ancient village by means of the lake, which the burden of the sins of the wicked will not enable them to cross.

At the time of Lewis and Clark's sojourn among these people, the Mandans numbered about 1250, and the Minnetarees 2500 souls.

The first mention made of the Mandans was by Verendrye, the father, who, with two of his sons, saw them on the Missouri in 1738. The sons again saw them in 1732, on what is now assumed to have been the first expedition to attempt to explore the Rocky Mountains. David Thompson visited them in 1797, and Alexander Henry the younger was among the Mandans in 1806; George Catlin, the celebrated Indian painter and collector of Indian handiwork, visited them in 1832; Maximilian, Prince of Wied, with Bodmer, an artist, went among, described, and painted them in 1833, and others have added to the literature of the subject. These Indians were well known to the northwestern fur traders in the period centring around the year 1800.

Lewis and Clark were really the discoverers of the Mandan Indians, so far as general knowledge of them goes, and there can be little, if any, doubt that Catlin and Maximilian were led to visit these tribes by the interest excited by their narrative. The Mandans were not like the other plains Indians − hostile, nomadic, improvident, etc. It has been their boast − I am not sure how true it may be − that, like the Flatheads, the blood of the white man has never been spilled by them. They lived, as our story reveals, in stockaded villages of earthen huts, made war on other tribes defensively only, cultivated the ground, raising corn, pumpkins, squashes, beans, etc., and were, all in all, deserving in most ways of the high opinions formed of them by Lewis and Clark. In a rough way these Mandans were, probably, more nearly comparable to the peaceful, town-living Pueblos of the Southwest than any other tribes,

The explorations of the Verendryes, considering their historical importance, seem to have received scant attention from those best qualified to translate their journals and interpret them. The senior Verendrye was at Lake Nepigon in 1727, and died in 1749; between those years, he and his three sons and a nephew – La Jemerays – were engaged in constant exploration in the Northwest, south and west of the Lake Winnipeg country. In 1736, one of the sons was killed by Indians and the nephew died. There have been fourteen spellings of the name Verendrye, the one here given seeming to be the approved form at the present time, although there exist reasons for believing that the form Véranderie is the proper one.

The father's full name and title was Pierre Gaultier de Varennes, Sieur de la Verendrye, while the son upon whose shoulders the father's mantle principally fell was the Chevalier de la Verendrye.

At this period the Sea of the West was a lodestar of exploration and Verendrye, incited thereto by the Canadian authorities, and indeed, under their orders, undertook what proved a thankless task of exploration.

Verendrye's experience was that of many another French explorer. Urged into undertakings where exposure, hardship, danger, nay even death itself lay in wait for him, he toiled and labored only to be neglected and left in the lurch at the end.

As Capt. E. L. Berthoud, a well-known American engineer and explorer, has said:

The neglect of Canada, and the abuses of its officials in the reign of Louis XV, hastened the loss of the Canadas in North America; and, coupled with the extravagance and waste of the Government of France, was a forerunner of the French Revolution, ending the corruption and misgovernment of one Hundred and Fifty years.

In pursuance of his plan to discover the Western Sea, Verendrye the elder, with his two sons, some Frenchmen,

and Indians, thirty-four persons in all, left Fort la Reine –
now Portage la Prairie – in Manitoba, in the fall of 1738, and
reached the Mandans after a trip of much toil and hardship.
Here he purposed remaining during the winter, but his interpreter deserted him and, after prevailing upon two
Frenchmen to remain and learn the Mandan language,
Verendrye, utterly disgusted and broken-hearted, returned
with the rest to Fort la Reine, reaching there February 11,
1739. The state of his feelings may be discerned from his
cry that, "death alone can deliver us from such miseries."

Going to Montreal, in 1739, Verendrye returned to Fort
la Reine in 1741, and found that his eldest son, the Chevalier,
had just reached there from another trip to the Mandans,
where he had obtained a cotton blanket said to have come
from white men (Spaniards?) near the Western Sea.

Another expedition was planned and, led by the Chevalier Verendrye and his brother, it left Fort la Reine April 29,
1742, and arrived at the Mandan towns on May 18th. There
they remained until late in July waiting for the "Gens des
Chevaux" – People of the Horses – Indians who were to act
as their guides. But these not appearing, they obtained
two Mandan guides and started for the Western Sea. After
a summer and fall of varying adventures, on January 1,
1743, they came in sight of the Rocky or Shining Mountains, and in the latter part of the month they reached
them, in the neighborhood of the Snake tribe of Indians.
The Indians with whom they were journeying now became
senselessly panic-stricken, and a homeward stampede followed. On May 18, 1743, they reached the Mandans, on
their return, and on July 2d were once more at Fort la Reine.

The route pursued by Verendrye on this journey has
been the subject of some conjecture. One statement as-
sumes that he went up the Missouri River to the Gates of
the Mountains, thence southward to the Yellowstone and

Stinking-water rivers, and to the Wind River Mountains. But this is an utterly impossible route. At that period, it must be remembered, the Mandans were living well down the Missouri, where Mandan and Bismarck now are, and the Chevalier's course, after leaving the Indian villages, was, with scarcely an exception, W. S. W., S. S. W., and S. W. This would have carried him across the Bad Lands of North Dakota, which he really seems to have described, and across the southeastern corner of Montana to the vicinity of the Big Horn Mountains and perhaps around and beyond them. But never a sight of the Western Sea did he have, nor did he even ascend the mountains.

The return route was E. S. E., until he reached the Missouri, where, on an eminence near the Indian "fort" of the "Gens de la Petite Cerise," – People of the Little (Choke?) Cherry, – Verendrye placed "a plate of lead with the arms and inscription of the King." Then turning N. N. E. and N. W., he journeyed up the river to the Mandan towns.

The data upon which to reconstruct Verendrye's trail is meagre and lacks definiteness, and would require deep study to work out the problem. Captain Berthoud thinks that the party reached the Wasatch Mountains, and that the Western Sea which they sought was, beyond doubt, the Great Salt Lake – which is surely a plausible conjecture.

Two things are certain: Chevalier Verendrye was the first white man who saw the Rocky Mountains, so far as our knowledge goes at the present time, and the Verendrye family gave us our first information regarding the Mandans. Verendrye stated that the Mandans were very "crafty in trade and all other relations," that they were also finer leather dressers than any other tribes, "and do very fine work on furs and feathers."

On Lewis's map of 1806, sent to President Jefferson in

NOTE. – Verendrye discovered the northern part of the Rocky Mountains.

the spring of 1807, when leaving Fort Mandan, and also on Clark's map of 1814, the position of the five villages into which the tribes had then become consolidated is shown, as is also Fort Mandan. Their location was about fifty-five miles above Mandan and Bismarck, N. D., and seven miles below the mouth of Knife River.

These tribes, like some others of the Missouri Valley, instead of living in the usual skin tepee, were domiciled in earthen huts of large size, warm and well built, and grouped in stockaded villages.

A Mandan Village and "Bull" Boats. From Maximilian.

Gass, who describes these earth lodges, might really have given us a much better picture of them than the hazy, indefinite one he draws, and so might Lewis and Clark. Alexander Henry, the younger, who was familiar with the Mandans in the days of Lewis and Clark, has written the most complete description, perhaps, of these ancient and interesting structures, and I reprint a part of it here:

A Mandane's circular hut is spacious. I measured the one I lodged in, and found it 90 feet from the door to the opposite side. The whole space is first dug out about 1½ feet below the surface of the earth. In the centre is the square fireplace, about five feet on each side, dug out about two feet below the surface of the ground flat. The lower part of the hut is constructed by erecting strong posts about six feet out of the ground, at equal distances from each other, according to the proposed size of the hut, as they are not all of the same dimensions. Upon these are laid logs as large as the posts, reaching from post to post to form the circle. On the outer side are placed pieces of split wood seven feet long, in a slanting direction, one end resting on the ground, the other leaning against the cross-logs or beams. Upon these beams rest rafters about the thickness of a man's leg, and 12 to 15 feet long, slanting enough to drain off the rain, and laid so close to each other as to touch. The upper ends of the rafters are supported upon stout pieces of squared timber, which last are supported by four thick posts about five feet in circumference, 15 feet out of the ground and 15 feet asunder, forming a square. Over these squared timbers others of equal size are laid, crossing them at right angles, leaving an opening about four feet square. This serves for chimney and windows, as there are no other openings to admit light, and when it rains even this hole is covered over with a canoe [bull boat] to prevent the rain from injuring their gammine [*sic*] and   earthen-pots.   The whole roof is well thatched with the small willows in which the Missourie abounds, laid on to the thickness of six inches or more, fastened together in a very compact manner and well secured to the rafters. Over the whole is spread about one foot of earth, and around the wall, to the height of three or four feet, is commonly laid up earth to the thickness of three feet, for security in case of an attack and to keep out the cold. The door is five feet broad and six high, with a covered way or porch on the outside of the same height as the door, seven feet broad and ten in length. The doors are made of raw buffalo hide stretched upon a frame and suspended by cords from one of the beams which form the circle. - Every night the door is barricaded with a long piece of timber supported by two stout posts set in the ground in the inside of the hut, one on each side of the door.

Henry then describes the interior and the surroundings of the huts at length, but lack of space prevents repetition here.

George Catlin – 1832 – describes in much detail, and most interestingly, the lodges and villages of the Mandans, and a few brief excerpts from his writings will not be out of place. There were, in Catlin's and Maximilian's time, two villages of the Mandans, as in Lewis and Clark's day. Writing of the principal village, Catlin says:

The ground on which the Mandan village is at present built, was admirably selected for defense; being on a bank forty or

A Mandan Hut on the Fort Berthold Reservation in 1904. Primitive ladder reclines at side of the covered entrance.

fifty feet above the bed of the river. The greater part of this bank is nearly perpendicular, and of solid rock. The river, suddenly changing its course to a right-angle, protects two sides of the village, which is built upon this promontory or angle; they have therefore but one side to protect, which is effectually done by a strong piquet, and a ditch inside of it, of three or four feet in depth. The piquet is composed of timbers of a foot or more in diameter, and eighteen feet high, set firmly in the ground at sufficient distances from each other to admit of guns and other missiles to be fired between them. The ditch (unlike that of civilized modes of fortification) is inside of the piquet, in which their warriors screen their bodies from the view and weapons of their enemies, whilst they are reloading and discharging their weapons through the piquets. . . .

Their village has a most novel appearance to the eye of a stranger; their lodges are closely grouped together, leaving but just room enough for walking and riding between them; and appear from without, to be built entirely of dirt. . . .

The floors of these dwellings are of earth, but so hardened by use, and swept so clean, and tracked by bare and moccasined feet, that they have almost a polish, and would scarcely soil the whitest linen. . . . They all sleep on bedsteads similar in form to ours, but generally not quite so high; made of round poles rudely lashed together with thongs. A buffalo skin, fresh stripped from the animal, is stretched across the bottom poles, and about two feet from the floor; which, when it dries, becomes much contracted, and forms a perfect sacking-bottom. The fur side of this skin is placed uppermost, on which they lie with great comfort, with a buffalo-robe folded up for a pillow, and others drawn over them instead of blankets. These beds, . . . are uniformly screened with a covering of buffalo or elk skins, oftentimes beautifully dressed and placed over the upright poles or frame, like a suit of curtains; leaving a hole in front, sufficiently spacious for the occupant to pass in and out, to and from his or her bed. Some of these coverings or curtains are exceedingly beautiful, being cut tastefully into fringe, and handsomely ornamented with porcupine's quills and picture writings or hieroglyphics.   .   .   .

Maximilian also gives considerable space to descriptions of their villages and the life in them, and I quote from him as follows:

Their villages are assemblages of clay huts, of greater or less extent, placed close to each other, without regard to order. Mih-Tutta-Hang-Kush, the largest of the Mandan villages, was about 150 or 200 paces in diameter, the second was much smaller. The circumference forms an irregular circle, and was anciently surrounded with strong posts, or palisades, which have, however, gradually disappeared as the natives used them for fuel in the cold winters. At four places, at nearly equal distances from each other, is a bastion built of clay, furnished with loop-holes, and lined both within and without with basket-work of willow branches. They form an angle, and are open towards the village; the earth is filled in between the basket-work; and it is said that these bulwarks, which are now in a state of decay, were erected for the Indians by the whites.

These Indians, poor and uncultivated as they were, yet maintained both summer and winter residences. On their relative use of these Maximilian says:

> In winter, that is, at the beginning or middle of November, these Indians remove, with the greater part of their effects, to the neighboring forest, where their winter huts are situated. These consist of precisely similar huts, of rather smaller dimensions. Their departure from the summer huts is determined by the weather, but, as beforesaid, is generally about the middle of November; and their return, in the spring, is usually about the latter end of February, or the beginning of March, so that we may reckon that they pass above eight months in their summer quarters. Inside of the winter huts is a particular compartment, where the horses are put in the evening, and fed with maize. In the daytime they are driven into the prairie, and feed in the bushes, on the bark of poplars.

Maximilian calls attention to the fact that the lodges of the "Konza" – Kansas – Indians were similar to those of the Mandans and Minnetarees, the differences being "slight" ones.

Dr. Washington Matthews, who lived among these Indian tribes on the Fort Berthold Reservation in North Dakota from 1865 to 1872, and who, through his exhaustive investigations, is an authority upon the subject, states[1] that the earth lodge, in closely allied forms, has been found from North Dakota to Kansas, in the Missouri Valley, and that, at a very early day, they undoubtedly existed "in the Mississippi Valley as far south as Louisiana and as far east as East Tennessee." The only ones in existence to-day are those found on the Berthold Reservation.

In my visit to the reservation in the fall of 1902 I saw

---

[1] "The Earth Lodge in Art," *American Anthropologist,* January - March, 1902

two of these lodges and obtained photographs of them. If there were any differences between these and those of one hundred years ago, except the substitution of wooden for skin doors, they were so slight as not to be noticeable offhand.

At one of them, the owner being absent, I was unable to enter it, but through a wide crack in the door I obtained a good view of the interior and it fitted well with the descriptions here given of the old lodges. It was evidently used at the present time for a storage house, at least to some extent, and was not a regular residence, for the log cabin home of the owner stood alongside of it.

At the other hut, across the Missouri River and several miles distant from the first one, the owner refused me permission to invade it, stating that it was used for ceremonial purposes.

Mrs. Baker, a daughter of Two Chiefs, an old Mandan who has seen seventy-two snows, and a graduate of the Indian School at Santee, Neb., and who converses and writes well in English, stated that there were not more than five or six earth lodges to be found on the reservation to-day.

The word "circular" used by the writers quoted in describing these huts must be taken in its larger, general meaning. The huts were really irregularly polygonal in shape. Those I saw were forty feet in diameter, perhaps, and the first had nine sides and the second eleven. In one case one of the sides was double the length of the others.

Catlin's pictorial representations of these huts are not true to nature. The lodges were of a much more squatty appearance than he depicts them and without any such high arched, dome-like, hemispherical roof as he places upon them. He evidently adopted a conventional, and largely imaginary, figure for his huts, and pushed artistic license to the extreme. At a little distance the general effect was sufficiently that of a "circular" structure to justify the use of the word when not used in a restrictive sense.

When at Fort Berthold, I was informed that the very aged Mandan Chief, Rushing Eagle, or more commonly, Bad Gun, descended from the great chief Four Bears, – whom, I regret, I was not able to see, – had kept standing

Two Chiefs and Daughter Relating the Story of the Mandans.

until recently a very old lodge in which he kept some ancient relics, and that among these were some of the identical articles that Catlin had painted into his pictures in 1832. I was not able to verify this. The lodge had but lately been destroyed because of its age and decaying condition.

After my inspection of the two earthen houses mentioned, I could not but be impressed with the fact that these old Mandan and Arikara lodges were practically the prototypes of the settler's sod house of the prairies of recent time. The sides and roofs of these huts were covered with sod chunks of regular shapes and sizes, just such as we would cut out of the prairie for the same purpose. The porch, covered entrance, or passage-way mentioned was and is a characteristic, standing feature of these earthen lodges, and one which Catlin persistently ignored both in his paintings and text. Maximilian brought out this peculiarity of the Mandan hut in his work.

In one of the illustrations of an earth hut there can be seen a notched pole leaning against a scaffold, the latter used now, as in old days, for drying corn, etc. This pole is one of the primitive ladders anciently used by these Indians, and, evidently, not yet entirely discarded.

The monuments of these tribes, in the shape of abandoned and ruined huts and towns, are to be found, as has been stated, on the banks of the upper Missouri from about Heart or Cannon-ball River, below Mandan and Bismarck, to Knife River or beyond. The Indians seem, notwithstanding the great labor involved in so doing, to have moved quite frequently, not necessarily, however, for long distances. As the Sioux harassed them continually, these removals were due in part to a desire to protect themselves more effectually, and another reason was the scarcity of fuel and timber which in time was felt in each neighborhood. In making these removals, it was quite common, as Lewis and Clark mention, for two small villages to combine in one at the new location. Owing to the immense difficulty of cutting timbers with their crude stone axes, in making these changes of residence they undoubtedly carried with them the timbers of the abandoned huts and used them in rebuilding, wherever possible. The Indians left Knife River because of the scarcity of timber and the attacks of the Sioux. When the trading post of Fort Berthold — so

called in honor of Bartholomew Berthold, a fur trader of St.
Louis – was established, about 1844 or 1845, the Indians
"drew the logs [of which it was built] with lariats of rawhide
over their shoulders."

The dirt mounds, ruins of their former homes, have often
been mistaken for the ancient burial-grounds of these tribes,
which is not surprising unless one has studied the history
of this interesting people. About ten miles above Bismarck
one of the best of these collections of mounds is found, on
a bluff overlooking one of the most beautiful stretches of the
Missouri, just below Square Butte. There are eighteen or
twenty of the mounds, most of them well-defined, and
generally more or less circular in form. They form a semi-
circular arc, with the river as a chord, and are now more or
less merged together into an irregular ridge. These mounds
have been dug over and over, yet I was able to find among
them many shards and arrow-points and knives when I
visited them.

From the writings of Bradbury, Brackenridge, and
Catlin; Maximilian's admittedly reliable work; Dr. Matthews's *Ethnography and Philology of the Hidatsa Indians:*
and Powell's *Indian Linquistic Families of America,* etc.,
principally, supplemented by observations of my own, I
summarize additional matter of interest relating to the
tribes among whom our explorers wintered in 1804-5, and
thereby made historic.

The Arikara Indians belong to the Caddoan family, as
do the Pawnees, with whom they habited a century ago;
the Mandans and the Minnetarees, Grosventres, or, correctly, Hidatsa Indians, are each a part of the large Siouan
family, as are also the Crows, with whom the Hidatsa were
formerly closely affiliated.

The word "Arikara" seems to be a Mandan word; Minnetaree is a Hidatsan word applied to these people by the

Mandans, while Hidatsa was the name of the village on Knife River which Lewis and Clark considered the abode of the Minnetarees proper, and Mandan is a corruption of a Dakotan word. The French word *Grosventures* – Big-bellies – by which the Hidatsa are commonly known, is not applicable in any way to these people; it is a misnomer entirely.

The Mandans call themselves Métutahanke, *the Lower Village* as Dr. Matthews gives it, or Miti-Untanhanke, *the Village on the East,* as it was given to, and partially written for, me by Mrs. Baker, both referring to the same village, the one called Ma-too-tón-ha by Lewis and Clark. Maximilian calls this village Mih-Tutta-Hang-Kush, and these different readings of the same word well indicate the difficulties experienced in obtaining correct Indian vocabularies.

These people have always been farmers, and both men and women have for years, now, shared the labors of the field. In early days they raised corn, tobacco, squashes, beans, the wild sunflower, etc., and now they grow, in addition, potatoes, turnips, and various vegetables. The Arikara seem to be the best farmers. Each tribe now raises cattle and horses, but they do not seem to grasp the idea that cattle raising, if attended to properly, will enrich them, a scrub lean steer being as valuable in their eyes as a fat, blooded one. These Indians are virtually self-supporting, as they receive very little from the Government,

The Berthold Reservation is at present good only for stock raising. If it is practicable to irrigate it from the waters of the Missouri it should be done, and I have little doubt that it would almost revolutionize the character of these Indians in a short time, for it would make certain the regular maturing of crops and banish the discouragements consequent upon repeated failures.

It should be remarked concerning the words Minnetaree and Grosventre that Lewis and Clark used these words with respect to two distinct tribes both ethnographically and geographically. The Grosventres of the Missouri, those confederated with the Mandans, have no connection with the Grosventres of the prairie, who live far west from the former on the Marias River in Montana. These latter are the real "Fall" Indians to whom Lewis and Clark refer, so called from the falls of the Saskatchewan River, whence they came.

The five villages mentioned by Lewis and Clark in 1804, were still in existence in 1833, when Maximilian visited these Indians. One important change had, he states, occurred. The Missouri River had characteristically changed its channel and in Maximilian's day flowed on the eastern side of Rooptahee, or Ruhptare, the second Mandan town of our narrative, so that both the Mandan villages were then on the western – south – bank.

Although at the time that Lewis and Clark sojourned near these tribes the "Ricaras" were at war with the Mandans and were living much farther down the Missouri, they had before lived in proximity to the other tribes and subsequently removed again to their neighborhood. When Lewis and Clark ascended the river the Arikara were among the most tractable and friendly of the Indians whom they met. Soon afterward, in consequence of difficulties with the traders, possibly, or perhaps goaded thereto by the Sioux, they became hostile and for years were among the worst and most combative tribes the whites had to contend against.

Our explorers refer to the ravages of the smallpox. This scourge of savages as well as of civilized peoples has indeed wrought havoc among these tribes. Maximilian states that the two Mandan villages mentioned by Lewis and Clark were established by the Mandans – in or before the year 1800 – after a visitation of this disease which, with an attack of the

Sioux soon after, wiped out so many of their people that the remnant consolidated in these two towns.

The worst infliction of this sort was subsequent to the visits of Catlin and Maximilian, and it almost completely annihilated the Mandans, if the old accounts are fairly trustworthy.

In 1837[1] the smallpox was carried among them from the Missouri River steamboat, St. Peter's, owned by the American Fur Company, and out of 1600 Mandans, only about 31 or 32 families were left; 500 Minnetarees out of 1000 fell victims to the pestilence, and 1500 of the 3000 Arikara also died. The epidemic spread to the other tribes of the north, and Schoolcraft estimates that before its ravages had ceased it claimed at least 10,000 victims; Catlin and Maximilian make the number very much larger. Kenneth McKenzie of the American Fur Company, in a letter to Catlin, written in June, 1839, states that there were 7000 Crees and 15,000 Blackfeet wiped out by the disease. In some instances the losses were undoubtedly much exaggerated.

I quote from Schoolcraft:

An eye-witness of this scene, writing from Fort Union on the 27th of November, 1837, says: "Language, however forcible, can convey but a faint idea of the scene of desolation which the country now presents. In whatever direction you turn, nothing but sad wrecks of mortality meet the eye; lodges standing on every hill, but not a streak of smoke rising from them. Not a sound can be heard to break the awful stillness, save the ominous croak of ravens and the mournful howl of wolves fattening on the human carcasses that lie strewed around."

Another writer says:

Many of the handsome Arickarees, who had recovered, seeing the disfiguration of their features, committed suicide; some by

[1] See Henry R. Schoolcraft, Catlin's *Opeeka,* Chittenden's *Fur Trade of the Northwest,* etc.

throwing themselves from rocks, others by stabbing and shooting. The prairie has become a graveyard; its wild flowers bloom over the sepulchres of Indians.

There can be no question, from all the reports, that this visitation was one of the most awful, widespread, decimating scourges that ever afflicted any people, not excepting the Egyptians who were made to suffer for Pharaoh's hardness of heart. In telling me about this scourge, Two-Chiefs, an old Mandan who shows marks of the disease, stated that the Grosventres ran away when the disease appeared, – they didn't run fast enough nor far enough to escape it, however, – and that when the pestilence had run its course the Arikara moved into the Mandan villages and boldly appropriated the huts and all their belongings. The Mandans were gone, wiped out, and there were none to use the dwellings or to object to such forced occupancy. Some accounts state that even the few surviving Mandans were driven from their own huts. Subsequently these tribes were again thus afflicted, and from one who was then stationed at Fort Clark and an eye-witness of the fact, I am informed that suicide was committed by the victims throwing themselves over the bluffs of the river to the rocks below. De Smet states that both the smallpox and cholera created havoc among the northern Indians in 1851.

The Lewis and Clark narrative for March 16th describes it process for making glass beads known to the Mandans.

The Indians did not make the glass itself. This they obtained from the whites, but there is evidence that, prior to the appearance of the traders, they used obsidian, or natural glass, for this purpose. Dr. Matthews, as late as 1870, had flat triangular blue glass pendants made to order by an Arikara woman, he furnishing the glass.

These people also made unglazed pottery, mats, and baskets, ladles and spoons, from the horns of the Rocky

Mountain sheep *(Ovis montana)* and the buffalo, and from the shoulder-blades of the bison they fashioned the hoes with which they hoed the ground in very early time. Since the whites came, the crude implements of the old days have been mostly supplanted by our household, garden, etc., utensils; but, in 1902, I purchased a fine sheep-horn ladle apparently in daily use still.

The tradition relating to the origin of the Mandans given by Lewis and Clark, according to Dr. Matthews, relates, not only to the Mandans, but to the Hidatsa, as well. This tradition, I find, is current at the present day and the lake from which the tribe emerged is said to be Minnewakan, or Devil's, Lake in North Dakota, the Hidatsa name for this lake – Midihopa – meaning sacred or mysterious water. Dr. Matthews thinks that "one nation borrowed its legend from the other," so that both have a common source.

As to the religious beliefs of these people, Bradbury well remarks, "There is nothing relating to the Indians so difficult to understand as their religion." The Mandans and Arikara in Dr. Matthews's day still used the ark and medicine lodge, and performed their ceremonies there, as Catlin and Maximilian have described.

Bradbury, referring to the sacred lodge of the Arikara, says:

> This is called the *Medicine Lodge,* and in one particular corresponds with the sanctuary of the Jews, as no blood is on any account whatsoever to be spilled within it, not even that of an enemy; nor is any one, having taken refuge there, to be forced from it.

These people had a belief in a "Great Spirit," or "Old Man Immortal," or "Great Mystery," and Dr. Matthews discusses it quite fully in his paper. Their ancient belief appears to have been, on the whole, a species of Polytheism. Religious missionary work on the Fort Berthold Reservation began in 1876, and since then there has been a marked change in their religious ideas. The leaven acted but slowly at first, but when its results were apparent it seemed to work with cumulative effect. "Only a small minority of the people now hold to the wreck of their old paganism." Carlisle, Santee, and other schools have had their influence in producing this uplift. The younger generations see things with a new and broader vision and their moral and religious notions are cast in a new mould.

Mr. Hall, the missionary among these people, in discussing their general condition, past and present, says:

> Twenty-five years ago the old Indian community was like Sodom; now the Indians live decently on the allotments, with their wives, and none of them have more than one. There is vice to fight, but only as in every white community. Religiously the phenomena of growth are seen here as elsewhere. Form and ritual are in sight, and are adopted before the inner power is felt. The old beliefs have largely passed away from the younger generation. The Christian teaching answering to all that was of higher aspiration and better living in the old religion, has saved them from infidelity and won their intellectual faith. The church is more a social centre to them than a spiritual.

Both the Congregationalists and Catholics now have religious organizations on the reservation. The former have three churches, and the latter a church and a school combined, but this was unused at the time of the writer's visit. One of the Congregational chapels is largely the work of the Arikara Indians. It cost nine hundred dollars, and of this the Indians contributed more than one third. They hewed the logs and hauled the stone and lumber, the latter from a distance of sixty miles. There are also a few Episcopalians among these people.

In considering the moral excellencies and delinquencies of the old Mandans and allied tribes, we must necessarily, I take it, consider in connection therewith their ideas of entertainment and hospitality. And we must remember that we are reviewing the ethical acts and beliefs of an uncivilized, uncultivated people, touched with the frost of savagery and barbarism, and a hundred years removed, as well, from the canons of moral conduct at present taught them.

Mandan Indian of 1833
From "Travels to the Interior of North America," etc, by Maximilian.

On the way up the river the expedition, as will be recalled, had been importuned by Indian women for the opportunity of affording the men the privilege of connubial pleasures – for a consideration. This was with the approval, too, of their fathers, husbands, and brothers. This importunity was continued when the party arrived at the Mandan villages, although scarcely any reference is made to it in the regular narrative; as a matter of fact it was an incident of the exploration from beginning to end. In the journal for January 16, 1805, we read:

Kagohami visited us and brought us a little corn, and soon afterward one of the first war-chiefs of the Minnetarees came, accompanied by his squaw, a handsome woman, whom he was desirous we should use during the night.

That these offers were quite generally accepted was not disguised, and the itinerary for November 22, 1804, relates an instance where serious trouble occurred for the "woman in the case," her husband stabbing her three times and seeking to kill her.

In his journal for April 5, 1805, just as the party were ready to resume their trip westward, Gass indulges in a little moralizing on this matter, and covertly reveals a good deal regarding the habits of the members of the expedition during that memorable winter at Fort Mandan.

He says:

> It may be observed generally that chastity is not very highly esteemed by these people, and that the severe and loathsome effects of *certain French principles* are not uncommon among them. The fact is, that the women are generally considered an article of traffic and *indulgencies* are sold at a very moderate price. As a proof of this I will just mention, that for an old tobacco box, one of our men was granted the honour of passing a night with the daughter of the head-chief of the Mandan nation. An old bawd with her punks, may also be found in some of the villages on the Missouri, as well as in the large cities of polished nations.

Bradbury remarks, in this connection:

> It scarcely requires to be observed, that chastity in females is not a virtue, nor that a deviation from it is considered a crime, when sanctioned by the consent of their husbands, fathers, or brothers.

While there were, surely enough, "certain lewd fellows of the baser sort" among these people, just as there were and are among the Caucasian race, it seems incontrovertible that, among many of them at least, this proffer of women was a part of their customary hospitality, at least to the whites.

Bradbury draws this picture of Indian entertainment:

> No people on earth discharge the duties of hospitality with more cordial good-will than the Indians. On entering a lodge I was always met by the master, who first shook hands with me, and immediately looked for his pipe; before he had time to light it, a bear-skin, or that of a buffalo, was spread for me to

sit on, although they sat on the bare ground. When the pipe was lighted, he smoked a few whiffs, and then handed it to me; after which it went round to all the men in the lodge. Whilst this was going on, the squaw prepared something to eat, which, when ready, was placed before me on the ground. The squaw, in some instances, examined my dress, and in particular my mockasons; if any repair was wanting, she brought a small leather bag, in which she kept her awls and split sinew, and put it to rights. After conversing as well as we could by signs, if it was near night, I was made to understand that a bed was at my service; and in general this offer was accompanied by that of a *bedfellow*.

The worst indictment in this respect that I have seen drawn against these tribes is by Henry; his story is truly a disgusting one and, in many of its details, unquotable. Of the Mandans he says in part:

Both men and women make it a rule to go down to the river and wash every morning and evening. . . . Modesty in the female sex appears to be a virtue unknown. The women wear a kind of leather shift which reaches down to the calves of their legs; this they slip off at some distance from the shore and walk deliberately into the water, entirely naked, in the presence of numbers of men, both old and young, who pay no attention to them. . . . The river being very shallow for some distance from shore, they make no scruple of standing only knee deep, and thus wash themselves before going out further to swim; and in coming out they pass close by you as unconcernedly as if they had on a petticoat or shift. They sometimes bundle up their leather garment under the arm or in one hand and walk deliberately into the village to their own huts, where they sit by the fire to dry themselves in the presence of everyone; and then, having chatted for some time with their families, they go to bed entirely naked. The men wear no other covering in summer than buffalo robes, and even those are seldom worn within doors, being only thrown on when they go out to visit or walk about the village.

And again:

They seem to be a very lascivious set of people. The men make no scruple in offering their wives to strangers without solicitation, and are offended if their favors are not accepted, unless convinced that there is some good reason for your refusal, and that it is not out of contempt. They expect payment for their complaisance, but a mere trifle will satisfy them – even one single coat button.

Concerning the Grosventres, or Hidatsa Indians, he remarks: "Upon the whole they appeared to me to be a fierce and savage set of scoundrels, still more loose and licentious than the Mandanes."

This word-painting by Henry is, assuredly, not a pleasant one to contemplate. Whether it is a brutally frank, true-to-nature picture, or an overdrawn one, may not be easy to determine, for while there is reason for believing the former to be the case, still Henry was predisposed to look askance upon everything connected with these people, to magnify and exaggerate their faults, and to minimize and belittle their virtues, according to the testimony of Charles MacKenzie, a fellow-trader of the Northwest Company to the Mandans and Grosventres, given in his journal, *The Missouri Indians.* Among other things he says:

Mr. Henry avowed his disappointment and did not disguise his detestation of the Indians; he was displeased with himself, dissatisfied with his "equal" [Chaboillez, junior, one of his traveling companions] and disgusted with his inferiors. Mr. Chaboillez was at his ease, . . . sat in the throng, smoked the pipe when it came his turn . . . as if he were bred a *Gros Ventre,* but Mr. Henry kept at a distance from the crowd and smoked his pipe alone.

In such a mood the victim would surely "nothing extenuate," even though he may not have "set down aught in malice." John McDonnell, another of the Northwest Company traders, comments in a general way on these people in his journal – about 1797. He pronounces them the best husbandmen in the Northwest, and adds: "They are the mildest and most honest Indians upon the whole continent and, withal, very fond of the white people."

Catlin, who spent much time in the Mandan country and who describes these people in great detail, pictures them in no such sombre tones as does Henry. He found them most warmly hospitable, and if he observed in his day – 1832 – any such lascivious practices as Henry mentions, I cannot find that he refers to them. It is true that if Henry was disposed to see and describe events of doubtful character, Catlin was ever ready to praise and laud, and now and then he overshot the mark. And yet he has faithfully portrayed much that he witnessed, if subsequent writers are to be believed.

As an offset to Henry's description of the Indians' manner of bathing, Catlin has this to say:

At the distance of half a mile or so above the village, is the customary place where the women and girls resort every morning in the summer months, to bathe in the river. To this spot they repair by hundreds, every morning at sunrise, where, on a beautiful beach, they can be seen running and glistening in the sun, whilst they are playing their innocent gambols and leaping into the stream. They all learn to swim well, and the poorest swimmer amongst them will dash fearlessly into the boiling and eddying current of the Missouri, and cross it with perfect ease. At the distance of a quarter of a mile back from the river, extends a terrace or elevated prairie, running north from the village, and forming a kind of semicircle around this bathing-place; and on this terrace, which is some twenty or thirty feet higher than the meadow between it and the river, are stationed every morning several sentinels, with their bows and arrows in hand, to guard and protect this sacred ground from the approach of boys or men from any direction.

At a little distance below the village, also, is the place where the men and boys go to bathe and learn to swim.

While, according to Catlin, the marriage and divorce laws of these people were of a flimsy character, he says of the women:

Such, then, are the Mandans – their women are beautiful and modest, – and amongst the respectable families, virtue is as highly cherished and as inapproachable, as in any society whatever; yet at the same time a chief may marry a dozen wives if he pleases, and so may a white man; and if either wishes to marry the most beautiful and modest girl in the tribe, she is valued only equal, perhaps, to two horses, a gun with powder and ball for a year, five or six pounds of beads, a couple of gallons of whiskey, and a handful of awls.

All through Catlin's letters he pays tribute to the modesty and virtue of the Mandan women and maidens and to the general good and manly attributes of the men.

The Bison Dance of the Mandans.
From "Travels to the Interior of North America," etc, by Maximilian.

Maximilian says, "Prudery is not a virtue of the Indian women," and according to him the ethical ideas of both men and women were of a very low order and fashioned a good deal on the French style of moral architecture.

Whether he considered this due to virgin and innate innocence or to natural or acquired depravity, he does not state. He dismisses the subject in a few words and apparently found other matters to discuss which were much more congenial and interesting. In 1843, Audubon, the great naturalist, saw the Mandans and Arikara, but he found nothing to admire in them – all the poetry about them he thought was contained in books.

Brackenridge remarks at some length upon what he observed among the Arikara, and handles the subject in such a plain, yet refined, dignified, broad, and instructive way, that I cannot refrain from quoting him also:

To give an account of the vices of these people, would only be to enumerate many of the most gross which prevail amongst us, with this difference, that they are practised in public without shame. The savage state, like the rude uncultivated waste, is contemplated to most advantage at a distance. . . . They have amongst them their poor, their envious, their slanderers, their mean and crouching, their haughty and overbearing, their unfeeling and cruel, . . . their generous and magnanimous, their rich and hospitable, their pious and virtuous, their kind, frank, and affectionate, and in fact, all the diversity of characters that exists amongst the most refined people; but as their vices are covered by no veil of delicacy, their virtues may be regarded rather as the effect of involuntary impulse, than as the result of sentiment. . .

Amongst others of their customs which appeared to me singular, I observed that it was a part of their hospitality, to offer the guest, who takes up his residence in their lodges, one of the females of the family as a bedfellow; sometimes even one of their wives, daughters, or sisters, but most usually a maid-servant, according to the estimation in which the guest is held, and to decline such offer is considered as treating the host with some disrespect; notwithstanding this, if it be remarked that these favors are uniformly declined, the guest rises much higher in his esteem.

This want of chastity among the Arikara was by no means universal – perhaps a more minute acquaintance with them might have enabled me to explain the phenomenon: indeed, from the remains of a singular exhibition, which several of us witnessed, I was induced to believe that Diana had not altogether yielded to the dominion of her rival goddess. On one of their festive days, as we drew near the medicine lodge or temple, we saw in front of the entrance, or door, a number of young girls tricked out in all their finery. . . . We observed a cedar bough fixed in the earth on the top of the lodge. Prizes of beads, vermillion, and scarlet cloth. were exhibited: and the old men who live in the temple to the number of five or six, now proclaimed, as I was informed, that whosoever amongst the young girls of Arikara had preserved unsullied her virgin purity, might then ascend the temple and touch the bough, and one of the prizes would be given to her; that it was in vain to think of deceiving, for the Manitou, or Spirit, knowing all things, even their secret thoughts, would most certainly reveal the truth; and moreover, the young men were enjoined under the severest denunciations, to declare all that might be within their knowledge. Curiosity was now much excited. In a few moments, the daughter of the interpreter (a Frenchman who had resided upwards of twenty years), a beautiful girl of sixteen came forward, but before she could ascend to touch the bough, a young fellow stepped forth, and said something, the amount of which I easily conjectured from its effect, for the young lady instantly shrunk back confused and abashed, while the surrounding crowd was convulsed with laughter. A pause ensued, which lasted for some considerable time. I began to tremble for the maidens of Arikara, when a girl of seventeen, one of the most beautiful in the village, walked forward, and asked, "Where is the Arikara who can bring any accusation against me?" then touched the bough, and carried off the prize. I feel a pleasure in adding, for the honor of the ladies of Arikara, that others followed, though I did not take the trouble of noting the number.

However one may decide the question as to whether the vices of these – and, indeed other – aboriginal people were in large part the natural results of their uncultivated condition, and, particularly as connected with the rites of hospitality, were little, or in no wise, prompted by conscious lasciviousness, in a general way they have arrived at a much higher moral plane since Lewis and Clark cantoned with them.

As against the gloomy word picture drawn by Henry let me close this part of my narrative with a brief but more cheerful one, nearly a century later, by Mr. Hall:

Just before last Thanksgiving day I was going through the bottomland, two miles away from the church site. The air was clear and still after a shower. Among the bushes I heard what seemed to be a continuous ringing note of music. It was the sound of axes striking hard, dry wood. Through the still air and among the bushes it was blended into one note. A company of the men of our church were hewing logs for the frame of the new chapel. I went on with a note of thanksgiving in my heart. . . . The heathen dance-lodge, the place of religious ceremony and center of social life, went to ruin three years ago, and as the church arose near by, the wind blew down the remnant of it and it is gone.

After all, if we condemn these ignorant beings of a century ago, what can we say of the civilized whites who accepted the favors offered by the Mandan and Arikara belles?

Among the traditions of these people is one of an ark and deluge, not unlike our own Soachian story. Another was of a supernatural birth, of a man who performed miracles, one of which was not unlike that of Chirst's miracle of the loaves and fishes.

Their great medicine festival was the *Okeepa,* described at length by Catlin and Maximilian. It lasted several days and in some respects was not unlike the now well-known Indian Sun-dance of the Sioux and other tribes, and it included fearful tortures and sufferings.

These tribes, with the exception of the Arikara, formerly buried their dead on scaffolds, and these formed a striking feature of the landscape near their villages. The Arikara mode of sepulture was like our own and all these people now generally use this form of burial. Near the present Fort Berthold agency at Elbowoods, there is a spot in the hills where many dead are buried among the rocks. The coffins were crude affairs, had no earth covering, and are now quite decayed and burst open, exposing the skeletons, with their old bed-quilt wrappings and household dishes and utensils, which were entombed with the corpses.

Mandan Indian Graves in 1904, in the Hill near Fort Berthold Indian Agency, North Dakota.

239

In the early days the Mandans were noted for their long light hair and fair complexions. This caused Catlin to exploit a notion that these people were descended from a colony of Welshmen who were supposed to have landed on the Florida coast or thereabouts in very early days and then mysteriously to have disappeared. The hair of the men often trailed on the ground, and Henry, Catlin, and others refer to this in much detail. Now they wear their hair cut short, of their own volition, and in my brief visit I noticed no peculiarities of complexion or in color of hair. All of them, Mandans, Arikara, and Minnetarees, seem to be a sturdy, manly set of fellows, with frank and intelligent countenances. I am inclined to think they have not had the best of supervision in the past, nor been treated with sufficient liberality and consideration by the Government.

Catlin was effusive in his praise of these Indians, and both he and Maximilian appear to have found some individuals who savored strongly of the Chingachgook type of Indian, and whose memories and virtues are venerated to day. Such a man, for one, was the old Mah-to-toh-pah, or Four Bears, of Catlin, the Meto-Topé of Maximilian, and I can easily believe that Lean, or Poor Wolf, a Grosventre of to-day, now blind and infirm with the weight of his eighty-three years, has been a man that one could trust and respect. De Smet says that Four Bears was "the most civil and affable Indian" that he ever met on the Missouri. Two-Chiefs, and Leggings, Mandans, and now old like Poor Wolf, must also have been men of dignity and character.

Probably the most admirable character among all these Indians, in recent years, was Son of the Star, an Arikara Chief. In answer to a recent inquiry of mine regarding this estimable chieftain, a prominent and well-known lecturer, who had known Son of the Star well, replied that he was the finest man he had ever known, white or Indian.

Leggings, a Mandan Indian of 1904.

Son of the Star was a warrior, orator, logician, philosopher, statesman, diplomat, and above all, a *man* in the highest and broadest sense of the word. He was the pride and idol of his tribe, and one of those men whose existence proved that Cooper drew his finer Indian characters from living examples, and not from imagination.

Son of the Star saw that the way of the white man was the way the Indian must follow, and he educated and directed his tribe in consonance with that idea.

The Berthold Reservation occupies both sides of the Missouri River, the mouth of the Little Missouri River touching the reservation at about the middle of the south side. The Arikara, or "Rees," occupy the lower part of the reservation on the north side of the Missouri, the Grosventres, or Hidatsa, are found above the "Rees," while the Mandans are settled almost wholly on the south side of the stream.

As a pure race "the polite and friendly Mandans," as they were known to the traders, are slowly but surely declining, and it will not be long before the last one will have departed for the happy hunting grounds. The reservation rolls call for two hundred and fifty Mandans. In talking with Two-Chiefs, I asked him how many full-blood, pure Mandans he thought still remained. The old man, seventy-two years of age, stood in deep thought for several moments, and then replied, "Not more than ten families; all the others are mixed blood." Numerically, the tribe as a whole seems to be holding its own.

The visitor to the reservation will ordinarily see little difference among these various tribes. Each, however, retains its own language, but while there are some of each tribe who cannot converse in the other tongues, there are many who can. Maximilian stated that the Mandans were natural linguists and that, in his day, the most of the Mandans spoke the Minnetaree tongue, but that few Minnetarees could use the language of the Mandans. Dr. Matthews says that it is not unusual for a conversation to be carried on in two tongues, the Mandan using his own language and the Grosventre or Arikara, in reply, speaking in his tongue.

There are several things on this reservation that will at once attract attention. The tepee and blanket are seldom seen, though I understand that the tepee is used in summer, on camping trips, and I presume the blanket is in cold weather. Log huts have succeeded the old earth lodges and both sexes dress after the manner of white people, even, at least in some cases, to fur overcoats for the men.

The Indians use agricultural machinery, ride about in buggies and wagons, husband and wife sitting beside each other on the seats, – rather unusual among Indians, – and they shelter their implements and wagons fairly well when not in use. They receive the instructions from the agency farmers in good part and are quite apt in applying their teachings.

Brackenridge refers to the fact that the Indian youth received no training. To-day he could not make such a charge. Besides the many non-reservation schools, such as Carlisle, Santee, etc., to which many students are sent from this reservation, there are five schools upon the reservation itself, placed at convenient points. Four of these are Government schools and the fifth is a mission school under the care of the American Missionary Association of the Congregational Church. The system of instruction at these schools seems to be similar to that used in our regular public schools. An effort is also made, where possible, to instruct the scholars in the practical affairs of life, the girls in various household matters, and the boys in the usual "chores" incident to a large establishment. The school at the agency, the Browning Boarding-school, is named after ex-Commissioner Browning, and it accommodates about one hundred pupils. It is a new brick, three-storied structure, steam-heated and lighted by acetylene gas. The third story is a dormitory, and the building is a school and home together.

I was in the dining-room during a dinner hour, and was surprised to see how few pupils there were who appeared to be less than full bloods. I saw many having light hair and fair complexions, but to a much less extent than at other Indian reservation schools. The food supplied the pupils was good and wholesome, and there was plenty of it, and the young Indians' table-manners were as correct as those of white children of the same grade and conditions.

The children at all the schools appeared to be thoroughly happy and to enjoy their school life. Samples of work which I saw and which were taken at random from a collection of papers prepared by Indian scholars of various grades at the boarding-school, illustrate the advances made by these people since Lewis and Clark and Brackenridge saw them, and are quite suggestive of what may be accomplished by patient and steady work among them. In 1900, the total enrolment of school children was 275, being nearly 78 per cent. of the children on the reservation between six and eighteen years of age. It was stated to me by the Principal of the Browning School, who has had experience on other reservations, that these Indians support the school better than any other Indians of whom he has knowledge and cause no trouble whatever.

Henry A. Boiler, in *Among the Indians,* gives a very complete picture of life among these people in the '60's. Boller was a trader among them for many years, and his description of an Indian bull-boat is one of the best I have seen of this interesting craft, and I give it here:

A School Building, Teacher and Family, and Indian Scholars on the Fort Berthold Reservation, in 1904.

245

These boats, which are necessary adjuncts to every Gros Ventre lodge, are made of the fresh hide of a buffalo-bull stretched over a frame work of willow. As the hide dries, it shrinks, binding the whole together with great strength. In shape they resemble large wash-tubs, and will bear astonishing loads, considering the frail manner of their construction.

They are ticklish craft to navigate, however, and unless the voyager is extremely careful to preserve an equilibrium, he will suddenly and most unexpectedly find himself treated to a cold plunge. These bull-boats are always paddled by the squaws, and very laborious work it is, since the paddle is thrust into the water only about two feet in advance and drawn towards the boat, thus impelling it slowly forwards.

In embarking in one of these frail canoes, the saddles, guns, and other equipments are carefully placed in the bottom; the hunter next steps in, holding the ends of his horses' lariats, which are fastened with a double running noose around their lower jaws.

The squaw then pushes the boat off, and wades out with it until the water becomes sufficiently deep, when, steadying herself with her paddle, she carefully takes her place, and the horses, two or three of which are usually crossed at once, being urged into the river by the shouts and cries of the bystanders, slowly and reluctantly yield themselves to the guidance of their master. For a while, although the squaw paddles with all her might, the boat makes no headway, but whirls around like a top. The struggles and plunges of the unwilling and refractory horses retard its progress and momentarily threaten to upset the frail vessel, until the very violence of their exertions carries them out into deep water. The strong current bears them swiftly along, and the horses, guided and supported by their master, swim after, only their heads and elevated tails being visible.

The occupations of the winter kept the explorers busy. One of the principal diversions was hunting. Day after day the narrative recounts the sending forth of hunting parties. Sometimes these hunters were accompanied by Indians and together they dashed upon the great herds of buffalo that covered the hills; or, if occasion required, still-hunted them. Again they went out by themselves, led by Lewis or Clark, or a sergeant, often going from thirty to sixty miles from the fort to find the game. The regular journal of December 7 and 1804, runs thus:

Shahaka [Big White], the chief of the lower village, came to apprise us that the buffalo were near, and that his people were waiting for us to join them in the chase. Captain Clark with fifteen men went out and found the Indians engaged in killing buffalo. The hunters, mounted on horseback and armed with bows and arrows, encircle the herd and gradually drive them

An Old Indian "Bull-Boat". Made from a buffalo hide stretched over a framework of willow poles.

into a plain or an open place fit for the movements of horse; they then ride in among them, and singling out a buffalo, a female being preferred, go as close as possible and wound her with arrows till they think they have given the mortal stroke; when they pursue another till the quiver is exhausted. If, which rarely happens, the wounded buffalo attacks the hunter, he evades his blow by the agility of his horse, which is trained for the combat with great dexterity. When they have killed the requisite number they collect their game, and the squaws and attendants come up from the rear and skin and dress the animals. Captain Clark killed ten buffalo, of which five only were brought to the fort; the rest, which could not be conveyed home, being seized by the Indians, among whom the custom is that whenever a buffalo is found dead without an arrow or any particular mark, he is the property of the finder.

DECEMBER 8th. The thermometer stood at 12° below zero — that is, 42° below the freezing point; the wind was from the northwest. Captain Lewis, with 15 men, went out to hunt buffalo, great numbers of which darkened the prairies for a considerable distance; they did not return till after dark, having killed eight buffalo and one deer. The hunt was, however, very fatiguing, as they were obliged to make a circuit at the distance of more than seven miles; the cold, too, was so excessive that the air was filled with icy particles resembling a fog; the snow was generally six or eight inches deep and sometimes eighteen, in consequence of which two of the party were hurt by falls, and several had their feet frost-bitten.

The entry for December 10th gives a picture of what they endured on these outings:

DECEMBER 10th. Captain Clark who had gone out yesterday with 18 men, to bring in the meat we had killed the day before, and to continue the hunt, came in at twelve o'clock. After killing nine buffalo and preparing those already dead, he had spent a cold, disagreeable night on the snow, with no covering but a small blanket, sheltered by the hides of the buffalo they had killed. We observe large herds of buffalo crossing the river on the ice. The men who were frost-bitten are recovering.

Strangely enough, with perhaps one exception, the journals of Lewis and Clark and of Gass absolutely contradict each other, from December 7th to December 15th, as to who led these hunting parties. Where the regular journal says Clark, Gass says Lewis, and *vice versa*.

On December 10th, where the regular narrative says that Captain Clark and some men had camped out overnight, Gass, under December 9th, says, "Captain Lewis

Indians Hunting the Bison in the Days of Lewis and Clark. From a water-color painting by C. M. Russell

249

and the rest of us encamped out and had tolerable lodging with the assistance of the hides of the buffalo we had killed." As Gass was one of the party, he certainly should have known who his leader was.

Father De Smet, in his *Western Missions and Missionaries,* – and Audubon also, – gives a lengthy description of the old method of hunting the bison by the Indians before they were generally supplied with firearms. It was by means of a large circular pen, an acre or more in area, with two radial wings extending from the narrow entrance, or throat of the circle, and the whole was made of rocks, brush, and trees. The bison were driven into the circle, being led by an Indian disguised in a buffalo robe and simulating the cry of a young buffalo calf, and also guided thereto by the wing fences, and once inside they were slaughtered at will amid the shouts and cries of the men, women, and children, who worked themselves into a frenzy as the killing progressed. This method, essentially, is used by some of the tribes, to-day, in hunting rabbits and other game.

Another method was to drive the animals over a moderately high cliff below which the hunters were gathered. Here, as the bison came thundering onward and pitched down over the precipice, the hunters would shoot their arrows into the maimed and crippled beasts. At the base of such a cliff, in Paradise Valley on the Yellowstone River, near Emigrant station, just north of the Yellowstone Park boundary, within two or three years I picked up a number of arrow-heads that had been thus used. Boller gives a good account of a winter bison hunt made by the Grosventres and Mandans in the late fifties or early sixties, in which he took part.

The hospitable people among whom the explorers were quartered were surely friends in need. Now, we were visited by several Indians, with a present of pumpkins; [and] one of the Ahnahaways brought us down the half of an antelope; [again], a woman brought a child with an abscess in the lower part of the back, and offered as much corn as she could carry [and these squaws had strong backs] for some medicine; . . . a number of squaws and men dressed like squaws [either berdashes, or hermaphrodites, or men adjudged cowards] brought corn to trade for small articles for the men; . . . the Indians brought corn, beans, and squashes, which they readily gave for getting their axes and kettles mended.

Barter and exchange were carried on the winter through, even the most trivial articles the men possessed bringing rich returns.

We were fortunate enough to have among our men a good blacksmith, whom we set to work to make a variety of articles. His operations seemed to surprise the Indians who came to see us, but nothing could equal their astonishment at the bellows, which they considered as very great medicine.

This man was, presumably, John Shields, one of the most reliable of their men and of particular utility to them at Fort Mandan in the manner here indicated. From pieces of sheet iron he made arrow-points, hide-scrapers, etc., a piece of iron four inches square being worth seven or eight gallons of corn. Coal (lignite) was abundant in the vicinity, so that the blacksmith was easily supplied.

The journal entry for January 1, 1805, will show what some of their diversions were:

TUESDAY, JANUARY 1, 1805. The new year was welcomed by two shots from the swivel and a round of small-arms. The weather was cloudy but moderate; the mercury, which at sunrise was at 18°, in the course of the day rose to 34° above zero. . . . In the morning we permitted 16 men with their music to go up to the first village, where they delighted the whole tribe with their dances, particularly with the movements of one of the Frenchmen, who danced on his head. In return they presented the dancers with several buffalo-robes and quantities of corn.

We were desirous of showing this attention to the village, because they had received an impression that we had been wanting
in regard for them, and because they had in consequence cir-
culated invidious [sic] comparisons between us and the northern
traders. All these, however, they declared to Captain Clark,
who visited them in the course of the morning, were made in
jest.

Gass relates on Wednesday, 2d:

This day I discovered how the Indians keep their horses
during the winter. In day time they are permitted to run out
and gather what they can; and at night are brought into the
lodges, with the natives themselves, and fed upon cotton wood
branches; and in this way are kept in tolerable case.

The following statement, taken from Boller, will prove
of interest in this connection:

Cottonwood bark is very nourishing, and if judiciously fed, a
horse will fatten on it. A tree is cut down, the tender boughs
lopped off, and after warming it to take out the frost, the bark
is peeled and torn into strips of various lengths, resembling pine
shavings; the knots and rough pieces are carefully thrown away,
and it is then ready for use.

The Indians of the upper villages had been more or less
suspicious of the mission of Lewis and Clark, and had not
received them with the wide-open hospitality of the Mandans.
Tribal jealousy was probably somewhat responsible for this,
On November 30, 1804, an opportunity occurred of very
effectually quelling all this distrust, and furthermore, of
actually placing the Ahnahaways, or Wattasoons, in a somewhat equivocal position. As the narrative tells the whole
story, I quote it as follows:

NOVEMBER 30th. About eight o'clock an Indian came to
the opposite bank of the river, calling out that he had something
important to communicate. On sending for him, he told us
that five Mandans had been met about eight leagues to the
southwest by a party of Sioux, who had killed one of them,

wounded two, and taken nine horses; that four of the Wattasoons were missing, and that the Mandans expected an attack.
We thought this an excellent opportunity to discountenance the
injurious reports against us, and to fix the wavering confidence
of the nation.

Captain Clark therefore instantly crossed the river with 23
men strongly armed, and circling the town approached it from
behind. His unexpected appearance surprised and alarmed the
chiefs, who came out to meet him and conducted him to the
village. He then told them that having heard of the outrage
just committed, he had come to assist his dutiful children; that
if they would assemble their warriors and those of the nation,
he would lead them against the Sioux and avenge the blood of
their countrymen. After some minutes' conversation, Oheenaw
the Chayenne arose: "We now see," said he, "that what you
have told us is true, since as soon as our enemies threaten to
attack us you come to protect us and are ready to chastise those
who have spilt our blood. We did indeed listen to your good
talk, for when you told us that the other nations were inclined to
peace with us, we went out carelessly in small parties, and some
have been killed by the Sioux and Ricaras. . . . Four of the
Wattasoons whom we expected back in 16 days have been absent 24, and we fear have fallen. But, father, the snow is now
deep, the weather cold, and our horses cannot travel through
the plains; the murderers have gone off. If you will conduct us
in the spring, when the snow has disappeared, we will assemble
all the surrounding warriors and follow you."

Captain Clark replied that we were always willing and able
to defend them; that he was sorry that the snow prevented
their marching to meet the Sioux, since he wished to show them
that the warriors of their great father would chastise the enemies
of his obedient children who opened their ears to his advice. . . .

After two hours' conversation Captain Clark left the village.
. . . He then crossed the river on the ice and returned on
the north side to the fort.

The effect of this military demonstration was most
happy, and it proved to the Indians that if Clark and his
companion officer were good talkers in council, they were
also a good deal more than that when the pinch came. In
February the party had occasion to make another expedition
of this sort on their own account. By February 1st their

supply of meat became exhausted, and Captain Clark with eighteen men, including Sergeant Gass, started down the river on February 4th, with the thermometer at 18° below zero, to replenish their larder. They hunted down the river some sixty miles or more to the Cannon-ball River, and Gass tells the story of the trip:

MONDAY [Feby.] 4th. A fine day. Captain Clarke and 18 more went down the river to hunt. . . .
TUESDAY 5th. We proceeded on to some Indian camps and there we killed three deer. The next day we went on to more Indian camps and killed some deer. On the 7th we encamped in a bottom on the south side of the Missouri, . . . killed 10 elk and 18 deer, and remained there all night. On the 9th we built a pen to secure our meat from the wolves, which are very numerous here. . . . On the 12th we arrived at the fort; and found that one of our interpreter's wives had in our absence made an ADDITION to our number. On the 13th we had three horses shod to bring home our meat.
THURSDAY 14th. Four men set out early with the horses and sleds to bring home our meat; and had gone down about 25 miles when a party of Indians . . . came upon them and robbed them of their horses one of which they gave back, and went off without doing the men any further injury. The same night the men came back and gave information of what had happened. At midnight Captain Lewis called for twenty volunteers who immediately turned out. Having made our arrangements, we set out early accompanied by some Indians. . . .
SATURDAY 16th. . . . Having proceeded twelve miles we discovered fresh smoke arising at some old camps, where we had hid some meat before when Captain Clarke was down. . . . Having arrived at the place we found the savages were gone; had destroyed our meat, burnt the huts and fled into the plains. . . . We hunted the 17th and 18th and got a good deal of meat which we brought to a place where some more had been secured. The 19th we loaded our sleds very heavy, and fifteen men drew one and the horse the other, which was a small one. On the next day we arrived at the fort much fatigued.

Both hunting parties had good luck, Clark's outfit killing forty deer, three buffalo, and sixteen elk; and Lewis's party thirty-six deer, fourteen elk, and one wolf. Much of the meat was too lean for use, but they brought back a goodly and welcome supply, for they were now living on corn procured from the Indians through the efforts of their blacksmiths.

The birth of the papoose mentioned by Gass must be noticed. Its mother was the grand little Bird-woman, Sacágawea, the wife of Chaboneau the interpreter. The birth of this papoose furnishes an interesting instance in the practice of Indian obstetrics. The narrative states that:

> This being her first child she was suffering considerably, when Mr. Jessaume told Captain Lewis that he had frequently administered to persons in her situation a small dose of the rattle of the rattlesnake, which had never failed to hasten the delivery. Having some of the rattle, Captain Lewis gave it to Mr. Jessaume, who crumbled two of the rings of it between his fingers, and mixing it with a small quantity of water gave it to her. What effect it may really have had it might be difficult to determine, but Captain Lewis was informed that she had not taken it more than ten minutes before the delivery took place.

Several times during the winter the Indians and the explorers were visited by traders of the Northwest Fur Company from their post on the Assiniboin River to the north. Up to this time the British Fur Companies had practically had a monopoly of the fur trade in this region, and they could not but feel that the Louisiana Purchase and this exploration was an entering-wedge, as it was, into their traffic. Whatever they might have felt, they were courteous and friendly and evinced no disposition to misconduct themselves, and their visits seem to have been pleasurable ones to the Captains

A possible exception to this general statement may have to be made in connection with Lafrance, a clerk of Larocque, and also in respect to an entry under date of March 17th in the journal, which reads as follows:

Our Minnetaree interpreter Chaboneau, whom we intended taking with us to the Pacific, had some days ago been worked upon by the British traders, and appeared unwilling to accompany us, except on certain terms – such as his not being subject to our orders, and his doing duty or returning whenever he chose. As we saw clearly the source of his hesitation, and knew that it was intended as an obstacle to our views, we told him that the terms were inadmissible, and that we could dispense with his services. He had accordingly left us with some displeasure.

Clark's statement of the reconciliation, taken from the codex, literally, runs thus:

Mr. Chabonah Sent a frenchman of our party [to say] that he was Sorry for the foolish part he had acted and if we pleased he would accompany us agreeabley to the terms we had perposed and doe every thing we wished him to doe &c. he had requested me Some thro our French inturpeter two days ago to excuse his Simplicity and take him into the cirvice, after he had taken his things across the River we called him in and Spoke to him on the Subject, he agreed to our tirms and we agreed that he might go on with us &c. &c.

The "British traders" referred to I suspect were Hudson's Bay Company men and not those of the Northwest Company, from the following reference to this Company on January 13th:

Chaboneau, who with one man had gone to some lodges of the Minnetarees near Turtle mountain [on the Little Missouri River], returned with their faces much frost-bitten. . . . He informs us that the agents of the Hudson's Bay Company at that place had been endeavoring to make unfavorable impressions with regard to us on the mind of the great chief, and that the Northwest Company intended building a fort there. The great chief had in consequence spoken slightingly of the Americans, but said that if we would give him our great flag he would come and see us.

I do not find that the Captains mention being visited at Fort Mandan by any of the Hudson's Bay Company people

An Old French-Canadian Trapper. From a drawing by Paxson.

VOL. I. - 17.

– although Larocque states there was one of them among the Mandans at this time – who may thus have been outwardly inimical and have shown it. The narratives of the Northwest Company traders themselves – Larocque and MacKenzie – indicate that the relations between the Americans and these traders were entirely pleasant and reciprocal. Lewis spent a day in repairing Larocque's compass, and also had the horses of the latter placed in the American herd for their better protection, while Larocque apparently made no effort to prejudice the Indians against the Americans.

MacKenzie says:

Mr. La Rocque and I having nothing very particular claiming attention, we lived contentedly and became intimate with the gentlemen of the American expedition, who on all occasions seemed happy to see us, and always treated us with civility and kindness. It is true, Captain Lewis could not make himself agreeable to us. He could speak fluently and learnedly on all subjects, but his inveterate disposition against the British stained, at least in our eyes, all his eloquence.
Captain Clark was equally well informed, but his conversation was always pleasant, for he seemed to dislike giving offence unnecessarily.

Harmon of the Northwest Company, who was wintering at Fort Alexandria, on the upper Assiniboin River, in 1804-05, in his journal for November 24, 1804, after referring to the arrival at the Mandan towns of Lewis and Clark, and stating that Mr. Chaboillez had received their letter of October 31st, adds: "Mr. Chaboillez writes, that they behave honourably toward his people, who are there to trade with the Natives."

The narrative of December 16 and 17, 1803, mentions the visits of "a Mr. Haney" of the Northwest Fur Company, and again – to anticipate – on July 1, 1806, he is referred to, this time as "Henry." Dr. Coues erroneously assumed, yet quite naturally, perhaps, that this was the explorer, Alexander Henry, the nephew and the younger. The latter, however, was at this time at his post at the junction of the Red and Pembina rivers, in the Red River Valley, as appears from his own journal and those of others.

Strangely enough though, Henry did visit the Mandan country in July, 1806, leaving the villages about two weeks before Lewis and Clark reached them on their return voyage from the Pacific, but he was not there in 1804-05.

When Dr. Coues came to edit the Alexander Henry journal, and in so doing consulted other and contemporaneous narratives, he discovered and corrected his own error. The Larocque journal and the "Liste" of Northwest Company employees, both found in Masson, I – 1889, disclose that "Mr. Haney" was *Hugh Heney,* a clerk of that Company, Department of Upper Red River.

Among the Mandan Indian chiefs recognized by the explorers were some who deserve special attention. Shahaka, or Big White, a Mandan, was "a man of mild and gentle disposition;   .   .   .   rather   inclining   to   corpulency;   a little talkative, regarded amongst the Indians as a great defect; not . . . much celebrated as a warrior," according to Brackenridge. He was evidently of a kindly nature, and he visited the fort often during the winter. When the expedition returned in 1806, he was the only chief who volunteered or was willing to venture the trip to the United States, a tale that is recounted in the story of Sergeant Pryor's life. Shahaka is pleasantly spoken of by Bradbury and Brackenridge, and also by other early writers.

Ompschara, or Black Moccasin, was made first chief of the Hidatsa village Metaharta by Lewis and Clark. They say little about him, but Catlin wrote interestingly of him and he painted his portrait. He says:

> The chief sachem of this tribe is a very ancient and patri-
> archal looking man, by the name of Eeh-tohk-pah-shee-pee-shah

(the black moccasin), and counts, undoubtedly, more than an hundred *snows*. I have been for some days an inmate of his hospitable lodge, where he sits tottering with age, and silently reigns sole monarch of his little community around him, who are continually dropping in to cheer his sinking energies, and render him their homage. His voice and his sight are nearly gone; but the gestures of his hands are yet energetic and youthful, and freely speak the language of his kind heart. . . .

This man has many distinct recollections of Lewis and Clarke, who were the first explorers of this country, and who crossed the Rocky Mountains thirty years ago. . . . He enquired very earnestly for "Red Hair" and "Long Knife" (as he had ever since termed Lewis and Clarke), from the fact, that one [Clark] had red hair (an unexampled thing in his country), and the other wore a broad sword which gained for him the appellation of "Long Knife." . . .

About a year after writing the above, and whilst I was in St. Louis, I had the pleasure of presenting the compliments of this old veteran to General Clarke; and also of showing to him the portrait, which he instantly recognized amongst hundreds of others; saying, that "they had considered the Black Moccasin quite an old man when they appointed him chief thirty-two years ago."

The most conspicuous of these chiefs was the Minnetaree brute, Le Borgne, the one-eyed. The journal for March 9, 1805, says:

The grand chief of the Minnetarees, who is called by the French Le Borgne, from his having but one eye, came down for the first time to the fort. He was received with much attention, two guns being fired in honor of his arrival. . . . In the course of the conversation, the chief observed that some foolish young men of his nation had told him there was a person among us who was quite black, and he wished to know if it could be true. We assured him that it was true, and sent for York. Le Borgne was very much surprised at his appearance, examined him closely, and spit on his finger and rubbed the skin in order to wash off the paint; nor was it until the negro uncovered his head and showed his short hair, that Le Borgne could be persuaded that he was not a painted white man.

This modern copper-colored Cyclops was a self-willed,

capricious, despotic tyrant. His character is well depicted by this excerpt from the journal of March 10th:

> One of the wives of Le Borgne deserted him in favor of a man who had been her lover before the marriage and who after some time left her, and she was obliged to return to her father's house. As soon as he heard it Le Borgne walked there and found her sitting near the fire. Without noticing his wife, he began to smoke with the father; when they were joined by the old men of the village, who, knowing his temper, had followed in hopes of appeasing him. He continued to smoke quietly with them till, rising to return, he took his wife by the hair, led her as far as the door, and with a single stroke of his tomahawk put her to death before her father's eyes. Then turning fiercely upon the spectators, he said that if any of her relations wished to avenge her, they could always find him at his lodge; but the fate of the woman had not sufficient interest to excite the vengeance of the family.
>
> The caprice or the generosity of the same chief gave a very different result to a similar incident which occurred some time afterward. Another of his wives eloped with a young man, who not being able to support her as she wished, they both returned to the village, and she presented herself before the husband, supplicating his pardon for her conduct. Le Borgne sent for the lover. At the moment when the youth expected that he would be put to death, the chief mildly asked them if they still preserved their affection for each other; and on their declaring that want, and not a change of affection, had induced them to return, he gave up his wife to her lover, with the liberal present of three horses, and restored them both to his favor.

Bradbury and Brackenridge both relate a story of cruelty similar to the first one here told. Le Borgne was a man of tremendous influence and of great bravery, and all early writers and traders had much to say of him, and of the terror he inspired.

York's experience with Le Borgne was an amusing one, but I can match it with another almost identical in its nature, occurring three quarters of a century later and one thousand miles distant from the Mandan towns.

In the winter of 1874-75, with J. K. Hillers of Powell's

Survey, I travelled overland to the Moki Indian villages in northern Arizona, by way of Santa Fé, Albuquerque, and Fort Wingate. From the last-named point our means of transportation were two heavily loaded army wagons and one of the teamsters was a large, black, splendidly built negro. John was as great a curiosity to the Moki as York was to the Mandans. The second day after our arrival, as John, the interpreter, and myself were talking, surrounded by a crowd of Indians, a bright-eyed, intelligent, comely Navajo squaw visiting there said something to the interpreter. Turning to us, he laughingly remarked, "John, she wants to know if you were made black or are only painted?"

John replied that he was *not* painted. Then another Navajo sentence and:

"John, she asks if you are black all over?"

"Yes," replied the negro.

The squaw looked at him intently for a moment or two, evidently doubting, and then, after more Navajo jargon:

"She does not believe you, and wants you to take your clothes off so she can see if you are black all over."

John, I doubt not, blushed, but at all events he drew the line at disrobing. The woman was perfectly sincere, and her inquiry was, I presume, in the true spirit of scientific investigation from a Navajo squaw's standpoint. Seeing is believing the world over, and it is apparently not confined to the Caucasian race.

In contrast to Le Borgne, the journal eulogizes Poscopsahe, or Black Cat, the "grand chief of the whole Mandan nation." This chief was a very brave as well as an intelligent man – evidently one of those who were wise in council and undaunted in battle, and the early traders all admired him as much as they feared Le Borgne.

One chief visited by Captain Lewis had evidently the innate instincts that belong to modern polite society, termed, however, by the Captains, "civilized indecorum." Mahpah-paparapassatoo, or Horned Weasel for short, when Captain Lewis made his call, was "not at home." Perhaps his hut was too small to hold more than his name and himself.

As the winter waned, preparations began for the continuation of their voyage. The time had passed, seemingly, in a pleasant and satisfactory manner. There was enough of earnest labor, hunting, dancing, and music with their fiddles to vary the monotony, and, thank God! no serious illness nor death had invaded their ranks. But now, as the days lengthened and the snow-banks began to melt and the winds softened, it was time to turn to the future and be ready, betimes, to go about their business. To this end, their boats, which had all winter lain in the encasing ice, were cut out with great difficulty, and hauled up on the bank of the river preparatory to overhauling. The codex reveals a serious state of affairs in this connection:

the situation of our boat and perogue is now allarming, they are firmly inclosed in the Ice and almost covered with snow – the ice which incloses them lyes in several stratas of unequal thicknesses which are separated by streams of water. this [is] peculiarly unfortunate because so soon as we cut through the first strata of ice the water rushes up and rises as high as the upper surface of the ice and this creates such a depth of water as renders it impracticable to cut away the lower strata which appears firmly attached to, and confining the bottom of the vessels, the instruments we have hitherto used has been the ax only, with which, we have made several attempts that proved unsuccessfull from the cause above mentioned. we then determined to attempt freeing them from the ice by means of boiling water which we purposed heating in the vessels by means of hot stones, but this expedient proved also fruitless, as every species of stone which we could procure in the neighbourhood partook so much of the calcarious genus that they burst into small particles on being exposed to the heat of the fire. we now determined as the dernier resort to prepare a parsel of Iron spikes and attach them to the end of small poles of convenient length and endeavour by means of them to free the vessels from the ice. we have already prepared a large rope of Elk-skin and a windless by means of which we have no doubt of being able to draw the boat on the bank provided we can free [it] from the ice.

Sixteen men, presumably under direction of Sergeant Gass, were sent up the river near to the mouth of Knife River to construct canoes, with which to ascend the Missouri. Gass's itinerary says:

FRIDAY 1st MARCH, 1805. The same party encamped out to make the canoes, and continued until six were made.

On the 20th and 21st we carried them to the river about a mile and a half distant: There I remained with two men to finish them, and to take care of them, until the 26th, when some men came up from the fort, and we put the canoes into the water. . . . We got three of them safe to the fort; but the ice breaking before the other three were got down, so filled the channel, that we were obliged to carry them the rest of the way by land. . . . We found they would not carry as much as was expected, and Captain Lewis agreed to take a large periogue along.

Cottonwood canoes were frail barks with which to navigate the raging Missouri, nevertheless they seem to have answered fairly well.

The ducks now began to fly northward, the rain to fall, and the ice to break up and run out. On March 28th the original journal says that the ice was gorged, "owing to Som Obstickle." The "obstickle" gave way on the 29th, and

the ice came down in great quantities, . . . Every spring, as the river is breaking up, the surrounding plains are set on fire, and the buffalo are tempted to cross the river in search of the fresh grass which immediately succeeds the burning. On their way they are often insulated on a large cake or mass of ice, which floats down the river. The Indians now select the most favorable point for attack, and, as the buffalo approaches, dart with astonishing agility across the trembling ice, sometimes pressing lightly a cake of not more than two feet square. The animal is of course unsteady, and his footsteps are insecure on this new element, so that he can make but little resistance; and the hunter, who has given him his death-wound, paddles his icy boat to the shore and secures his prey.

One of the important matters of preparation for departure was the packing of their specimens of various sorts in cases, to be forwarded to the President by the large batteau or barge manned by Corporal Warfington and the watermen who had accompanied them thus far.

The list of articles sent to Jefferson was, in part, made up of a pair of stuffed antelopes, skins of the white weasel, red fox, yellow bear, squirrels, white hare, and marten; mountain sheep, deer and elk horns; articles of Indian dress, a Mandan bow and arrows, some "Ricara" tobacco seed, an ear of Mandan corn, and a few live specimens of squirrels, magpies, etc.

The batteau returned to St. Louis, accompanied by thirteen persons all told, ten of them attached of the expedition. With the batteau and its precious cargo went a letter from Captain Lewis to the President, and a copy of this letter was sent by Jefferson to the Senate and House of Representatives.

Portions of these letters are reprinted here:

MESSAGE

TO THE SENATE AND HOUSE OF REPRESENTATIVES OF THE UNITED STATES

"In pursuance of a measure proposed to congress by a message of January 18th, one thousand eight hundred and three, and sanctioned by their appropriation for carrying it into execution, captain Meriwether Lewis, of the first regiment of infantry, was appointed, with a party of men, to explore the river Missouri, from its mouth to its source, and, crossing the highlands by the shortest portage, to seek the best water communication thence to the Pacific ocean; and lieutenant Clark was appointed second in command. They were to enter into conference with the Indian nations on their route, with a view to the establishment of commerce with them. They entered the Missouri May fourteenth, one thousand eight hundred and four, and on the first of November took up their winter quarters near the Mandan towns.

A letter of . . . April seventh, from captain Lewis, is herewith communicated. During his stay among the Mandans, he had been able to lay down the Missouri, according to courses and distances taken on his passage up it, corrected by frequent observations of longitude and latitude; and to add to the actual survey of this portion of the river, a general map of the country between the Mississippi and Pacific, from the thirty-fourth to the fifty-fourth degrees of latitude. These additions are from information collected from Indians with whom he had opportunities of communicating, during his journey and residence with them. Copies of this map are now presented to both houses of congress. With these I communicate also a statistical view, procured and forwarded by him, of the Indian nations inhabiting the territory of Louisiana, and the countries adjacent to its northern and western borders; of their commerce, and of other interesting circumstances respecting them. . . .

TH: JEFFERSON.

February 19, 1806

Extract of a Letter from Captain Meriwether Lewis, to the President of the United States, dated

FORT MANDAN, April 7th, 1805.

DEAR SIR,

HEREWITH enclosed you will receive an invoice of certain articles which I have forwarded to you from this place.

You will also receive herewith enclosed, a part of Capt. Clark's private journal; the other part you will find enclosed in a separate tin box. This journal will serve to give you the daily details of our progress and transactions.

I shall dispatch a canoe with three, perhaps four persons from the extreme navigable point of the Missouri, or the portage between this river and the Columbia river, as either may first happen. By the return of this canoe, I shall send you my journal, and some one or two of the best of those kept by my men. I have sent a journal kept by one of the sergeants, to captain Stoddard, my agent at St. Louis, in order as much as possible to multiply the chances of saving something. We have encouraged our men to keep journals, and seven of them do, to whom in this respect we give every assistance in our power. . . .

By reference to the muster rolls forwarded to the war department, you will see the state of the party; in addition to which we have two interpreters, one negro man, servant to Capt. Clark; one Indian woman, wife to one of the interpreters, and a Mandan man, whom we take with a view to restore peace between the Snake Indians, and those in this neighbourhood, amounting in total with ourselves to 33 persons. By means of the interpreters and Indians, we shall be enabled to converse with all the Indians that we shall probably meet with on the Missouri.

From this place we shall send the barge and crew early tomorrow morning, with orders to proceed as expeditiously as possible to St. Louis; by her we send our dispatches, which I trust will get safe to hand. Her crew consists of ten able bodied men, well armed, and provided with a sufficient stock of provision to last them to St. Louis. I have but little doubt but they will be fired on by the Siouxs; but they have pledged themselves to us that they will not yield while there is a man of them living. Our baggage is all embarked on board six small canoes, and two peroques; we shall set out at the same moment that we dispatch the barge. One, or perhaps both of these peroques, we shall leave at the falls of the Missouri, from whence we intend continuing our voyage in the canoes, and a peroque of skins, the frame of which was prepared at Harper's Ferry. This peroque is now in a situation which will enable us to prepare it in the course of a few hours.

As our vessels are now small, and the current of the river much more moderate, we calculate upon traveling at the rate of 20 or 25 miles per day, as far as the falls of the Missouri. Beyond this point, or the first range of rocky mountains, situated about 100 miles further, any calculation with respect to our daily progress, can be little more than bare conjecture. The circumstance of the Snake Indians possessing large quantities of horses, is much in our favour, as by means of horses the transportation of our baggage will be rendered easy and expeditious over land, from the Missouri to the Columbia river. Should this river not prove navigable where we first meet with it, our present intention is, to continue our march by land down the river, until it becomes so, or to the Pacific ocean. The map, which has been forwarded to the secretary of war, will give you the idea we entertain of the connexion of these rivers, which has been formed from the corresponding testimony of a number of Indians, who have visited that country, and who have been separately and carefully examined on that subject, and we therefore think it entitled to some degree of confidence. Since our arrival at this place, we have subsisted principally on meat, with which our guns have supplied us amply, and have thus been enabled to reserve the parched meal, portable soup, and a considerable proportion of pork and flour, which we had intended for the more difficult parts of our voyage. If Indian information can be credited, the vast quantity of game with which the country abounds through which we are to pass, leaves us but little to apprehend from the want of food.

We do not calculate on completing our voyage within the present year, but expect to reach the Pacific ocean, and return as far as the head of the Missouri, or perhaps to this place, before winter. You may therefore expect me to meet you at Montachello in September, 1806. On our return we shall probably pass down the Yellow Stone river, which, from Indian information, waters one of the fairest portions of this continent.

I can see no material or probable obstruction to our progress, and entertain, therefore, the most sanguine hopes of complete success. As to myself, individually, I never enjoyed a more perfect state of good health than I have since we commenced our voyage. My inestimable friend and companion, captain Clark, has also enjoyed good health generally. At this moment every individual of the party is in good health and excellent spirits, zealously attached to the enterprise, and anxious to proceed; not a whisper of discontent or murmur is to be heard among them; but all in unison act with the most perfect harmony. With such men I have every thing to hope, and but little to fear.

Be so good as to present my most affectionate regard to all my friends, and be assured of the sincere and unalterable attachment of

Your most obedient servant,
MERIWETHER LEWIS,
Captain of 1st U. S. regiment of infantry.

TH: JEFFERSON,
President of the United States

Certain references in Jefferson's message to Dr. Sibley and Mr. Dunbar are not pertinent to this work, and are therefore not quoted.

Regarding Lewis's letter and plans, it will be seen that he did not "dispatch a canoe" from the portage between the Missouri and the Columbia to St. Louis.

An Upper Missouri River Steamer in 1904

It is to be regretted that his references to those who were keeping journals were not definite and explicit, and that particular efforts were not subsequently made, as it appears, to preserve the journals in some central portion of the Government archives.

It appears from Lewis's letter that he hoped to reach the Pacific and return to the Three Forks of the Missouri, or even to Fort Mandan, before the winter of 1805-06. But he found that,

> The best laid schemes o' mice and men
> Gang aft a-gley.

A great change has taken place in the country since Lewis and Clark and the Mandans lived there. The few Indians that are left are now on a reservation farther west, as has been shown, at Fort Berthold; farms and towns, flocks and herds, dot the prairie where the Indians then lived and hunted, and steamboats and railways have succeeded the Indian bull-boats and the pirogues of Lewis and Clark.

At the very point, near Bismarck, where there was a buffalo ford in the olden time, the Northern Pacific steel and iron railway bridge now spans the Missouri, the railway engineers merely following the lead of the buffalo engineers in selecting the point for crossing the stream.

Not a vestige of Fort Mandan remains. On the return of the expedition in 1806, under date of August 17th, the Lewis and Clark itinerary says: "In reaching Fort Mandan we found a few pickets standing on the riverside, but all the houses except one, had been burnt by an accidental fire."

What the "accidental fire" left, the remorseless river took long ago. The character of the Missouri along here for the rapid cutting of its banks has been abundantly shown. A century has given ample opportunity for that one hut and those few pickets to have been insidiously

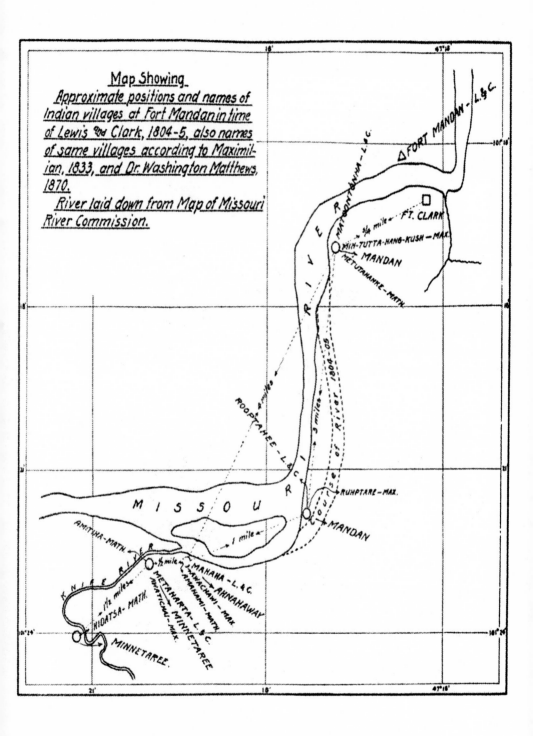

Map Showing
Approximate positions and names of
Indian villages at Fort Mandan in time
of Lewis & Clark, 1804-5, also names
of same villages according to Maximilian, 1833, and Dr. Washington Matthews,
1870.
River laid down from Map of Missouri
River Commission.

undermined and carried away by the stream, and we know from Maximilian that this had been done in 1833.

As I stood on the high bluffs of the river at this point in 1899, and overlooked the scene, I was profoundly impressed. To the north the distant valley of Knife River, deep green with heavy foliage, leads down to the Missouri; to the south the rough, bluffy ground near me grows rougher and bluffier

The Old Mandan Earth Lodge – in the Distance – and the Newer Log Cabin, Fort Berthold Reservation, 1804 vs. 1904.

as it reaches a big bend, and the irregular, grayish, ash-colored cut bank seems like that of a prodigious railway cut; the great river, in a wide, swollen flood, rolls on as it did a hundred years ago, and in broad, massive curve sweeps around a low point on the opposite shore, when, in a mood of inconstancy, it whirls back again in the other direction, and, at the beginning of the curve, is that "bluff of coal" mentioned by the explorers, standing out strong and plain as a guide to us. Those were the limits – the "bluff of coal" to the south, the Knife River to the north, and between them were the old Mandan villages, now gone forever.

There extends for one and one half or two miles a flat, heavily timbered bottom – Elm Point it is now called, and down near the lower end of it was where old Fort Mandan stood, and with our glasses we can make out, on the opposite shore, all that is left of Fort Clark, the trading post named after Captain Clark, and of which but a trace remains.

Another important change in this region should be noted. On the way up the river the explorers frequently remarked on the banks or bluffs of coal to be seen. To-day the lignite beds underlying a wide area of this region are supplying a satisfactory fuel to the dwellers on these treeless hills and prairies. There is probably no one feature of change or development in this northland that will have a more vital and economic value in the future than this of an unlimited and easily obtained supply of good fuel at the very doors of the people.

CHAPTER VI

FORT MANDAN TO MARIA'S RIVER

ON Sunday, April 7, 1805, Fort Mandan was abandoned at five o'clock P.M., and the westward journey resumed. At the same hour the large barge, or batteau, under charge of Corporal Warfington and with a company of thirteen persons, all told, started down the river for St. Louis. We can believe that that forced breaking of companionships and severance of social relationships with each other and with the friendly Mandans was not without its pangs.

Those homeward bound, while glad to return, possibly, to the privileges of frontier civilization, may well have felt that it was a hardship of one kind to be debarred from the hardships of another sort, and the prospective honor which awaited their west-bound comrades.

The party now consisted of thirty-two persons. Besides ourselves were Sergeants John Ordway, Nathaniel Pryor, and Patrick Gass; the privates were William Bratton, John Colter, John Collins, Peter Cruzatte, Robert Frazier, Reuben Fields, Joseph Fields, George Gibson, Silas Goodrich, Hugh Hall, Thomas P. Howard, Baptiste Lapage, Francis Labiche, Hugh M'Neal, John Potts, John Shields, George Shannon, John B. Thompson, William Werner, Alexander Willard, Richard Windsor, Joseph Whitehouse, Peter Wiser, and Captain Clark's black servant, York. The two interpreters were George Drewyer and Toussaint Chaboneau. The wife of Chaboneau [Sacágawea, the Bird-woman] also accompanied us with her young child, and we hope may be useful as an interpreter among the Snake Indians. She was herself one of that tribe, but was taken in war by the Minnetarees, by whom she was sold as a slave to Chaboneau, who brought her up and afterwards married her.

As the boats turned their prows to meet the stiff current and the oars flashed in the sunlight, doubtless the rousing chorus of some Western boatman's song broke forth and sounded across the wave. They sailed onward, from day to day, in much the usual way and with much the same experiences that they had in the previous year. Shallow water, rapids, head winds, sand-banks were encountered and overcome. Creeks were passed and many of them named, The system of nomenclature adopted by the Captains, if system it can be called, was like that of most explorers. Where there were well-defined Indian or French names for streams, bluffs, and buttes, these were usually accepted; where there were none, names were applied dependent upon local occurrences or peculiarities or, when these failed, the names of their men, friends, and sweethearts were drawn upon. In some cases the explorers were not fortunate in the names selected, and applied those which were certain to fall into disuse. In a great many instances their nomenclature should have been retained, and that it has not been reflects no credit on our sense of geographical propriety and fairness. Strangely enough, they made little attempt to name mountain ranges or peaks. There was also a lack of definiteness and discrimination in referring to mountain ranges. The term mountain – in the singular – was quite as apt to be used by them in respect to a massive range as it was to a particular mountain, and Rock or Rocky mountain or mountains was applied to any and everything in the Rocky Mountain region without, I think, having in mind the Rocky Mountains as a chain.

In the time of Lewis and Clark the Spanish word *cañon,* which later came into such general use through the entire West, had not progressed beyond the sunny regions of the Southwest, else their nomenclature would have been more varied. This word *cañon,* meaning, literally, a tube or hollow, is now very generally used to characterize all gorges and ravines, both large and small, deep and shallow, smooth and jagged.   One of the finest examples of a cañon along the route pursued by Lewis and Clark, is that water-gap or gorge through the mountains in Montana, called by them the "Gates of the Rocky Mountains," through which the Missouri River flows.

Steadily the little fleet swept up the river past the future sites of Fort Stevenson and Fort Berthold; past Elbowoods, where is now located the agency of the tribe of Indians from whom they had just parted, to the mouth of the Little Missouri River, where they remained a day to make observations for latitude and longitude.

The region through which they were passing was and is an interesting one. It is the fringe of the well-known *Mauvaises Terres* to the south, through the heart of which the Little Missouri flows, – a land weird, spectacular, fantastic, unique. Buttes and hills and bluffs and cliffs, richly and warmly colored and gracefully moulded, greet the eye in bewildering fashion, and as the band of adventurers journeyed westward, they caught something of this scenic feast as they approached the mouth of the Little Missouri. The country is underlaid with vast beds of lignite coal, which has burned out over wide areas, and is even yet burning in places; and the residuum, the scoria, in the shape of these parti-colored buttes and hills sculptured by the elements, forms a kaleidoscopic landscape of rare interest. Coal veins form lines plainly distinguishable in the hills bordering the river, and the explorers note that some of these veins are burning and emit sulphurous odors, as is the case to-day.

In recounting the story of the Mandans, Hidatsa, etc., in the previous chapter, reference was necessarily made to Forts Stevenson and Berthold.

Fort Berthold[1] was the older post, and was built in 1845 by the American Fur Company, according to Dr. Matthews.

The Hidatsa Indians removed up the river from Knife River in that year; the Mandans soon followed the Hidatsa, and the Arikara followed them both in 1862. The fort was a stockaded post on the edge of the bluff on the north side of the river. An opposition post, constructed in 1859, was merged with the former in 1862, when the old stockade was abandoned for the latter. On Christmas Eve, 1862, the Sioux attacked the post, burned the old, and almost captured the new one.

Military occupancy began in about 1864, when Iowa volunteer cavalry were sent there, the regulars appearing two years later.

Fort Stevenson was established in 1867, some miles down the river from Berthold, at which time the latter was abandoned as a military post and has since been used as part of an Indian reservation. Fort Stevenson was abandoned in 1883 by the military, and for a time was used as an Indian school. Nothing now remains of the old Fort Berthold, and scarcely anything is left of Stevenson. The Indian agency at Elbowoods is about as far above the old Berthold as Stevenson was below it. Both of these posts were historical landmarks in the development of the region, although practically unknown to most persons of the present generation.

---

[1] Larpenteur, in *Forty Years a Fur Trader*, etc., by Coues, published by Francis P. Harper, New York City, makes many references to Fort Berthold, and Boller, in *Among The Indians*, – a book hard to find, – gives his experiences as a trader at that post. Jos. H. Taylor, Washburn, N. D., in two little books, *Frontier and Indian Life* and *Kaleidoscopic Lives*, recounts many stories of this region in the early years Taylor is his own editor and publisher, as well as an author, and his work, done at odd times and under disadvantages, is necessarily fragmentary and unfinished, but of considerable interest.

Old Fort Berthold, Dakota Territory, in 1865. (Courtesy of Dr. Washington Matthews.)

On the 10th of April the explorers overtook three French-men on the way to the Yellowstone River, trapping beaver *en route,* the advance guard of a mighty army to follow. They found large quantities of wild onions on the hills – saw alkaline (sulphate of soda) flats, many brant, geese, bald eagles, and the corpses of buffaloes drowned by break-ing through the ice. Goose, or Goose Egg Creek - now

Mandan Indian Ferry on the Upper Missouri River, Fort Berthold Reser-vation 1904

Shell Creek, near the upper end of the Berthold Reservation – was named because of the geese found there, which made their nests in trees. Gass says a man climbed a tree sixty feet high and found one egg in a goose nest. On the 14th they named an island Sunday Island, which name it still appears to bear. They also honored Chaboneau by naming a creek near this island, and on which he had once camped, after him. This is probably Indian Creek of to-day. An addition was made to their numbers this day in the shape of a wandering black Assiniboin Indian dog which joined them.

It should here be particularly noted that, although the expedition passed through the territory of several presumably hostile or treacherous Indian tribes, and at points along the river where they were now journeying they found evidences of the proximity of Assiniboins, yet, after leaving the Mandan country they never saw an Indian until they reached the Continental Divide between the headwaters of the Missouri (Jefferson) and the Columbia (Lemhi) rivers.

Lewis and Clark distinctly state, under date of April 14th, that they have now passed beyond the highest point on the Missouri heretofore explored by white men. Chaboneau had been as far as the creek named for him, and Lepage, another recruit from the Mandan towns, had, with one other Frenchman, gone a few miles farther, but beyond that they were entering virgin territory. Chaboneau was a former Northwest Fur Company *engagé,* and Lepage and he would have known what territory had been covered by the traders. The American fur trade certainly followed the American flag.

The explorers now saw large quantities of game: buffalo, elk, deer, antelope, geese, ducks, beaver, prairie chickens swans, frogs, and bears, and they lived like epicures so far as choice meats went.

If the journal remarks quite often concerning the game and their enjoyment of it, we must remember that in such an outdoor life, as the writer can attest from happy experience, the appetite is an important function, and the enjoyment of these wild meats-delicate, tender, juicy, fresh, cooked and eaten in the open air – is something that must be experienced really to be understood.

The party are very much afflicted with sore eyes, which we presume are occasioned by the vast quantities of sand which are driven from the sand-bars in such clouds as often to hide from

us the view of the opposite bank. The particles of this sand are
so fine and light that it floats for miles in the air like a column of
thick smoke, and is so penetrating that nothing can be kept free
from it, and we are compelled to eat, drink, and breathe it very
copiously.

The phenomenon recorded here is a common one along
this part of the Missouri. On my trip to the Fort Berthold
agency, the valley of the river, as seen from the hills, appeared at times to be covered or filled with just such sand
clouds as annoyed Lewis and Clark in 1805.

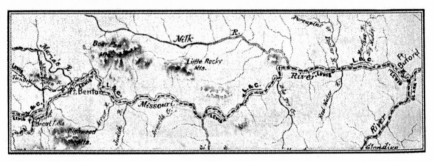

*Route of Lewis and Clark, from Mouth of Yellowstone River to the Great
Falls of the Missouri*

On April 26th the expedition reached the junction of the
Missouri and Yellowstone rivers.

The wide plains watered by the Missouri and the Yellowstone spread themselves before the eye, occasionally varied with
the wood of the banks, enlivened by the irregular windings of the
two rivers, and animated by vast herds of buffalo, deer, elk and
antelope . . . This river, which had been known to the
French as the Roche jaune, or as we have called it the Yellowstone, rises according to Indian information, in the Rocky mountains; its sources are near those of the Missouri and the Platte
[not very near those of the Platte], and it may be navigated in
canoes almost to its head. . . . In the upper country its
course is represented as very rapid, but during the two last and
largest portions its current is much more gentle than that of the
Missouri, which it resembles also in being turbid, though with less
sediment.   .   .

At two and a half miles above the junction, and between the high and low plain, is a small lake two hundred yards wide, extending for a mile parallel with the Missouri along the edge of the upper plain. At the lower extremity of this lake, about four hundred yards from the Missouri, and twice that distance from the Yellowstone, is a situation highly eligible for a trading establishment; it is in the high plain which extends back three miles in width, and seven or eight miles in length, along the Yellowstone, where it is bordered by an extensive body of woodland, and along the Missouri with less breadth, till three miles above it is circumscribed by the hills within a space four yards in width. A sufficient quantity of limestone for building may easily be procured near the junction of the rivers; it does not lie in regular strata, but is in large irregular masses, of a light colour, and apparently of an excellent quality. Game, too, is very abundant, and as yet quite gentle. Above all, its elevation recommends it as preferable to the land at the confluence of the rivers, which their variable channels may render very insecure.

The exact origin of the word "Yellowstone" is not known. Lewis and Clark seem to have been the first to anglicize the French *Roche juane* – Yellow Rock – river, rendering it, as shown, the Yellowstone River, which form it has since retained. *Roche juane* is without much doubt a French form of an Indian name meaning Yellow rock, or stone, but from what tribe – Mandan, Crow, Bannock, Blackfeet, etc. – the French took it, has not, to my knowledge, been ascertained. The Sioux called the Yellowstone the Elk, and Maximilian says that that is the meaning of most of the Indian names for the stream. If Verendrye thus named the river, he seems to have made no record of it. Naturally, the name should have sprung from the Grand Cañon of the Yellowstone, whether it came from Indian sources or from some wandering trapper of whom all traces have perished. Aside from this vividly yellow feature, which would most wonderfully impress any Indian or white man who saw it, there is nothing on the river itself to account for this particular name.

The suggestion by Lewis and Clark that the junction of these streams was an advantageous site for a trading establishment was acted upon. In 1822 Ashley and Henry built a fort, or post, on the land between and about a mile above the junction of the streams, but it was abandoned in 1823.

Fort Union, the best built and most important of all the Missouri River posts, was a noted one in its day and time;

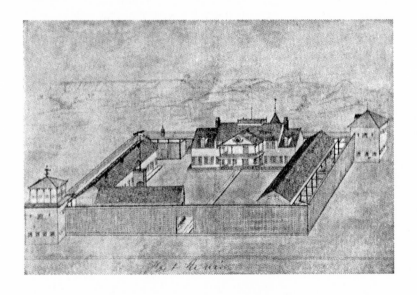

Fort Union at Junction of Missouri and Yellowstone River, Built in 1828 Or 1829 (Courtesy of Dr. Washington Matthews.)

it was begun, Maximilian says, in 1829, and, according to Governor Stevens, it was situated on the left bank of the Missouri, about two and three quarter miles above the mouth of the Yellowstone. The fort was quadrangular in shape, 240 by 220 feet in size, palisaded with heavy pickets squared and placed close together, from seventeen to twenty feet high, and it had two two-storied bastions built of stone, containing small cannon. It was a finely appointed fort, the centre and headquarters, really, of the upper Missouri fur trade of the time, and here the agents lived in a sort of barbaric splendor with a great retinue of clerks and *engagés,* with bright blanketed Indians coming and going, trading and carousing.

Fort William, named for William Sublette, was established below the mouth of the Yellowstone in 1833 as an opposition post, but it was short-lived, being abandoned in 1833.

In 1866, Fort Buford, a military post, was erected nearly on the site of old Fort William, and with that the decline of Fort Union began. Fort Buford is still occupied as a military establishment, and Lewis and Clark's judgment regarding this locality has been vindicated. Judging from the maps of the Missouri River Commission, there has been much change at this point since Lewis and Clark described the conditions as they found them.

On the 26th, Joseph Fields was sent up the Yellowstone on a trip of inspection. Fields was probably the first white man to ascend this river.

The explorers left the Yellowstone on April 27th, and on the 29th Captain Lewis and a hunter, while walking on the shore, met "two white bears." Gass says of them: "The natives call them white, but they are more of a brown-gray." The species was the now well-known grizzly *(Ursus horribilis),* which was unknown to science until discovered by the Lewis and Clark expedition. Their encounter wiith these beasts is thus reported:

Captain Lewis, who was on shore with one hunter, met about eight o'clock two white bears. Of the strength and ferocity of this animal the Indians had given us dreadful accounts; they never attack him but in parties of six or eight persons, and even then are often defeated with the loss of one or more of the party Having no weapons but bows and arrows, and the bad guns with which the traders supply them, they are obliged to approach very near to the bear, and as no wound except through the head or heart is mortal, they frequently fall a sacrifice if they miss their aim. . . . On approaching these two, both Captain Lewis and the hunter fired and each wounded a bear; one of them made his escape; the other turned upon Captain Lewis and pursued him seventy or eighty yards, but being badly wounded he [the beast] could not run so fast as to prevent him [Lewis] from reloading his piece, which he again aimed at him, and a third shot from the hunter brought him to the ground; he was a male, not quite full grown, and weighed about three hundred pounds.

With game of all sorts abundant, they went on, reaching, on May 8th a stream which, from "a peculiar whiteness, such as might be produced by a tablespoonful of milk in a dish of tea, . . . induced us to call it Milk River," which name it retains. This is one of the largest rivers in the Northwest and the greatest northern tributary of the Missouri. On May 9th they passed a "most extraordinary river," the Big Dry, which, like many Western streams, may at times be a rolling flood and again be completely dry. It was now in the latter state.

On the 11th of May, Bratton had an adventure which shows how each man really carried his life in his hand upon all occasions, and shows also what remarkable luck attended them throughout their long wanderings.

About five in the afternoon one of our men, who had been afflicted with biles and suffered to walk on shore, came running to the boats with loud cries and every symptom of terror and distress; for some time after we had taken him on board he was so much out of breath as to be unable to describe the cause of his anxiety, but he at length told us that about a mile and a half below he had shot a brown bear, which immediately turned and was in close pursuit of him; but the bear being badly wounded could not overtake him. Captain Lewis with seven men immediately went in search of him and having found his track followed him by the blood for a mile, and found him concealed in some thick brush-wood, and shot him with two balls

I certify that the within named Wm Bratton
has received from me all arrears of pay
(clothing and rations due him by the United
States) from the date of his enlistment to the
present date

October 10th 1806

Meriwether Lewis Capt.
1st U.S. Regt Infty
M——

Reverse Side of Discharge Paper of Wm. Bratton. (See page 113.)

285

through the skull. Though somewhat smaller than that killed a few days ago, he was a monstrous animal and a most terrible enemy; our man had shot him through the center of the lungs, yet he had pursued him furiously for half a mile, then returned more than twice that distance, and with his talons had prepared himself a bed in the earth two feet deep and five feet long, and was perfectly alive when they found him, which was at least two hours after he received the wound.

May 14th was a noted day in their calendar, when many lives were in jeopardy, and excitement, confusion, and terror stalked across the theatre of their little world and, for a time, threatened to close summarily the careers of many of them and end the exploration. A bear and Chaboneau performed star parts in the drama which came near being tragedy.

Towards evening the men in the hindmost canoes discovered a large brown bear; . . . six of them, all good hunters, . . . concealing themselves by a small eminence came unperceived within forty paces of him. Four of the hunters now fired, and each lodged a ball in his body, two of them directly through the lungs. The furious animal sprang up and ran openmouthed upon them; as he came near, the two hunters who had reserved their fire gave him two wounds, one of which, breaking his shoulder, retarded his motion for a moment; but before they could reload he was so near that they were obliged to run to the river. . . . Two jumped into the canoe; the other four separated, and concealing themselves in the willows fired as fast as each could reload. . . . At last he [the bear] pursued two of them so closely that they threw aside their guns and pouches and jumped down a perpendicular bank of twenty feet into the river. The bear sprang after them, and was within a few feet of the hindmost when one of the hunters on shore shot him in the head and finally killed him; they dragged him to the shore, and found that eight balls had passed through him in different directions.
At camp . . . we had been as much terrified by an accident of a different kind. This was the narrow escape of one of our canoes containing all our papers, instruments, medicine, and almost every article indispensable for the success of our enterprise. The canoe being under sail, a sudden squall of wind

struck her obliquely and turned her considerably. The man at
the helm, who was unluckily the worst steersman of the party,
became alarmed, and instead of putting her before the wind
luffed her up into it. The wind was so high that it forced the
brace of the square-sail out of the hand of the man who was attending it, and instantly upset the canoe, which would have been
turned bottom upward but for the resistance made by the awning. Such was the confusion on board, and the waves ran so
high, that it was half a minute before she righted, and then
[was] nearly full of water; but by baling out she was kept from
sinking until they rowed ashore. Besides the loss of the lives
of three men who, not being able to swim, would probably have
perished, we should have been deprived of nearly everything
necessary for our purposes, at a distance of between two and
three thousand miles from any place where we could supply the
deficiency.

To a creek near the point where the bear incident took
place they gave the name, "Brown-bear-defeated Creek,"
which name very naturally "died a-bornin'." Maximilian
relates numerous bear hunts in 1833 on this part of the Missouri, his experiences being similar to those of Lewis and
Clark.

The pirogue incident was owing to Chaboneau being at
the helm and completely losing his head as well as the helm.
When the squall struck them, this individual, instead of
doing the proper thing, began "calling to his God for mercy,"
and not until Cruzatte, the bowsman, "threatened to shoot
him instantly if he did not take hold of the rudder and do
his duty," did the witless Frenchman act. Lewis, who
came near jumping into the river and swimming for the
boat, was filled "with the utmost trepidation and terror,"
and concluded when it was all over that it was a "proper
occasion to console ourselves and cheer the sperits of our
men," and so they "took a drink."

But if Chaboneau was a craven upon this occasion, his
spouse was a heroine. She did n't lose her head-quite
the contrary! Notwithstanding that she had that precious

papoose to care for, she calmly reached out and grabbed this and that article as the water set it afloat, and thus preserved much of value. Lewis ascribed to this little woman "equal fortitude and resolution with any person on board," and credited her with having "caught and preserved" most of the lighter articles which were washed overboard.

On the night of the 18th a tree in camp caught fire and was discovered and the men warned just in time to prevent a catastrophe, for scarcely had they removed from its vicinity when it fell "precisely on the spot" they had occupied.

May 20th, they reached and camped at the mouth of the Musselshell River, one of the large tributaries of the Missouri from the south. This stream rises in the mountains between the Missouri and Yellowstone rivers, flows eastwardly in rather erratic course, quite uncertain, for a time, whether it will join its fortunes to the Yellowstone or Missouri. But at last, "with two dips and a flirt," it swings to the north to the Missouri.

Creek after creek along here was named after some one of their men; Bratton, Gibson, Warner, and Wiser being thus honored. A large creek five miles up the Musselshell, on the "north side" – probably Crooked Creek – was also named in honor of Sacágawea.

The voyage from the Musselshell to Judith's River was devoid of special feature. They killed their first mountain sheep *(Ovis montana),* not goat, on this stretch of river, and saw many of these interesting animals, but the bison now became scarce. An amusing occurrence which, again, might have had serious results happened on the night of May 28th.

[WEDNESDAY] May 29th. Last night . . . a buffaloe swam over from the opposite side and to the spot where lay one of our canoes, over which he clambered to the shore; then taking fright, he ran full speed up the bank toward our fires, and passed within eighteen inches of the heads of some of the men, before the sentinel could make him change his course; still more alarmed, he ran down between four fires and within a few inches of the heads of a second row of men, and would have broken into our lodge if the barking of the dog had not stopped him. He suddenly turned to the right and was out of sight in a moment, leaving us all in confusion, every one seizing his rifle and inquiring the cause of the alarm. On learning what had happened, we had to rejoice at suffering no more injury than the damage to some guns which were in the canoe which the buffaloe crossed.

The country through which they had been passing since before reaching the Musselshell River partook, more or less, of the character of the *Mauvaises Terres*. While they say nothing really to indicate the fine scenic nature of it, it is a fact that it is extremely interesting. Maximilian, a sober, scientific traveller of the world, compared it at several points with the scenery of Switzerland. Before reaching the Musselshell, Maximilian noted "a remarkable place," which, "when seen from a distance, so perfectly resembled buildings raised by art, that we were deceived by them, till we were assured of our error." These he called "The White Castles." At another place, mountains "with singular pinnacles look like the Glacier des Bossons in the valley of Chamouny." West of the Musselshell this traveller was reminded "of the Mettenberg and the Eiger, in the Canton of Berne," and, again, the Rhine Valley was brought to mind. Characteristic names have been given to many points along this cañon, such as Citadel bluff, Cathedral rock, Eagle rock, Castle rock, Burned butte, Haystack butte, etc. Between Fort Buford and Milk River, on the "north" bank of the Missouri, the rails of the Great Northern Railway are now laid.

Judith's River (it will be noted that Lewis and Clark used the possessive form in applying their names) was named by Captain Clark in honor of Miss Julia Hancock of

Fincastle, Virginia, who, in 1808, became the Captain's first wife. He at the time supposed her name to be Judith.

It was the intention of Captain Lewis to call the Judith River – as it is now known – the Big Horn, and this name appears on Clark's map of 1814 as the next stream above the Judith on the south. Coues shows, however, that this map and the text are utterly inconsistent with each other. In the text, Big Horn – now Arrow Rive – is Slaughter River, and there is no Big Horn River named.

Clark evidently made the map without consulting the text or refreshing his mind on this point at the time. Maximilian refers to Big Horn River as located on Clark's map, but he makes a singular error in the same connection. He says:

The part of the country called the Stone Walls, which now opened before us, has nothing like it on the whole course of the Missouri. . . . Lewis and Clark have given a short description of this remarkable tract, without, however, knowing the name of Stone Walls which has since been given to it.

In the text neither Big Horn River nor the Stone Walls, as descriptive titles, is mentioned, but both are shown by name on Clark's map, and consequently the name "Stone Walls" is of the latter's coining.

Maximilian has a great deal to say about this twelve or fifteen miles of sandstone region. This cañon, with its "colonnades, pulpits, organs with their pipes, fortresses, castles, churches," etc., impressed the Prince of Wied, and he had Mr. Bodmer, his artist, devote several sketches to it.

The narrative thus describes this cañon:

These hills and river cliffs exhibit a most extraordinary and romantic appearance; they rise in most places nearly perpendicular from the water, to the height of between two and three hundred feet, and are formed of very white sandstone, so soft as to yield readily to the impression of water. . . . In trickling

An Old-Time Frontier Scout (From a drawing by Paxon.)

down the cliffs, the water has worn the soft sandstone into a thousand grotesque figures, among which with a little fancy may be discerned elegant ranges of freestone buildings, with columns variously sculptured, and supporting long and elegant galleries, while the parapets are adorned with statuary. . . .

In the midst of this fantastic scenery are vast ranges of walls, which seem the productions of art, so regular is the workmanship; they rise perpendicularly from the river, sometimes to the height of one hundred feet, varying in thickness from one to twelve feet, being equally [as] broad at the top as below.

And now, on June 2, 1805, our explorers reach a point of importance which begets both much agitation and cogitation. It is only a river, but *what* river is the question, and a momentous one. It may be stated at once that it was Maria's River, and so named by Captain Lewis in compliment to his cousin, Miss Maria Wood:

I determined to give it [the river] a name, and in honor of Miss Maria W—d called it Maria's River. It is true that the hue of the waters of this turbulent and troubled stream but illy comport with the pure celestial virtues and amiable qualifications of that lovely fair one; . . .

The gallant Captain was human, and he set a fashion that many explorers and geographers have since followed. The river is now charted as Marias, without the possessive. The information which the expedition possessed of the region had been necessarily gathered from the Indians. These had mentioned a northern branch of the Missouri called by them "the River which scolds at all other Rivers," which was presumably the Milk River, but of this new northern stream the explorers were ignorant. They were therefore greatly perturbed as to which direction to take — whether to follow Maria's River, which ran from the northwest, or the other stream, from the southwest. They were making geography, and with their scanty knowledge it was a difficult and serious matter to decide which of these streams

was the true Missouri. The northern branch was the nar-
rower but deeper stream.

We determined, therefore, to examine well before we decided on our future course; and for this purpose despatched two
canoes with three men up each of the streams, with orders to
ascertain the width, depth, and rapidity of the current, so as to
judge of their comparative bodies of water. At the same time
parties were sent out by land to penetrate the country, and discover from the rising grounds, if possible, the distant bearings of
the two rivers; and all were directed to return toward evening.

Gass headed the party that explored the south branch,
or true Missouri, and his narrative reads:

Myself and two men went up the south branch, and a serjeant and two more up the north. The parties went up the two
branches about 15 miles. We found the South branch rapid
with a great many islands and the general course South West.
The other party reported the North branch as less rapid, and not
so deep as the other. The North branch is 186 yards wide and
the South 372 yards.
The water of the South branch is clear, and that of the
North muddy. About a mile and a half up the point from the
confluence, a handsome small river falls into the North branch,
called Rose river. [This is now the Teton River.]

Gass and his comrades were therefore the first known
white men to ascend the Missouri above Maria's River.

This examination settled nothing; it only confused them
the more, as the nature of the two streams was such that it
required a more extended exploration of each to solve the
problem. Accordingly, on June 4th, Captain Lewis, with
six men, started up the north fork, and Captain Clark, with
five men, went up the south fork, to be gone a day and a
half, or longer if necessary, to examine the streams thoroughly and settle the vexed question.

Clark explored the south fork for forty-five miles and
returned to camp in two days, making the acquaintance of

the ferocious grizzly of this region on this trip. Lewis was gone four days, ascended Maria's River for fifty-nine miles, and he and Windsor nearly lost their lives in the following manner:

In passing along the side of one of these bluffs, at a narrow pass thirty yards in length, Captain Lewis slipped, and but, for a fortunate recovery, by means of his espontoon, would have been precipitated into the river over a precipice of about ninety feet.

The "White," or Grizzly Bear of Lewis and Clark – Ursus Horribilis.

He had just reached a spot where, by the assistance of his espontoon, he could stand with tolerable safety, when he heard a voice behind him cry out, "Good God! Captain, what shall I do?" He turned instantly and found it was Windsor, who had lost his foothold about the middle of the narrow pass, and had slipped down to the very verge of the precipice, where he lay on his belly, with his right arm and leg over the precipice, while with the other leg and arm he was with difficulty holding on to keep himself from being dashed to pieces below. His dreadful situation was instantly perceived by Captain Lewis, who, stifling his alarm, calmly told him that he was in no danger; that he should take his knife out of his belt with the right hand, and dig a hole in the side of the bluff to receive his right foot. With great presence of mind he did this, and then raised himself on his knees. Captain Lewis then told him to take off his moccasins and come forward on his hands and knees, holding the knife in one hand and his rifle in the other. He immediately crawled in this way till he came to a secure spot. The men who had not attempted this passage were ordered to return and wade the river at the foot of the bluff, where they found the water breast-high. This adventure taught them the danger of crossing the slippery heights of the river; but as the plains were intersected by deep ravines almost as difficult to pass, they continued down the river, sometimes in the mud of the low grounds, sometimes up to their arms in the water, and when it became too deep to wade, they cut footholds with their knives in the sides of the banks.

The results of these explorations convinced both Lewis and Clark that the south branch was the true Missouri. They arrived at this conclusion first, independently of each other, and then concurrently, by an exceedingly strong course of reasoning which, under the circumstances, reflects the greatest credit upon them. Strangely enough, all their men had reached an exactly opposite conclusion, but they cheerfully and loyally acquiesced in the decision to proceed up the south branch.

In preparation for this move it was determined to *cache* – French, from *cacher,* to hide – some of their supplies in order to lighten their loads, and as they were to return to this point the following year, they were also thus assured of reserve provisions for their homeward trip, provided the Indians did not discover the *cache.* This method of storage was a common one among the old mountaineers and plains-men, and as the description of the process by Lewis and Clark is as good as any, I give it:

Our *cache* is built in this manner: In the high plain on the north side of the Missouri, and forty yards from a steep bluff, we chose a dry situation, and then describing a small circle of about twenty inches in diameter, removed the sod as gently and carefully as possible; the hole is then sunk perpendicularly for a foot deep, or more if the ground be not firm. It is now worked gradually wider as they descend, till at length it becomes six or seven feet deep, shaped nearly like a kettle or the lower part of a large still, with the bottom somewhat sunk at the centre. As the earth is dug it is handed up in a vessel and carefully laid on a skin or cloth, in which it is carried away and usually thrown into the river or concealed so as to leave no trace of it. A floor of three or four inches in thickness is then made of dry sticks, on which is thrown hay or a hide perfectly dry. The goods, being well aired and dried, are laid on this floor, and prevented from touching the wall by other dried sticks in proportion as the merchandize is stored away. When the hole is nearly full, a skin is laid over the goods, and on this earth is thrown and beaten down until, with the addition of the sod first removed, the whole is on a level with the ground, and there remains not the slightest appearance of an excavation. In addition to this we made another, of smaller dimensions, in which we placed all the baggage, some powder, and our blacksmith's tools, having previously repaired such of the tools we carry with us as require mending. To guard against accident, we hid two parcels of lead and powder in the two distinct places. The red periogue was drawn up on the middle of a small island at the entrance of Maria's river, and secured, by being fastened to the trees, from the effect of any floods.

In succeeding years this immediate locality became a central one for the fur trade among the Blackfeet Indians of this region. As the trade pushed up the Missouri, posts were established as the necessity for them became apparent, at the mouths of the Poplar and Judith rivers, and in the early thirties successive forts were constructed near the mouth of Maria's River. Forts Piegan, or Pickann, in 1831-32; McKenzie, 1832; Fort Lewis, 1845, named in honor of Captain Lewis; and, finally, Fort Benton, named for Senator Thos. H. Benton, in 1850, were the posts which, succeeding each other in the order named, served as outposts of advancing civilization and *entrepôts* for the fur trade.

This was probably the point of greatest danger among the fur trading posts. As will be seen later, a difficulty between these Indians and Captain Lewis in 1806, coupled with the scrimmage still later, wherein Colter fought them, so incensed the Blackfeet and allied bands that for years every Blackfoot, Grosventre, or Blood Indian carried in his heart an implacable hostility toward the whites, and no

The Remains of Old Fort Benton, Montana, Built in 1850.

man's life was really safe outside the protecting walls of a fort, and sometimes not even within those walls.

Fort Benton was long the head of Missouri River navigation and a most important point. Intimately connected with it is the name of Alexander Culbertson, one of the chief men of the fur trade in its later years, and a familiar figure in the history of this region.

Fort Benton was built in 1850, of adobe, and around it has grown up the town of the same name. In 1902 one of the bastions of the old fort was still standing. It is, perhaps, the last standing monument of those old and strenuous days, and this remnant should be preserved.

The three largest Indian linguistic families were the Algonquian, Siouan, and Shoshonean. We have already met the Siouan in the Omaha, Otoe, Sioux, Mandan, Hidatsa, etc., tribes; we now touch the northwestern lobe of the Algonquian territory, and we shall soon traverse, latitudinally, the Shoshonean. A study of Powell's map of Indian linguistic stocks will prove interesting in connection with the narrative of Lewis and Clark.

The Blackfeet, or Siksika tribe, comprising the Blackfeet proper and the Bloods and Piegans, are of the Algonquian stock. There was, at the time of the Lewis and Clark exploration and afterward, another tribe, the Atsina, or Minnetarees or Grosventres, of the Prairies — also known as the Falls Indians — affiliating with these tribes, and the remnant of them is still found on the Blackfeet reservation. The Maria's River Valley was about the centre or heart of the country over which these tribes roamed, and accounts seem to agree that these Indians, who were all roughly grouped under the general name Blackfeet, were then the devils of the prairies and mountains. Not alone the whites, but Indians also suffered from their hatred and bloodthirstiness. The religious Flatheads, or Salish, the proud Nez Percés, or Chopunnish, the thieving Crows, or Absaroka, the wandering Snakes, or Shoshoni, and others, all were at feud with the Blackfeet because the latter persisted in being the copper-colored Ishmaelites among the tribes.

There are two or three traditions as to the origin of the name Blackfeet. The most interesting, perhaps, states that, after separating from the main tribe on the Saskatchewan River in their migration southward, they traversed a wide district over which a prairie fire had swept, and that their moccasins thus became much blackened, and the Crows, upon seeing them in this plight, called them *Blackfeet.*

W. A. Ferris, in his journal of the early thirties, while an employee of the American Fur Company, wrote a lengthy dissertation upon the Indians of the mountains, and refers to the utter incongruity and meaninglessness of the names of several of the tribes, thus:

> Several tribes of mountain Indians, it will be observed, have names that would be supposed descriptive of some national peculiarity. Among these are the Blackfeet, Flat-heads, Bored-noses, Ear-bobs, Big-belly's, &c., and yet it is a fact that of these, the first have the whitest feet; there is not among the next a deformed head; and if the practice of compressing the skull so as to make it grow in a peculiar shape ever did exist among them, it must have been many years since, for there is not *one* living proof to be found of any such custom. There is not among the Nez-percés an individual having any part of the nose perforated; nor do any of the Pen-d'oreilles wear ornaments in their ears; and finally the Gros-ventres are as slim as any other Indians, and corpulency among them is rare.

The country of the Blackfeet was a glorious one for an Indian. After leaving the cañon of the "Stone Walls," ascending the Missouri, the country undergoes a change; and about the Marias there extends to all points of the compass a noble, vast, and gently rolling plain, an ideal bison range. At long intervals only, this plain is punctuated by detached, isolated mountains or buttes; it is watered by the upper affluents of the Milk, the Marias, the Teton, and the Sun rivers, and the main range of the Rockies bounds its western horizon. In the early years of the nineteenth century, this country is said to have been the richest beaver country in the entire West.

The Blackfeet are now found upon a reservation on the extreme headwaters of the Milk and Marias rivers at the eastern base of the Rocky Mountains, and are, and have been for years, perfectly tractable and easily controlled. Governor Stevens, in 1853, found them congenial travelling companions, and experienced no trouble with them in his Northern Pacific Railway survey, made under Government direction.

One of the Blackfeet – Siksika – Indians.
(From a drawing by Paxson.)

If one desires to read the tale of these proud, haughty, warlike, roving Ishmaelites and see how the mighty have fallen from their high estate, one can find it in Geo. Bird Grinnell's volume, *Blackfoot Lodge Tales,* and he will there learn of the great change which has come to the only tribe against whom Lewis and Clark found it necessary to fire a gun in all their wanderings.

CHAPTER VII

MARIA'S RIVER TO THREE FORKS OF THE MISSOURI

THE most momentous stage of the journey thus far to our explorers now confronts them. That the importance of the disclosures of the next few days was understood, at least by the Captains and probably by all, and was looked forward to with anxiety, is well evidenced.

Had Captain Clark been as persistent in his exploration of the south branch and gone as far as did Captain Lewis on his tramp, all this suspense and anxiety would have been avoided. There had been one infallible sign given to them by the Indians by which they would know the true Missouri – the series of falls to be encountered before reaching the mountains. Clark stopped just short of making this discovery when he turned back on June 5th. The next day would have brought him to the falls, and Clark instead of Lewis would have been the discoverer of the Great Falls of the Missouri.

In proceeding up the stream from Maria's River, Clark now took charge of the boat party, and Lewis with four men went on land and afoot.

[TUESDAY], June 11th. This morning Captain Lewis, with four men, set out on their expedition up the south branch. They soon reached the point where the Tansy [Teton] River approaches the Missouri, and observing a large herd of elk before them, descended and killed several, which they hung up along the river, so that the party in the boats might see them as they came along. They then halted for dinner; but Captain Lewis, who had been for some days afflicted with dysentery, was now attacked with violent pains, attended by a high fever, and was unable to go on. He therefore encamped for the night under some willow-boughs; having brought no medicine, he determined to try an experiment with the small twigs of the choke-cherry, which, being stripped of their leaves and cut into pieces about two inches long, were boiled in pure water, till they produced a strong black decoction of an astringent bitter taste; a pint of this he took at sunset, and repeated the dose an hour afterwards. By ten o'clock he was perfectly relieved from pain, a gentle perspiration ensued, his fever abated, and in the morning he was quite recovered.

The Tansy River mentioned is now known as the Teton. A few miles below Fort Benton, after having run parallel to the Missouri for several miles, it approaches within "one hundred yards" of the latter. This spot is known as the *Cracon du Nez,* and it is a narrow ridge among the clay bluffs bordering the two streams. My visit to this spot in 1902 was unfortunate, in that the country was covered with a pall of smoke so thick that, as I stood on the ridge directly above the streams, it was with difficulty that the water could be seen. The streams are farther apart than Lewis and Clark estimated them to be – two hundred to three hundred yards at least, I thought, and Gass says two hundred yards – nd the angular, clay bluffs have been very much eroded. On the Missouri side the bluff is all scarred and broken as if by an upheaval, but it is really scarified by down-heavals, for there have been many landslides here. My guide, an intelligent man and an old-time resident, knew nothing of the "Grog Spring" of our explorers, and thought it had either dried up or been completely hidden by the slides.

Along the ridge once ran a wide, deep buffalo trail and, later, the Assiniboin-Benton freight road, and traces of each were distinctly visible.

The incident of Captain Lewis's illness and his extemporized cure shows how they met such emergencies, and also how often their lives, and consequently the fate of the expedition, hung in the balance.

After Lewis had departed from the camp on June 11th, Clark and the main party completed the *cache,* which contained "corn, pork, flour, some powder and lead," Gass says, to about one thousand pounds weight; this labor and the arrangements for the advance up the stream occupied the full day.

On the 12th, Lewis and his four men continued their tramp. In order to avoid the lateral ravines which, then as now, cut deeply into the bluffs along the river, they ascended to the open plain some two or three miles back. After a twelve-mile walk they felt like having some breakfast, and as the "buffaloe" which filled the plain in "vast he ds" discovered "them before they came within gunshot" and "took to flight," and as there was not a drop of water to be had, hungry and thirsty they were forced to return to the river.

Here they saw two large brown bears, and killed them both at the first fire. Having made a meal of a part and hung the remainder on a tree, with a note for Captain Clark, they again ascended the bluffs into the open plains.

They soon caught their first view of the Rockies all white with snow. That portion of the chain which first greeted their eyes was probably in the vicinity of the very pass where, in the following summer, Lewis was to break through the mountains on his way from the Bitter Root range to the Great Falls and its companion cataracts which he is now on the verge of discovering. There are two passes here, Lewis and Clark's, and Cadotte's – and, farther south, Mullan's; and as Lewis marched along up-stream he faced the Rockies and these passes, the latter, of course, then undiscovered and unnamed, except by Indians.

The scenery here is of a nature to delight a man of Lewis's impressionable temperament. Lacking the nobler grandeur and mightier aspects they were soon to find in the depths of the mountains, it yet has a characteristic beauty and sublimity of its own which at once arrest attention. In 1853 Governor Stevens rode across the same plain and faced the same scene. He said of it:

> The view at almost any point of the plateau between the Teton and Sun rivers is exceedingly picturesque and suggestive. The various minor upheavals and swales of ground, which here and there dot the surface of the country, have connected with them some story of Indian war, wrong, or suffering. This whole country was once occupied by the Snakes, and in later times by some of the tribes of the Flathead nation. It belongs now to the Blackfeet by conquest.

Again, a day or two later, he wrote:

> The stream is now full of beaver, and is much obstructed by their dams. The country is somewhat more broken to-day than it was yesterday; timber comes in view on the tops of the mountains, and the scenery becomes more grand with each mile as we proceed.

On this same day Captain Clark left Maria's River, passed the *Cracon du Nez* and the spring which they found there and "which the men called Grog spring," and stopped at night at an old Indian camp a few miles below the site of the future Fort Benton. Gass states that this spring was so named on Clark's reconnaissance, because at that point "we refreshed ourselves with a good drink of grog."

And now for an eventful day!

Captain Lewis and his men were up and off again at sunrise. At the end of a six-mile tramp, "they overlooked a most beautiful plain, where were infinitely more buffaloe than we had ever before seen at a single view. . . ." Finding that the river here bore considerably to the south,

and fearful of passing the falls before reaching the Rocky
Mountains, they now changed their course to the south.

> . . . In this direction Captain Lewis had gone about
> two miles when his ears were saluted with the agreeable sound of
> a fall of water, and as he advanced a spray, which seemed driven
> by the high southwest wind, arose above the plain like a column
> of smoke and vanished in an instant. Toward this point he
> directed his steps; and the noise, increasing as he approached,
> soon became too tremendous to be mistaken for anything but
> the Great Falls of the Missouri. Having travelled seven miles
> after first hearing the sound, he reached the falls about twelve
> o'clock. The hills as he approached were difficult of access and
> two hundred feet high; down these he hurried with impatience,
> and seating himself on some rocks under the centre of the falls,
> enjoyed the sublime spectacle of this stupendous object which
> since the creation had been lavishing its magnificence upon the
> desert, unknown to civilization.

No more uncertainty existed as to where they were and
what river they were ascending. The Indians had spoken
truly, not with forked tongues; the falls were before him in
all their tumultuous grandeur – *this was the Missouri!* After
spending some time in restful and satisfied contemplation of
the falls, Lewis endeavored to find a harbor for their canoes
– if by good luck Clark could bring them thus far! The
next morning – June 14th – a man was dispatched down the
stream, reaching Clark that afternoon and cheering him and
the men with the news of the discovery he carried to them.
While Clark was slowly forcing a passage up the swift current of the river, Lewis explored the stream above the falls
which he had just discovered. This carried him many miles
above the latter to the banks of the Medicine, or Sun River.

From the night of the 13th to the morning of the 16th
Lewis and his party camped under a tree near the fall,
doubtless in "the small plain" which he describes and
which I know from ocular inspection was well suited to
the purpose. While Lewis was exploring and writing, the

hunters were killing buffalo and jerking the meat to provide a supply for the entire party when they should again be united. They caught white fish and trout in the falls, and these, with the buffalo humps, tongues, and marrow bones, enabled them to live, literally, on the fat of the land.

During this exploration of the stream Lewis had a series of adventures that might well have caused him to feel that "all the beasts of the neighborhood had made a league to destroy him." His numerous hair-breadth escapes throughout the trip were truly marvellous.

After having reached the highest of the series of cataracts found here, Lewis ascended a hill – on which now stands a chimney that carries away the sulphur fumes from a smelter – and obtained his first view of Medicine, or Sun, River and its lovely valley.

Captain Lewis then descended the hill, and directed his course toward the river [Sun] falling in from the west. He soon met a herd of at least a thousand buffaloe, and being desirous of providing for supper, shot one of them; the animal immediately began to bleed, and Captain Lewis, who had forgotten to reload his rifle, was intently watching to see him fall, when he beheld a large brown bear which was stealing on him unperceived, and was already within twenty steps. In the first moment of surprise he lifted his rifle, but remembering instantly that it was not charged, and that he had not time to reload, he felt that there was no safety but in flight. It was in the open level plain, not a bush nor a tree within three hundred yards, the bank of the river sloping and not more than three feet high, so that there was no possible mode of concealment. Captain Lewis therefore thought of retreating in a quick walk, as fast as the bear advanced, toward the nearest tree; but as soon as he turned, the bear ran open mouth and at full speed, upon him. Captain Lewis ran about eighty yards, but finding that the animal gained on him fast, it flashed on his mind that by getting into the water to such a depth that the bear would be obliged to attack him swimming, there was still some chance for his life; he therefore turned short, plunged into the river about waist deep, and facing about presented the point of his espontoon.

The Great Falls of the Missouri Discovered by Captain Lewis, June 13, 1805

The bear arrived at the water's edge within twenty feet of him, but as soon as he put himself in this posture of defence, he [the bear] seemed frightened, and wheeling about, retreated with as much precipitation as he had pursued. . . .

He [Lewis] now resumed his progress in the direction which the bear had taken, toward the western river, and found it a handsome stream about two hundred yards wide, apparently deep, with a gentle current; its waters clear, and its banks. . . about the same height as those of the Missouri. . . . This river is no doubt that which the Indians call Medicine River, which they mentioned as emptying into the Missouri just above the falls.

. . . In going through the low grounds on Medicine River he met an animal which at a distance he thought was a wolf, but on coming within sixty paces it proved to be some brownish yellow animal standing near its burrow, which, when he came nigh, crouched and seemed as if about to spring on him. Captain Lewis fired and the beast disappeared in its burrow. . . . He then went on, but as if the beasts of the forest had conspired against him, three buffaloe bulls, which were feeding with a large herd at the distance of half a mile, left their companions and ran at full speed toward him. He turned round, and, unwilling to give up the field, advanced toward them. When they came within a hundred yards, they stopped, looked at him for some time, and then retreated as they came. He now pursued his route in the dark, reflecting on the strange adventures and sights of the day, which crowded on his mind so rapidly that he should have been inclined to believe it all enchantment, if the thorns of the prickly pear piercing his feet did not dispel at every moment the illusion.

On the following morning, on awaking from his night's sleep, "Captain Lewis found a large rattlesnake coiled on the trunk of a tree under which he had been sleeping." I have never found a rattlesnake coiled over my head, but I have killed many a one, have eaten fried rattlesnake, and have found Utah scorpions in my blankets upon arising in the morning. Such experiences are common to mountaineers and one becomes used to them. In 1872, Thomas P. Roberts made a reconnaissance of the upper Missouri River, and camped near the mouth of Sun River; in a letter written to Senator Paris Gibson, of which I hold a copy, Mr. Roberts details at length his experience with rattle-snakes at this place, and it almost surpasses belief. He was on horseback, separated from his party, and was following a narrow buffalo trail along the edge of the river, hoping that it would lead him to and past the Great Falls.

My horse, which was an exceedingly gentle beast, very fortunately for me, suddenly stopped and on the ground almost beneath his feet, a small rattler was making his escape from beneath a stone the horse's hoofs had overturned. The next moment I saw another snake ahead in the path and, more horrible, as I cast my eyes upward over the rocks which almost grazed my shoulder as I rode along, there were still other snakes. I stopped for a moment to consider whether I had not better turn back but, as there appeared to be no chance to turn the horse at this place, I continued a few rods further and now I discovered that every stone concealed a snake, not one of which, however, coiled or rattled. They appeared when I reached down and touched them with my whip, to clear the path for the horse's feet – only too glad to escape. My own sensations, it can be readily imagined, by this time were horrible beyond description. I had now come absolutely to the end of the buffalo trail The steep slope was all loose rocks and stones, with snakes sunning themselves in every direction. To add to my misery, at this juncture I heard faintly, pistol and rifle shots from the top of the bluff. At last! I thought, my men have met a band of Indians and will be exterminated.

I finally drew rein on the patient old horse, and watching carefully for snakes, driving several of them away with my riding whip, I dismounted. I had to place my back to the rocks and shove the hind quarters of the horse over the edge of the steep bank and then tugging on the bridle, with the animal plunging and pawing desperately to recover his foothold, I finally succeeded in getting him on the ledge and turned. . . . I had not proceeded far [on the return] until I espied "Scott" (one of my men) far above me but descending and coming in my direction. I supposed, of course, that he was the sole survivor of a fight and was hastening to rejoin me so that together, we might effect our escape. Finally we got within earshot of each other, and he had come back to tell me that it was impossible for me to ride along the water's edge, and further, to pilot me through a prairie dog village at the top of the bluff, which was alive with rattlesnakes. "Mr. Roberts," says he, "you won't believe how many snakes our men have seen and killed 'till you see them strung along our trail!" – "Don't tell me about rattlesnakes," I replied, "I have seen more in the last hour than you ever heard about."

In my own visits to this locality I neither saw nor heard of any snakes.

On the 13th, 14th, and 15th of June, Captain Clark and the boat party were ascending the river with the greatest of difficulty. On the 13th they passed the future site of Fort Benton, and when, on the 14th, they rolled into their blanket beds at night and looked up at the brilliantly spangled heavens and the lucent milky way, tired, worn, bruised, stiff, footsore, and weary in every muscle, they were yet content, cheerful, and happy, for Shields had come down to them from the Captain on ahead and shouted above the noise of the waters, "We have found the falls – we are on the true Missouri!"

Fiercer grew the current, more thickly strewn the rocks, more dangerous the rapids, which were now become really one continuous, never-ceasing rapid, but with gradations of rapidity and danger.

The narrative of June 15th and 16th tersely recounts their difficulties and progress and eulogizes their men.

The channel is constantly obstructed by rocks and danger- ous rapids. During the whole progress the men are in the water hauling the canoes, and walking on sharp rocks and round stones which cut their feet or cause them to fall. The rattlesnakes, too, are so numerous that the men are constantly on their guard against being bitten by them; yet they bear the fatigues with the most undiminished cheerfulness. We hear the roar of the falls very distinctly this morning. . . At six and three- quarter miles we reached a large creek on the south, which, after one of our men, we called Shield's Creek.

[SUNDAY], June 16. . . . We passed the rapid by doubly manning the periogue and canoes. . . . About a mile above where we halted was a large [Portage] creek falling in on the south, opposite which is a large sulphur spring falling over the rocks on the north. Captain Lewis arrived at two [o'clock] from the falls about five miles above us, and after consulting upon the subject of the portage, we crossed the river and formed a camp on the north, having come three-quarters of a mile to-day. From our own observation we had deemed the south side to be the most favourable for a portage, but two men sent out for the purpose of examining it reported that the creek and the ravines intersected the plain so deeply that it was impossible to cross it. Captain Clark therefore resolved to examine more minutely what was the best route. . . . Finding that the portage would be at all events too long to enable us to carry the boats on our shoulders, six men were set to work to make wheels for carriages to transport them. Since leaving Maria's River the wife of Chaboneau, our interpreter, has been dangerously ill, but she now found great relief from the mineral water of the sulphur spring. It is situated about two hundred yards from the Missouri, into which it empties over a precipice of rock about twenty-five feet high.

Of the lateral creeks along here mentioned by the explorers, Snow River is now called Shonkin Creek, Shields Creek is Highland Creek, and Portage Creek is Belt Mountain Creek. The name Portage should by all means be restored to the last-named creek if possible, for here it means something, decidedly, and should be used to perpetuate those days of 1805 which tried men's souls.

The narrative of Gass during these days affords some interesting details.

On the 15th of June, while they were navigating the rapids, he pays an indirect tribute to the determination and efficiency of the men: "we proceeded on as usual, but had the most rapid water I ever saw any craft taken through." On the 16th and 17th he records:

[SUNDAY] 16th. As we found the south side the best to carry our canoes up, we crossed over and unloaded our craft.

We then had to take the empty canoes to the side we had left, and to tow them up by a line about a mile, in order to get them up to the mouth of a small river on the south side, as a more convenient place to take them up the bank. This business was attended with great difficulty as well as danger, but we succeeded in getting them all over safe.

[MONDAY] 17th. Part of the men were employed in taking the canoes up the small river about a mile and an half; and some engaged in making small wagons to haul the canoes and loading above the falls.

Gass thus informs us that the overland portage found to be necessary began at a point one and a half miles up Portage, or Belt Mountain, Creek, thus making the argument for the restoration of this name a stronger one.

The illness of Sacagawea worried the Captains, as well it might. As Lewis frankly says, they were now about to enter the region where her people dwelt, and her friendly offices and interpretative abilities were expected to be of great value to them, and they watched over and doctored her with all the care possible. She gradually improved, thanks to the sulphur spring, as they lead us to suppose, but one day while yet convalescent, she ate too much of the *pomme blanche,* or white apple, and this brought on a relapse. She was again very sick, but by dint of heroic treatment and careful nursing by Drs. Lewis and Clark, irregular M.D.'s, the Bird-woman recovered. Her imprudence in eating provoked a sharp reprimand to Mons. Chaboneau, for he had been previously cautioned against this very thing.

We have now reached what may be termed an epoch in the progress of the exploration. They have met their first real difficulty – the absolute blocking of navigation – and in some way it must be overcome, or all their previous effort has been for naught, and failure confronts them, unless, perchance, friendly Indians might be found from whom horses could be purchased. Presumably, as has been fore-

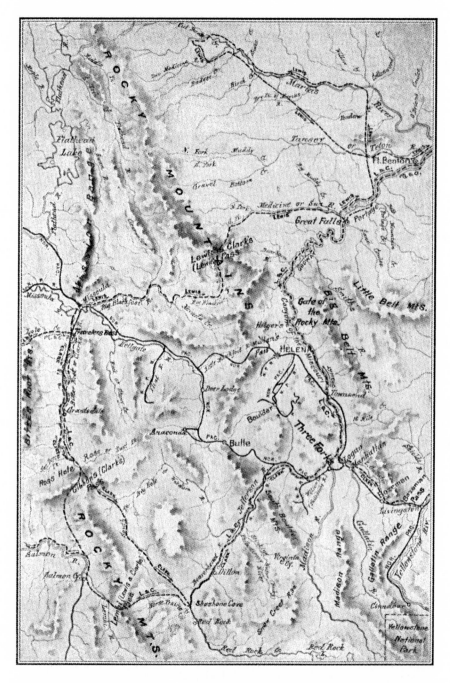

Route of Lewis and Clark from Maria's River to Traveller's Rest Creek and return, and also showing route of Captain Lewis from White Bear Islands to the headwaters of Maria's River and return to the mouth of that stream.

shadowed, a portage is the solution. But is it practicable? To determine this, on June 17th "Captain Clark set out with five men to explore the country," and while he is engaged in this work let us go back in time and with Captain Lewis explore the river and look upon its fine series of cataracts and cascades.

When Lewis, on the 13th, bent his steps toward that "column of smoke," as the Israelites once followed a pillar of cloud, and finally reached the falls and seated himself on the ledge of rock to view them, he was "filled with pleasure and astonishment."

He records his impressions in these words:

The river, immediately at its cascade, is 300 yards wide, and is pressed in by a perpendicular cliff on the left, which rises to about 100 feet, and extends up the stream for a mile; on the right the bluff is also perpendicular for 300 yards above the falls. For ninety or a hundred yards from the left cliff, the water falls in one smooth, even sheet. over a precipice of at least eighty feet. The remaining part of the river precipitates itself with a more rapid current, but, being received as it falls by the irregular and somewhat projecting rocks below, forms a splendid prospect of perfectly white foam, 200 yards in length and eighty [feet] in perpendicular elevation. This spray is dissipated into a thousand shapes, sometimes flying up in columns of fifteen or twenty feet, which are then oppressed by larger masses of the white foam, on all which the sun impresses the brightest colors of the rainbow. As it rises from the fall it beats with fury against a ledge of rocks, which extends across the river at 150 yards from the precipice. From the perpendicular cliff on the north, to the distance of 120 yards, the rocks rise only a few feet above the water. . . . A few small cedars grow near this ridge of rocks, which serves as a barrier to defend a small plain of about three acres, shaded with cottonwood, at the lower extremity of which is a grove of the same tree, where are several Indian cabins of sticks. . . At the distance of 300 yards from the same ridge is a second abutment of solid perpendicular rock about sixty feet high, projecting at right angles from the small plain on the north for 134 yards into the river. After leaving this, the Missouri again spreads itself to its usual distance of 300 yards, though with more than its ordinary rapidity.

The Captain was so "disgusted with the imperfect idea" of his description, that he "determined to draw his [my] pen across it and begin again," but I can vouch for the accuracy of the description, even to this day. I sat on an eminence on the east – Lewis's south – side of the stream for more than an hour, studying the scene with a copy of Lewis's description in my hands. I overlooked the entire fall and a long stretch of river below. There was the ledge of rock stretching across from the west – north – bank, on the high rock at the extremity of which Lewis sat and penned his description; just back of (below) the ledge still can be seen the "cottonwood plain," and yet farther down is the "second abutment of solid perpendicular rock." If Lewis could reseat himself there to-day he could not, probably, better his description. The rocks hold the river level, and there has been but slight erosion and change.

But this fall is only the first, in going up-stream, in a series of cascades, rapids, and falls that practically constitute the river for ten miles. It is much the largest and, in many respects, the finest, and its name, the Great Falls of the Missouri, is used in a collective sense for the entire series.

The Captain's story of his successive discoveries as, filled with amazement, he went on and on, is as follows:

After passing one continued rapid and three small cascades, each three or four feet high, he reached at the distance of five miles a second fall. The river is about four hundred yards wide, and for the distance of three hundred throws itself over to the depth of nineteen feet, and so irregularly that he gave it the name of the Crooked Falls. From the southern shore it extends obliquely upward about one hundred and fifty yards, and then forms an acute angle downward nearly to the commencement of four small islands close to the northern side. . . . Above this fall the river bends suddenly to the northward.

While viewing this place Captain Lewis heard a loud roar above him, and crossing the point of a hill for a few hundred yards, he saw one of the most beautiful objects in nature. The whole Missouri is suddenly stopped by one shelving rock, which, without a single niche, and with an edge as straight and regular as if formed by art, stretches itself from one side of the river to the other for at least a quarter of a mile. Over this it [the river] precipitates itself in an even uninterrupted sheet to the perpendicular depth of fifty feet, whence, dashing against the rocky bottom it rushes rapidly down, leaving behind it a spray of the purest foam across the river. The scene which it presented was indeed singularly beautiful, since, without any of the wild irregular sublimity of the lower falls, it combined all the regular elegances which the fancy of a painter would select to form a beautiful waterfall. The eye had scarcely been regaled with this charming prospect, when at the distance of half a mile, Captain Lewis observed another of a similar kind; to this he immediately hastened, and found a cascade stretching across the whole river for a quarter of a mile, with a descent of fourteen feet, though the perpendicular pitch was only six feet. . . . His curiosity being . . . awakened, he determined to go on, even should night overtake him, to the head of the falls.

At the distance of two and a half miles he arrived at another cataract, of twenty-six feet. The river is here six hundred yards wide, but the descent is not immediately perpendicular, though the river falls generally with a regular and smooth sheet; for about one-third of the descent a rock protrudes to a small distance, receives the water in its passage, and gives it a curve. On the south side is a beautiful plain [where the city of Great Falls now stands] a few feet above the level of the falls; on the north the country is more broken, and there is a hill not far from the river. Just below the falls is a little island in the middle of the river, well covered with timber. Here on a cottonwood tree, an eagle had fixed its [her] nest, and seemed the undisputed mistress of a spot to contest whose dominion neither man nor beast would venture across the gulfs that surround it, and which is further secured by the mist rising from the falls. This solitary bird could not escape the observation of the Indians, who made the eagle's nest a part of their description of the falls, which now proves to be correct in almost every particular, except that they did not do justice to their height. Just above this is a cascade of about five feet, beyond which, as far as could be discerned, the velocity of the water seemed to abate.

Being on the left bank – "north" side – of the stream, the Captain missed, this day, a fountain on the opposite bank which Captain Clark discovered later.

Black Eagle Fall from Below, Showing the Island where the Eagle had its Nest.

317

The traveller of to-day will find as much pleasure, and astonishment, too, perhaps, in visiting this series of cataracts as Lewis did. While there is, of course, none of the magnificent grandeur and magnitude of Niagara, nor the tremendous heights to be found among the falls of the Yosemite, nor the peculiar and wondrous effect produced by the Great Fall of the Yellowstone, there is, nevertheless, an influence and effect, both individually and collectively, formed by this extraordinary aggregation of cascades that profoundly impresses and moves one. In the distance of ten miles, from the first to the last fall, the total descent of the river is, by modern measurements, 412.5 feet. Probably 150 feet of this – Clark's measurements made it nearer 200 feet – is found in the four principal falls.

There are good roads leading down each bank of the river now, and no snakes, herds of bison, nor angry bears to attack one, so that the inspection of these waterfalls can be made in an easy and pleasurable manner.

Of the five falls which are known by name, Lewis and Clark seem to have named but two, Great Falls and Crooked Falls. The others are now known, successively, as Rainbow Fall, the one next above Crooked Falls; Colter Fall, just above Rainbow Fall, and Black Eagle Fall, the last one, ascending the stream, and lying within the corporate limits of the city of Great Falls.

The Great Falls completely fill the stream from shore to shore, but at somewhat of an angle, and pour over the declivity in a manner that means demolition to any craft or body unfortunate enough to be engulfed in the angry flood above, as the thirsty bison frequently were. One can sit on the rocky banks of the river, or perch oneself on the pinnacle of rock whereon Lewis sat, and gaze for hours, unwearied, watching the rush and play of the waters as they pitch and tumble over the rocks.

The Crooked Falls are most aptly named. To me, the Great Falls, although the highest, were less interesting, in some respects, than either the Crooked or the Rainbow Fall. The former runs in all directions, up-stream, down-stream, sideways, lengthways, and every other way. It is a most peculiar cascade, an irregular horseshoe in shape, and an uncommonly interesting and unusual type of its kind. Above the falls the water is brown – from the rocky bed – and quite clear; below it is foam and spray. The four islands mentioned by Lewis and Clark are still to be seen.

The Rainbow Fall is a noble cataract extending clear across the stream. It can be viewed full in front or in profile, as the fall is at the head of a bend. The extreme regularity of edge does not now exist, as Lewis described it, but the form, while more or less curved and indented, is still the most regular and dignified of any of those found here. The way in which Lewis wrote of this fall and the distinctions he drew between it and the Great or "Lower" Falls, show how singularly susceptible he was to the refinements of nature.

There are several points from which to see this fall, and a winding stairway enables one to go to the base of it and gain an upward view of it. On the left side, the one from which Lewis first beheld it, the rock of the stream bed and banks is probably harder than elsewhere at this cataract, for the rocky bed there throws a projection down-stream, and immediately below is a rock table over a part of which the water flows in some small cascades, that part of it bordering the central river rising in a green, bossy island above the waters. There is much spray, and a fine rainbow, extending across the river, is usually visible.

From the brink of the river below the fall, the effect of the huge wall of water as it comes over the ledge, brown and unbroken above, dashed to bits and torn into white spray below, is very fine.

The Colter Fall, so named by Hon. Paris Gibson, is a small, irregular one, somewhat dwarfed owing to its proximity to Rainbow Fall, but it worthily perpetuates the name of our friend, John Colter, the discoverer of Yellowstone Park.

Above Colter Fall there is a curve in the river to the left, or south, as one goes up-stream. Well around this bend there now stands a huge smelter. Down the grassy slope below the smelter and at the river's edge is the fountain already mentioned, which Lewis missed and Clark discovered when surveying the river.

This fountain, fan-shaped and between three hundred and four hundred feet wide, is now known as the Giant Spring, and it is truly a wonderful work of nature. Outside of Yellowstone Park I have seen but one spring to compare with it. The Park springs are of hot water, but the water of the Giant Spring is as cold and as pure and clear as one can conceive. The volume of water thrown out is enormous, being 680 cubic feet per second, and there is little or no variation. If the water could be utilized for irrigation on a desert, or could be made to furnish the city of Great Falls with its water-supply, without marring its present beauty, the useful and ornamental would be happily combined. Captain Lewis visited the spring on June 29th and thus describes it:

They proceeded to the fountain, which is perhaps the largest in America. It is situated in a pleasant, level plain, about twenty-five yards from the river, into which it falls over some steep irregular rocks, with a sudden ascent of about six feet in one part of its course. The water boils up from among the rocks and with such force near the center, that the surface seems higher there than the earth on the sides of the fountain, which is a handsome turf of fine green grass. The water is extremely

321

The Wonderful Fountain near Great Falls, Montanta, Discovered by Captain Clark on June 18, 1805, now Known as the Giant Spring.

pure, cold, and pleasant to the taste, not being impregnated with lime or any foreign substance. It is perfectly transparent and continues its bluish cast for half a mile down the Missouri, notwithstanding the rapidity of the river.

According to Captain Raynolds – in July, 1860 – the fountain covers a quarter of an acre in area, and its temperature is, or then was, 53° F. and that of the river 70° F. It is indeed a noble spring, boiling and bubbling in "giant" fashion and with a wonderful and extremely fascinating display of color – yellows and greens – formed by the vegetable growths at the bottom.

The last fall Captain Lewis found is now known as Black Eagle Fall, the name, a modern one, being based primarily and most appropriately upon the incident recorded by Lewis, of the eagle and its nest. It is strange that Lewis himself did not apply the name. The island, tree, and bird are gone now. Civilization has wrought its perfect work, and a dam, power-house, foot-bridge, and a huge smelter have usurped the eagle's erstwhile stronghold. The locality and fall bear scarcely any resemblance to what they were in 1805.

On July 12, 1860, Capt. W. F. Raynolds, – not Reynolds, as so often written, – United States Engineer Corps, passed here at the head of a Government exploring expedition. Referring to Lewis's incident of the eagle, he says:

A remarkable fact is that the eagle's nest, described in 1805, as above quoted, still remains in the cottonwood, on the island, in the stream, and as we came within sight a bald eagle of unusual size was perched in the tree by its side. This affords a very striking illustration of the habits of this peculiarly American bird, and from its known longevity it may have been the identical eagle that Captain Lewis made historical more than half a century ago.

In 1872, Thomas P. Roberts, already referred to, relates

the following, which I take from his letter to Senator Gibson[1]:

> My first view of the Black Eagle Falls was attended with a remarkable incident. I was riding ahead of the party, one man following at a short distance. When I rode out to the edge of the bluff, just below the falls, in order to obtain a good view of the situation, a large Black Eagle sailed out from an island below the falls, rising from a cottonwood tree, the top of which was broken off, and came directly towards me. I was interested in the bird, and it seemed also to be specially interested in me. Finally it alighted on the ground and walked along ahead of me, only a few yards distant, giving me some very sharp and, apparently, angry looks. After a few moments, however, it rose in the air and began to wheel in circles around me and finally, hovered in the air directly over my head and within ten feet, dangling its talons in a very threatening manner; I became alarmed and drew my revolver, intending to shoot, if it came a foot nearer. Just at this time the bird espied the man following me and flew in his direction, but not very far, for it was greeted with a pistol shot from my man, which caused the bird to fly off and return to its nest on the broken cottonwood tree. . . .
>
> What better or more appropriate name, under the circumstances, could therefore have been suggested than "Black Eagle" for your falls? I was told that the bird was alive several years after 1872.

On his reconnaissance Mr. Roberts named the Black Eagle and Rainbow falls. Whether these eagles may or may not have been the same that Captain Lewis saw fifty-five and sixty-seven years before, respectively, is a question for naturalists and ornithologists, probably, but certainly these accounts add interest to Lewis's narrative and form curious coincidences.

Former writers, after Lewis and Clark, seem to have been so much impressed with Lewis's eagle and his unrestricted dominion that little attention was paid to the Black Eagle Fall itself. It now appears much as any artificial dam and

---

[1] It is given more briefly in vol. i. of Montana Historical Society's *Contributions.*

cataract does, and not a vestige of the island and tree, apparently, remains, and of course all of the old individuality is gone.

Captain Clark's measurements of all these falls, carefully made with a spirit level, were:

Black Eagle Fall	26 feet 5 inches
Colter	6 feet 7 inches
Rainbow	47 feet 8 inches
Crooked	19 feet
Great	87 feet ¾ inches

These figures, according to more recent measurements, are somewhat over the real heights, I understand, but their close approximation, when it is remembered that the surveys were made a century ago, is evidence of the conscientious and reliable character of the work done by these men.

If the region about old Fort Mandan has been much changed since Lewis and Clark wintered there, the reverse is almost true of this spot. The geological conditions here are radically different, and, save as the city of Great Falls with its smelters, and the Great Northern railway bridge which spans the river just above Rainbow Fall, are now to be found here, there has been, with the exception of Black Eagle Fall, very little change.

If Lewis and Clark could revisit the locality, they would probably find that the lateral ravines were deeper and headed much farther back in the prairie than when they were making their portage. The tremendous cloud-bursts which occur here at times wash away the loose soil of the prairies, but the impression made upon the rocky bed beneath is not great from decade to decade, and the banks of the river, being rocky and precipitous, are slow to show the effects of erosion.

And how, during all the time of this exploration of the

Black Eagle Fall from Above, Showing the Smelter and Chimney on the Hill Referred to in the Text.

cataracts, has Captain Clark succeeded in his exploration for a portage?

The Captain left camp at the mouth of Portage-Belt Mountain-Creek on June 17th. That day and the next he measured "the heights and distances along the banks of the river" and, on the night of the 17th, "slept near a ravine at the foot of the Crooked Falls, having very narrowly escaped falling into the river . . . in descending the cliffs near the grand cataract."

The night of the 18th, after passing the junction of the Medicine – Sun – and Missouri rivers, and consequently, the spot where Great Falls, Mont., now stands, Clark and his little band camped at a spot memorable in the annals of the expedition, the Whitebear Islands. As may be supposed, the then ever-present "white bears," or grizzlies, were the inspiration for this name, which the islands still bear. The first night that the party camped at this spot they were attacked by bears, to whom the islands seemed to be a home and sanctuary. One of these animals chased Willard almost into the camp, and before it could be pursued had, in prowling around, discovered Colter and driven the future discoverer of Yellowstone Park and the hero of the adventure with the Blackfeet, in ignominious flight into the river, where he remained until Clark and three other men drove off the brute.

Captain Clark found, by an examination made on the 19th, that no insuperable obstacles to a portage existed and he roughly surveyed and staked out a portage line across the country, which he afterwards improved and shortened. The total length of the portage from Portage Creek to Whitebear Islands was seventeen and three quarter miles.

Everybody was now hard at work. One camp, which Clark looked after, was maintained at Portage Creek, and another, at the Whitebear Islands, was under charge of

Lewis. The best hunters were sent out in all directions, several of them up the valley of the Medicine River, where, in parties of one and two, they established bivouac camps and hunted, particularly for elk, which were very scarce-the skins of which they wanted for a special purpose. Some of the men remained at each camp, performing necessary labor, but all that could be spared were employed in conveying the canoes and stores from the lower to the upper camp.

At the lower camp they secured the pirogue "in a thick copse of willow bushes" and cached, besides, a goodly amount of miscellaneous supplies.

In order to lighten the work of transfer, they searched for trees large and round enough from which to make wheels to place under their canoes, so that they could be dragged across the plain. They, luckily, found ooze cottonwood tree – the only one within twenty miles – just below Portage Creek, measuring twenty-two inches in diameter, which answered the purpose.

The portage occupied the time of most of the party from June 21st to July 2d, nearly thirteen full days, and it was fatiguing work in the extreme, but was borne uncomplainingly. The axles and tongues of the so-called "waggons" being made of willow, cottonwood, and box-alder, were weak and some of them broke. These rude conveyances had to be dragged by hand across an uneven country, where the prickly pear abounded and the buffalo had so tramped the wet earth that it had dried into hard, sharp points, which caused great suffering to the men, their feet being protected only by moccasins.

A few brief extracts from the journals will afford some idea of their experiences:

There are vast quantities of buffaloe feeding on the plains or watering in the river, which is also strewed with the floating carcases and limbs of these animals. They go in large herds to water about the falls, and as all the passages to the river near that place are narrow and steep, the foremost are pressed into the river by the impatience of those behind. In this way we have seen ten or a dozen disappear over the falls in a few minutes.

The journal for the 19th records:

The wind blew violently to-day, as it did yesterday, and as it does frequently in this open country, where there is not a tree to break or oppose its force.

The narrative for the 21st deals with ornithology and botany as well as with the portage, and it exhibits the care with which the Captains observed everything about them.

On the 22d they had trouble:

We now set out to pass the portage, and halted for dinner at eight miles distance near a little stream. The axletrees of our carriage, which had been made of an old mast, and the cotton-wood tongues broke before we came there; but we renewed them with the timber of the sweet willow, which lasted till within half a mile of our intended camp, when the tongues gave way, and we were obliged to take as much baggage as we could carry on our backs down to the river, where we formed an encampment in a small grove of timber opposite the Whitebear islands.

Captain Lewis had brought with him from Harper's Ferry, Va., the iron frame of a boat which he put together at Whitebear Islands camp.

This boat frame, "36 feet long, 4½ feet wide and 2 feet 2 inches deep," was almost a fad of Lewis and it was for covering this that the elk-skins were wanted. All the men that could be spared were kept at work dressing the skins which the hunters brought in and setting up the iron frame of the boat. It required twenty-eight elk and four buffalo-skins to cover the craft, and after much tribulation they compounded a mixture of pounded charcoal, beeswax, and

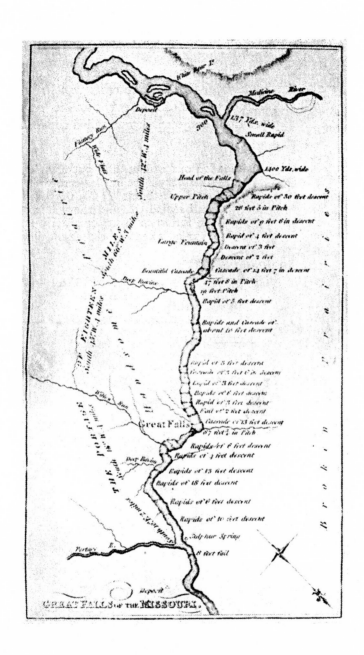

Lewis and Clark's Map of the Region about the Great Falls and Companion Cataracts, and Showing the Line of Portage.

329

buffalo tallow with which to smear the skins and seams so as to make the boat water-tight. The craft was launched on July 9th and Gass thus records the event and its results. The boat, it appears from his journal, was called the *Experiment.*

In the forenoon we loaded our canoes, and put the Experiment into the water. She rides very light but leaks some. . . . The tallow and coal were found not to answer the purpose; for as soon as dry, it cracked and scaled off, and the water came through the skins. Therefore for want of tar or pitch we had, after all our labour, to haul our new boat on shore, and leave it at this place.

The non-success of this scheme sat heavily on Lewis's mind and heart, and made it necessary once more to hunt for cottonwood trees suitable for canoes.

The Captain accepted the failure of the boat with true philosophic fortitude, *cached* the frame, – buried her, Gass puts it – and "after this we amused ourselves with fishing," a wise thing to do. In the meantime, Captain Clark, without loss of time, "set out by land with ten of the best workmen" for a spot on the Missouri some miles above them, where there was timber from which to make canoes.

In giving the full story of this boat we have advanced somewhat in time beyond other concurrent events.

The portage came near being the death of all of them. If it was n't heat, prickly pears, or bears, from which they suffered, it was hail, cloud-bursts, or something else. At one point on the portage.

they all repaired their moccasins, and put on double soals to protect them from the prickly pear and from the sharp points of earth which have been formed by the trampling of the buffaloe during the late rains. This of itself is sufficient to render the portage disagreeable to one who had no burden, but as the men are loaded as heavily as their strength will permit, the crossing is really painful. Some are limping with the soreness of their feet, others are scarcely able to stand for more than a few minutes from the heat and fatigue; they are all obliged to halt and rest frequently, and at almost every stopping place they fall, and many of them are asleep in an instant; yet no one complains, and they go on with great cheerfulness.

There was some variety, however, in the daily drudgery, and they managed to extract a little fun out of it all.

The party that went to the lower camp had one canoe and the baggage carried into the high plain to be ready in the morning, and then all who could make use of their feet had a dance on the green to the music of a violin.

Cruzatte, the waterman, was the violinist, and that violin, it is safe to assert, was worth more than its weight in gold during the long, weary months of the exploration, in the cheer and contentment that its tones put into the lives of the men.

Then, although their canoes were voyaging on cottonwood wheels across the prairie, they still retained their nautical habits.

The winds are sometimes violent in these plains. The men inform us that as they were bringing one of the canoes along on truck-wheels, they hoisted the sail and the wind carried her along for some distance.

Saturday, June 29th, was a day long remembered by some of them. Clark, Sacágawea, and Chaboneau, having sought shelter in a ravine from a cloud-burst, were all but swept down into the Missouri by a flood that came upon them without warning. The storm was widespread, almost a cyclone as it would popularly be called to-day.

Having lost some notes and remarks which he [Clark] had made on first ascending the river, he determined to go up to the Whitebear Islands along its banks, in order to supply the deficiency. He there left one man to guard the baggage, and went on to the falls, accompanied by his servant York, Chaboneau, and his wife with her young child. On his arrival there he observed a very dark cloud arising in the west which threatened rain, and looked around for some shelter, but could find no place where they would be secure from being blown into the river if the wind should prove as violent as it sometimes does in the plains. At length, about a quarter of a mile above the falls, he found a deep ravine where there were some shelving rocks, under which he took refuge. They were on the upper side of the ravine near the river, perfectly safe from the rain, and therefore laid down their guns, compass, and other articles which they carried with them.

The shower was at first moderate, and it then increased to a heavy rain, the effects of which they did not feel. Soon after a torrent of rain and hail descended; the rain seemed to fall in a solid mass, and instantly collecting in the ravine came rolling down in a dreadful current, carrying the mud and rocks, and everything that opposed it. Captain Clark fortunately saw it a moment before it reached them and springing up with his gun and shotpouch in his left hand, with his right clambered up the steep bluff, pushing on the Indian woman with her child in her arms; her husband too had seized her hand and was pulling her up the hill, but he was so terrified at the danger that but for Captain Clark, himself and his wife and child would have been lost. So instantaneous was the rise of the water that before Captain Clark had reached his gun and begun to ascend the bank, the water was up to his waist, and he could scarce get up faster than it rose, till it reached the height of fifteen feet, with a furious current which, had they waited a moment longer, would have swept them into the river just above the Great Falls, down which they must inevitably have been precipitated. They reached the plain in safety, and found York, who had separated from them just before the storm to hunt some buffaloe, and was now returning to find his master. They had been obliged to escape so rapidly that Captain Clark lost his compass and umbrella, Chaboneau left his gun, shotpouch, and tomahawk, and the Indian woman had just time to grasp her child, before the net in which it lay at her feet was carried down the current.

He now relinquished his intention of going up the river, and returned to the camp at Willow run. Here he found that the party sent this morning for the baggage had all returned to camp in great confusion, leaving their loads in the plain. On account of the heat they generally go nearly naked, and with no covering on their heads. The hail was so large, and driven so

333

Captain Clark, Chaboneau, Sacagawea and Papoose in the Cloud-burst near the Great Falls, on June 29, 1805 (From a drawing by Russell.)

furiously against them by the high wind, that it knocked several of them down; one of them particularly was thrown on the ground three times, and most of them bleeding freely and complained of being much bruised. Willow run had risen six feet since the rain, and as the plains were so wet that they could not proceed, they passed the night at their camp.

Any one who has travelled much across the Western plains, mountains, and deserts has seen such storms as this, or the effects of them. The writer has a vivid recollection of an experience, with a companion, in an *arroya* in southern Utah, when we all but rode into an advancing wall of water several feet high, as it suddenly appeared around a bend, which was born of a cloud-burst miles away.

The name of Whitebear, given to this island camp — although it was on the mainland — fitted it perfectly. The bears that infested the islands and their vicinage were of the most savage sort and apparently had not the least fear of man or his firearms. They harried the men day and night, and but for that strayed Assiniboin dog, might have played merry havoc with them. I know from experience what a boon a good camp dog is, and this derelict seems to have appreciated the company in which he found himself and to have wished to do even a dog's share to make the expedition a success.

J. Fields was sent up the Missouri to hunt elk; but he returned about noon and informed us that a few miles above he saw two white bears near the river, and in attempting to fire at them came suddenly on a third, which being only a few steps off immediately attacked him; that in running to escape from the monster he leaped down a steep bank of the river, where, falling on a bar of stone, he cut his hand and knee and bent his gun; but fortunately for him the bank concealed him from his antagonist, or he would most probably have been lost.

On the 27th the hunters out-manœuvred one of the brutes:

As they were hunting on the river they saw a low ground covered with thick brushwood, where from the tracks along shore they thought a bear had probably taken refuge; they therefore landed, without making a noise, and climbed a tree about twenty feet above the ground. Having fixed themselves securely, they raised a loud shout, and a bear instantly rushed toward them. These animals never climb, and therefore when he came to the tree and stopped to look at them Drewyer shot him in the head. He proved to be the largest we have yet seen;

Captain Clark and his Men Shooting Bears. From "A Journal of the Voyages and Travels," etc., by Patrick Gass.

his noise [nose] appeared to be like that of a common ox; his forefeet measured nine inches across; and the hind feet were seven inches wide and eleven and three-quarters long, exclusive of the talons.

The journal of July 2, 1805, says of the mountains:

They glisten with great beauty when the sun shines on them in a particular direction, and most probably from this glittering appearance have derived the name of the Shining mountains.

The Rocky Mountains are called by the explorers both the Snowy and the Shining Mountains, and still another name for them was the Stoney Mountains. As long ago as 1766-67, Jonathan Carver, a citizen of Connecticut, explored a portion of the Northwest, and in his book of travels refers to these mountains as the Shining Mountains.

The journal for July 4, 1805, is very interesting:

. . . We had intended to despatch a canoe with part of our men to the United States early this spring; but not having yet seen the Snake Indians, or knowing whether to calculate on their friendship or enmity, we have decided not to weaken our party, which is already scarcely sufficient to repel any hostility. We were afraid too that such a measure might dishearten those who remain; and as we have never suggested it to them, they are all perfectly and enthusiastically attached to the enterprise, and willing to encounter any danger to insure its success. . . .

Since our arrival at the falls we have repeatedly heard a strange noise coming from the mountains in a direction a little to the north of west. It is heard at different periods of the day and night, sometimes when the air is perfectly still and without a cloud, and consists of one stroke only, or of five or six discharges in quick succession. It is loud, and resembles precisely the sound of a six-pound piece of ordnance at the distance of three miles. The Minnetarees frequently mentioned this noise like thunder, which they said the mountains made; but we had paid no attention to it, believing it to have been some superstition, or perhaps a falsehood. The watermen also of the party say that the Pawnees and Ricaras give the same account of a noise heard in the Black mountains to the westward of them. The solution of the mystery given by the philosophy of the watermen is, that it is occasioned by the bursting of the rich mines of silver confined within the bosom of the mountain. . . .

We contrived . . . to spread, not a very sumptuous, but a comfortable table in honour of the day, and in the evening gave the men a drink of spirits, which was the last of our stock, after that the fiddle was produced and a dance begun, which lasted till nine o'clock, when it was interrupted by a heavy shower of rain.

The failure to send a boat and messengers to President Jefferson from this point caused much worry and concern to those interested, in the States, but the reasons assigned for not doing so will probably appear to most of us as logical and sound.

The phenomenon of explosions in the mountains is a somewhat unusual one, and in this day of scientific knowledge in general, and with the advances made in mineralogy, "the philosophy of the watermen" – Professor Cruzatte *et al.* – is amusingly interesting.

Roberts, when encamped at Sun River on the reconnaissance heretofore referred to, in 1872, heard these explosions and also other peculiar sounds. He writes:

> One day . . . a sharp and exceedingly swift whizzing sound was heard by all the party, high overhead, which we thought must have been caused by the passage of an aerolite through the air, but nothing of which was visible. Lewis and Clark spoke of a peculiar sound heard most frequently in this neighborhood, similar to that of a cannon fired at a great distance to the southwest. While we were in the Long Pool, above Sun, or Medicine river, as it is sometimes called, we heard a similar sound, exactly like the booming of a cannon some miles distant. We heard it three times, at intervals of about fifteen minutes. Altogether, there was something strange in the coincidence. It is not impossible that in some yet unexplored gulch on Smith river or elsewhere in the mountains, wherever the sound may have proceeded from, there may be a geyser similar to those in the fire-hole basin on the Upper Madison, some of which give an occasional salute of this sort before going into the regular spouting business. These sounds are occasioned, most probably, by the explosion of gases in these hot geysers.

Here we have the same reports that Lewis and Clark heard, with an added explanation based on the geyser phenomena of Yellowstone Park, in the knowledge of which Mr. Roberts had Lewis and Clark at a disadvantage.

I am informed by those resident in the country that these explosions are heard about the region of the falls and the Gate of the Mountains to this day, but no geysers have been discovered there nor has any one seen any "bursting of the rich mines of silver," although silver has been mined in many parts of that region and the mountains have been very thoroughly prospected.

The whizzing, humming sound heard by Roberts is an acoustic peculiarity which has never been explained, but it is no figment of the imagination, as many may think. The same phenomenon is heard in the region about Yellowstone and Shoshone lakes in Yellowstone Park. This strange sound has been heard and described by scientific men who have noted it in the Park, but they have been unable to give an adequate explanation or theory for it. As heard near Yellowstone Lake, it is likened to the vibrations of a harp high up above the tree-tops, or the sound of many telegraph wires swinging in the wind; to the humming of a swarm of bees, the echo of bells after repeated strokes of the hammer, voices faintly heard high overhead, and to various other sounds. It is a weird child of nature and doubtless may be heard, as are the explosions, in other places than those here named.

If there were glaciers in this portion of Montana, similar to those found on Mounts Hood, Adams, and Rainier, in Oregon and Washington, these explosions might be accounted for in the boom of avalanches, but there are none. Professor Winchell late of the University of Minnesota, and Professor Upham of the Minnesota Historical Society, both very able geologists, inform me that, to their knowledge, no explanation has ever been given for these reports.

The camp at Whitebear Islands was finally abandoned to the bears on Saturday, July 13th. On the morning of the 13th "the remaining baggage [was] embarked on board the six canoes," which with two men each, and in charge of Sergeant Ordway, left for Canoe Camp. Captain Lewis, with Lepage, who was ill, and Sacágawea, were put across the river by the canoes, and as the boats started for camp by water, these three walked across country. The pedestrians reached Canoe Camp within a few hours, but Ordway had head winds to contend with and did not reach there until noon of the 13th.

The city of Great Falls, Mont., is about three miles below the Whitebear Islands camp of Lewis and Clark, and a branch of the Great Northern Railway now runs along the bank of the river where their tents were pitched. Flattery Run, as the explorers called the stream near their camp, is now known as Sand Coulée Creek.

As the river at this point was and is quite sluggish, it is doubtful if there has been any very material alteration of the topography. The "small island in the middle of the river" mentioned by Lewis and Clark and shown on their map of the locality does not appear on the map of the Missouri River Commission and has probably been scoured away, but this is about the only noticeable change of any consequence.

Through the kind assistance of Hon. Paris Gibson, the "father" of the flourishing city of Great Falls, I was enabled, without loss of time, to find the coulée which the explorers descended from the plain to Whitebear Islands camp. There can hardly be any mistake made in the identification of this old roadway, for it naturally, so to speak, identifies itself. A slight depression, or "draw," as it is termed in the West, leads from the summit of the high prairie two or three miles back of the river, directly down to the stream opposite the islands, and forms a natural and good roadway.

The city of Great Falls, with its large smelters, constitutes the greatest change found hereabouts. The census of 1900 gave this young city a population of nearly fifteen thousand, and it and Missoula, another point visited by

Captain Lewis, are the two most promising among the smaller cities of Montana.

After leaving Canoe Camp the party would soon leave the buffalo range, and the question of subsistence would then become one of some moment. This leads them to remark that

It requires some diligence to supply us plentifully, for as we reserve our parched meal for the Rocky Mountains, where we do not expect to find much game, our principal article of food is meat, and the consumption of the whole, thirty-two persons belonging to the party, amounts to four deer, an elk and a deer, or one buffaloe, every twenty-four hours.

This seems to be the proper place to refer to a subject of national importance and interest, a corollary of the Lewis and Clark expedition and, apparently, having its inspiration largely in their report. This is the Pacific Railway idea, and an outline of what is here given was first published by the writer, upon his discovery of it, in *Wonderland* 1900.

The first promulgation of the idea of a Pacific Railway has been generally supposed to have been in a newspaper article by Dr. Samuel B. Barlow, a physician of Granville, Mass., in 1834 — perhaps earlier, as the date of the paper is not definitely known. Doctor Barlow advocated the northern route. Ten years later the idea was taken up in earnest by Asa Whitney, who espoused it with remarkable vigor in the face of much ridicule. He sank his fortune in the scheme and died a poor milkman, but not until he had seen the public aroused to the importance of the enterprise. A notable fact in connection with this advocacy of the railroad by Barlow and Whitney, especially so by Whitney, was the large prospective trade of the United States with China and Japan. This argument can now be thoroughly appreciated, for this trade, great as it is when compared

The White Bear islands and the Missouri River above the City of Great Falls. The Lewis and Clark portage from below the Great Falls, followed, approximately, the line of poles seen at the left centre of the illustration.

with Whitney's time, is a mere bagatelle to what it will become in the future expansion of commerce.

In 1835, Rev. Samuel Parker, a Presbyterian clergyman of Ithaca, N. Y., made a missionary trip across the continent and down the Columbia. In an interesting volume[1] recounting his adventures and observations he boldly says: "There would be no difficulty in the way of constructing a railroad from the Atlantic to the Pacific Ocean."

Certainly, however, the germ of this idea was publicly enunciated years before any of the above-named individuals gave expression to it. In the Twenty-ninth Congress, first session, House of Representatives, Document No. 173 (1846) there is printed a memorial by Robert Mills, Engineer and Architect, "submitting a new plan of roadway." This roadway was possessed of such advantages over other railroads and canals, "that it must eventually be substituted in their place," in the interests of economy, etc., in "a system of intercommunication with Oregon, and a commercial highway to the Pacific Ocean." In the Mills memorial occur these words:

> The author has had the honor of being perhaps the first in the field to propose to connect the Pacific with the Atlantic *by a railroad from the head navigable waters of the noble rivers disemboguing into each ocean* [italics mine]. In 1819, [nine years prior to the first railroad construction in this country] he published a work on the internal improvement of Maryland, Virginia, and South Carolina, connected with the intercourse of these States with the West.

Mills does not name this work and I have never seen it, but there is a lengthy extract from it in the memorial. It will be observed that Mills made his suggestion only thirteen years after Lewis and Clark returned from their exploration,

[1] *Journal of an Exploring Tour beyond the Rocky Mountains,* 1835-1837

and but five years after their report was first published, in 1814, and he quotes freely from their report in support of his proposition.

Mills's idea, in 1819, was to use a combination of a canal and connecting watercourses, starting from Charleston, S. C., to the Great Falls of the Missouri; "thence, passing through the plains and across the Rocky Mountains, to the navigable waters of the Kooskooskee River, a branch of the Columbia, three hundred and forty miles"; thence down the streams which we shall soon follow with the explorers, to Pacific tide-water The words between quotation marks are taken by Mills almost verbatim from Lewis and Clark's Summary Statement of distances, etc., and his proposed route is virtually the one that they followed.

Mills, still quoting from his memorial of 1819, continues:

> That eventually the internal communication with the Pacific ocean will be by the Missouri, there can be no question; and that our proposed canal, if executed, would constitute part of this grand route, must be evident, when we look at its position, both with respect to the seat of the general government and to the Ohio river. Would it be too extravagant to look forward to the period when our East India trade shall take this course, and the mouth of the Columbia river, or the head of its ship navigation, be the grand depot of articles going and coming? The safety and expedition of this channel would certainly lead us to form a conclusion favorable to this idea.

Then, after suggesting that other streams, among them the Platte and Yellowstone rivers east of the Rockies and the Multnomah and the south fork of Lewis River on the western side, may open satisfactory routes, he says:

> To calculate on the aid of steamboats upon these waters, and on an application of the same moving power to carriages upon railroads across the mountains, we may estimate an average progress of eighty miles per day on this route, which would enable us to accomplish the journey in little more than sixty-two days from Charleston to the Pacific ocean.

While this is by no means the Pacific Railroad idea in its entirety, it is here in embryonic form at least, and Mills should receive just credit as the originator of the idea so far as present records show.

The first agitation for a Pacific railway contemplated the northern route. Political exigencies during the Civil

View from the Summit of Bear's-tooth Mountain, just below the Gates of the Rocky Mountains, Showing the Missouri River.

War finally forced the first Pacific railway construction — the Union Pacific — to be along the Platte River, from the east, this road connecting with a companion road, the Central Pacific, from California and the West.

General Stevens, in his surveys for a northern route in 1853, *et seq.,* covered a wide range of country, including both the Missouri and the Yellowstone valleys, and portions of his surveys were eventually adopted by both the Northern Pacific and the Great Northern railways.

On July 15th, the canoes were completed and the explorers continued their journey.

Along this part of their course they were still inclined to name the affluent streams of the Missouri, to a great extent, after the members of their own party, and also for the members of Jefferson's Cabinet. We have examples of this in Smith's River, after the Secretary of the Navy; Dearborn's River, after the Secretary of War; the Gallatin and Madison rivers, after Secretaries Gallatin and Madison, and various creeks after Ordway, Potts, Pryor, Gass, Howard, etc.

Smith's, or Deep, River, passed on the 15th of June, rises between the Big Belt and Little Belt ranges of mountains east of Helena and in the vicinity of White Sulphur Springs and opposite to the sources of Shields and Musselshell rivers, and flows northwestward to the Missouri, joining it a few miles above Canoe Camp.

Dearborn River, on the contrary, has its sources in the main Rockies about Cadotte's and Lewis and Clark's passes and, flowing southeast, debouches into the Missouri in the heart of the fine cañon through which the latter stream here flows and along whose left bank and thence through Little Prickly Pear – Ordway's – River cañon, the tracks of the Great Northern Railway – Montana Central – are laid. This cañon is very winding, abounds in bold cliffs and vertical walls, and among its crags Lewis and Clark saw "many of the big-horned animals," or Rocky Mountain sheep.

The party were now approaching the country where they might expect at any time to encounter the Shoshone Indians, Sacágawea's people. It was important that all precautions possible be taken to avoid accidents or blunders at the first meeting with the Indians, for the success of the expedition now really rested upon their reception by the

Shoshoni and upon the result of their negotiations with them. To this end, Captain Clark, with J. Fields, Potts, and the sable York, left the canoes and proceeded by land along the left – north – bank to search for Indian trails, or roads as the explorers called them, or any other signs of Indians. The mountains were steep and their progress was slow, but toward evening of the second day that they thus progressed, the Captain found "a wide Indian road" which he followed across the mountains for thirty miles and camped on the river, when "Captain Clark's first employment on lighting a fire was to extract from his feet the briars [spines from the prickly pear] which he found seventeen in number." One who has, in the olden days, traversed the Western plains where the prickly pear abounds will fully appreciate Clark's condition.

In this trip Captain Clark followed up Ordway's – now Little Prickly Pear – Creek and then down Prickly Pear Creek to the river; being worn and bruised by the flinty character of the ground and by the prickly pear, they determined to await there the arrival of the main party. Clark and his little band had left the others on July 18th, and rejoined them on the 22d.

In the meantime, Captain Lewis and the boat party "proceeded on very well" through Ox Bow Bend, at the base of the Bear's-tooth Mountain, a noted landmark of the region, until after dark, when they camped in the heart of the "Gates of the Rocky Mountains."

This cañon deserves particular mention. It is one of the finest in the West and were it more accessible to the ordinary traveller and tourist it would long since have been one of the best known and most admired gorges in the country. The head of it is about eighteen miles north from Helena, and Hilger's ranch is located there.

The Heart of the Gates of the Rocky Mountains. (From a painting by De Camp.)

This ranch and the cañon have, in years past, been a pleasure-ground for Helena people, and a little steamer has enabled tourists to make the trip down through the cañon and return.

Lewis and Clark, or, more specifically Captain Lewis, for Clark never saw the Gates of the Mountains, was wonderfully impressed by this stupendous chasm and endeavored to describe it suitably:

A mile and a half beyond this creek, the rocks approach the river on both sides, forming a most sublime and extraordinary spectacle. For five and three-quarters miles these rocks rise perpendicularly from the water's edge, to the height of nearly twelve hundred feet. They are composed of a black granite near the base, but from their lighter color above, and from the fragments, we suppose the upper part to be flint, of a yellowish-brown and cream color. Nothing can be imagined more tremendous than the frowning darkness of these rocks, which project over the river and menace us with destruction. The river, of one hundred and fifty yards in width, seems to have forced its channel down this solid mass; but so reluctantly has the rock given way that, during the whole distance, the water is very deep even at the edges, and for the first three miles there is not a spot, except one of a few yards, in which a man could stand between the water and the towering perpendicular of the mountain. The convulsion of the passage must have been terrible, since at its outlet are vast columns of rock, torn from the mountain, which are strewn on both sides of the river – the trophies, as it were, of a victory. . . . We were obliged to go on some time after dark, not being able to find a spot large enough to camp on; but at length, about two miles above a small island in the middle of the river, we met with a spot on the left side, where we procured plenty of light wood and pitch-pine. This extraordinary range of rocks we called the Gates of the Rocky Mountains. . . .

July 20th. By employing the tow-rope whenever the banks permitted the use of it, the river being too deep for the pole, we were enabled to overcome the current, which is still strong. At the distance of half a mile we came to a high rock in the bend to the left in the Gates. Here the perpendicular rocks cease, the hills retire from the river, and the valleys suddenly widen to a greater extent than they have done since we entered the mountains.

Hilger's Ranch, Montana, at Head of the Gates of the Rocky Mountains. Source of Pott's Creek is just beyond the House, among the Trees.

349

Roberts and his party passed through the cañon in the opposite direction, and his description[1] does greater justice to the subject than Lewis's account:

For two miles ahead a wonderful vista now began to open out, and still there was visible no outlet to the turreted and pin-nacled walls which penned us in. . . .

For some moments the party was spell-bound, but very soon the adjectives began to flow rapidly, both in French and English. Yet how trite they sounded in the presence of this magnificent display of nature's wonderful handiwork. High up on either hand were colossal statues, carved by the master, Time, in the niches of this gigantic winding hall, five miles long. The walls rose majestically six hundred, eight hundred, and one thousand feet high, and in places appeared to rest against the white clouds above, which completed the arch over our heads. The sides afforded no foothold for man or beast, excepting occasionally, up through lateral fissures, in whose dark recesses lay tumbled in rare confusion huge broken pillars and angular rocks, jammed and forming natural bridges from chasm to chasm.

Down the river, midway in the cañon, at the principal turn to the left, the wall actually hung over the river, so that a plum-met-line six hundred feet long, dropped from the brow, would have struck our boat as we passed beneath it. Pine trees fringed the summit, and struggled for an existence in some of the crev-ices, some of their tops pointing downward, and many were broken off where the superincumbent growth was too weighty for the slight hold of their roots.

We long for the pencil of a Bierstadt or a Moran. Such gro-tesque forms, such heights, such depths, such lights and shades as here presented themselves, were far beyond the power of pen to illustrate. Words may exaggerate points, but no descriptive language can do justice to this scene. . . .

I have made two trips exploring the recesses and enjoying the glories of the Gates of the Mountains, as the cañon is now called, the word Rocky being usually discarded, and I can vouch for almost any description that can be written of this cañon − it would be hard to say too much. The warm, bright, vari-tinted colors of the red sandstone cañons

---

[1]   Hist. Soc. Mont. *Contributions,* vol. i.

Cañon of the Gates of the Rocky Mountains.

351

of the Colorado River system and those of the brilliant Cañon of the Yellowstone are entirely lacking here, but the effect is most impressive and indeed oppressive at times. There are wonderful and most varied carvings in the soft gray walls of almost immeasurable dimensions, and the grayish tone lends itself most harmoniously to this Gate of the Mountains sculpture.

I could wish no one a more pleasurable experience than to float with the current through the silent gorge, past its battlements, gigantic domes, caves, holes in the wall, overhanging precipices, cathedral towers, huge amphitheatres, and echoing walls. It would not be exaggeration to call this a lesser Yosemite, for in the season of melting snow and rain, waterfalls plunge down from the cliffs and add their beauty to the scene.

From the Gates of the Mountains to the Three Forks of the Missouri, the experiences we have already noted were simply repeated. Clark and his men followed the "Indian road," and the whole band of adventurers were cheered and encouraged by Sacágawea's pointing out familiar spots known in childhood. Smoke signals in the mountains, abandoned brush wickiup villages, an occasional though old moccasin track on the trail, and a lost and wild Indian horse informed them that the Indians knew of their presence and, supposing them to be the dreaded Blackfeet, were watching them from their mountain coverts and keeping themselves hidden.

In navigating the Missouri in its course southward through Montana, the pole and tow line were almost continuously in use. The men were exhausted when evening and camping-time came, and then for hours rest was impossible – until the nights grew cool – because of the gnats and mosquitoes. One who has not experienced the almost indescribable annoyances inflicted by these Western insects can scarce credit the unvarnished tales told by mosquito-bitten travellers in the West, even though one hails from the swamps of New Jersey.

As Captain Clark and his party reconnoitred ahead of Lewis and the others, they killed elk and deer and placed the carcasses on the banks of the stream where the boatmen could find them. Geese in great numbers, and many antelopes, cranes, ducks, and curlews were seen, and an occasional snake added variety to their observations in natural history. Otter and beaver abounded, the latter industriously damming the river and flooding the low lands. Botanically, they found wild onions, garlic, wild flax, the prickly pear, thistles, gooseberries, service-berries, wild currants of several species, – red, purple, yellow, and black, – the sumach and red willow and choke cherry, box alder and the narrow-leaved cottonwood trees, and the beautiful aspen. Along the bottoms the wild sunflower was in bloom. This was the bread-fruit tree to the Indians. The seed was parched, then pounded between stones and ground into meal which, when mixed with buffalo marrow-grease, made a very palatable dish. Or it was used as a gruel and to thicken their soups.

Lewis and Clark have been noted for the truthfulness of their descriptions and for the reasonable accuracy of their distances. In regard to the latter, the explorers seem to have had the tendency, well-nigh universal, to over-estimate in the long run. Instances of their remarkable accuracy in concrete cases are frequent, yet in their progress, day by day and week by week, the natural tendency to exaggerate the distances travelled manifested itself.

Dr. Coues, in studying the Captains' route along this particular part of the Missouri, noted apparent discrepancies which he attempted to harmonize. In *Wonderland 1900,* the writer pointed out that this had not been done. Dr.

Coues's mistake was a natural one, that any one unfamiliar with the situation by personal inspection would have fallen into.

Lewis and Clark say: "At a mile from the Gates [of the Mountains] a large creek . . . empties behind an island. . . ." They named this Potts, after one of their men and Hilger's ranch is now located at this point, as already mentioned. Dr. Coues identified this creek with (Big) Prickly Pear Creek farther along, but the island is there, and the creek is there, just as Lewis and Clark stated, even if the maps do ignore it, and it is *not* (Big) Prickly Pear Creek either. A visit to Hilger's ranch explains the mystery. Just below Hilger's house a magnificent spring bursts from the ground and pours forth an enormous quantity of water, making a large stream which flows into the Missouri. As it doesn't run for more than a quarter of a mile, perhaps, at the outside, and does not extend up the valley, the cartographers naturally do not plat it, but there it is, and the explorers were simply misled as to its extent by its appearance at the river. The question then arises, What was Prickly Pear Creek?

On July 18th, when Captain Clark and his land party left the others they followed up Ordway's, now Little Prickly Pear, Creek, and, crossing the divide, found themselves on the 19th in "a handsome valley, watered by a large creek." There is but one such stream in that locality, – Prickly Pear Creek, the headwaters of a branch of which are directly opposite those of Little Prickly Pear Creek, in the vicinity of Marysville, Mont., just north of Helena.

The main party on July 21st reached "a large and bold creek, twenty-eight yards wide, coming in from the north, where it waters *a handsome valley.* We called it Pryor's creek. . . ." Note the similarity to Clark's description!

A careful study of Clark's map of 1814, and of other

Head of the Gates of the Rocky Mountains, at Mouth of Potts's Creek, near Hilger's Ranch, Montana

maps, and of the journals of Gass and of Lewis and Clark, together with some knowledge of the "lay of the land," convince me that Prickly Pear Creek is none other than the *Pryor's* Creek of Lewis and Clark. The regular narrative, and apparently the original codices as well, have been bungled at this point in some manner, and an entanglement of descriptions, creeks, and names has resulted which is not easily unravelled. What has helped to cause this confusion is the fact that Prickly Pear Creek, in its relation to the river and to the cañon just below its mouth, is precisely a duplicate of Potts's Creek at Hilger's and the Gates of the Mountains.

The smoke that was seen up the valley by Lewis's party, and which the regular journal locates in the valley of Potts's Creek, was in fact up Prickly Pear Creek Valley, for Gass says plainly that this "smoke" valley, as Lewis and Clark first called it, was not reached until two o'clock P.M. of the day they left the Gates of the Mountains, and Lewis's original note-book seems to confirm this.

The name Smoke Creek, first given to Prickly Pear Creek — and correctly if the name was to be used — was changed to "Potts Valley creek," and then, whether by Lewis, Clark, or Biddle, through confusion or by intention we know not, it was finally plainly placed against the apparently large creek near the Gates of the Mountains and Pryor's name was given to the present Prickly Pear Creek. In connection with this matter I have prepared a table of distances from Lewis and Clark, from the Whitebear Islands camp to the Three Forks of the Missouri, for comparison with the later and very accurate measurements of the map of the Missouri River Commission.

The table throws no particular light on the problem under consideration, but it affords a valuable and instructive test of Lewis and Clark's work, not only in this immediate locality, but as a whole.

The terminal points used are well known and definitely established. The maps of the Missouri River Commission, splendid examples of their kind, show the topography immediately along the river, and, what is of special value, *every five miles of distance* as measured along the channel is marked.

For well-established reasons the river here has changed its bed but very little, if at all, since Lewis and Clark explored it, so that their distances are properly comparable with those of the map named.

TABLE OF COMPARATIVE DISTANCES BETWEEN LEWIS AND CLARK AND MISSOURI RIVER COMMISSION, WHITEBEAR ISLANDS TO THREE FORKS OF THE MISSOURI, MISSOURI RIVER.

NAMES OF POINTS OR STATIONS ACCORDING TO PRESENT-DAY NOMENCLATURE	LEWIS AND CLARK'S NAME OF UP-STREAM TERMINAL STATION	LEWIS AND CLARK'S DISTANCES MILES		MISSOURI RIVER COM DISTANCES MILES		LEWIS AND CLARK'S OVERMEASUREMENT	PER CENT OF OVERMEASUREMENT BETWEEN STATIONS
		Between Pts.	Totals	Between Pts.	Totals		
Whitebear Islands to Dearborn River...	Same..........	80	80	72	72	8	11 %
Dearborn River to Little Prickly Pear Creek..	Ordway's Creek	14¼	94¼	11	83	3¼	27 %
Little Prickly Pear Creek to Hilger's...	Potts's Creek...	27¾	122	26	109	1¾	8 %
Hilger's to Prickly Pear Creek........	Pryor's Creek. .	20½	142½	8	117	12½	150 %
Prickly Pear Creek to Sixteen Mile Creek.	Howard's Creek	89¾	232¼	75	192	14¾	20 %
Sixteen Mile Creek to Junc. Mad. and Jeff. rivers......	Same..........	20¼	252½	18	210	2¼	10 %

In taking the distances from the Commission's map, I have used, save in two instances, the five-mile points nearest the places under consideration, and have assumed Pryor's Creek to be Prickly Pear Creek.

It will be seen from the table that between Whitebear Islands and the Three Forks – the junction of the Madison and Jefferson rivers, to be precise – Lewis and Clark overrun the actual distance of 210 miles, more than 40 miles, or 20%. It will be seen, too, that with the exception of the locality between Hilger's, or Potts's Creek, and Prickly Pear, or Pryor's Creek, these distances overrun in a fairly uniform ratio.

According to Clark's map, the Commission's map, the streams of the region, and Gass's narrative, no other stream than Prickly Pear Creek will answer for Pryor's Creek, and even the United States General Land Office map, of extremely doubtful value in cases of this sort, evidences this.

Notwithstanding these occasional errors and the excessive distances, the general description is so plain and faithful that the narrative as a whole invariably enables us easily to identify localities.

For example, the camp of July 17th was "in a bend on the north . . . opposite to a very high cliff" – evidently the "Big Rock" of the Missouri River Commission map; the camp of July 19th in the Gates of the Mountains is perfectly plain as to its site, but wild as to distance: the region at the mouth of Potts's Creek is accurately described, the point where "a small run" is reached on the 24th is "Indian Creek" of to-day, just below Townsend, Mont., and exactly where the main – Helena – line of the Northern Pacific Railway, which follows the right bank of the Missouri from the Three Forks to Townsend, crosses the Missouri River; the "number of fine bold springs which burst out near the edge of the river under the cliffs," of July 25th, form the Mammoth Spring of to-day; Howard's Creek of the 26th is now Sixteen Mile Creek and a railway junction

Cathedral Bluff, in the Canon of the Gates of the Rocky Mountains.

point – Lombard; the camp of the 26th, "on the left shore near a rock . . . of a bend . . . opposite two . . . islands," was at the base of "Eagle Rock." Other points are equally identifiable.

We are told that in 1849, after Marshall's discovery of gold in California, four hundred ships lay idly at anchor in San Francisco Bay – the sailors had deserted and run away to the gold placer diggings.

Had the men with Lewis and Clark, in 1805, as they waded the cold waters in the shallows of the Missouri between the Gates of the Mountains and the Three Forks, known that every twist of the foot stirred golden flecked sands, and each motion of the pushing pole loosened tiny nuggets of yellow gold worth their weight in coin of the realm just as they lay on the gravel bars, what might have been the result? Would discipline, loyalty to a cause, pride of achievement, have restrained them to a later time, or would desertion and the collapse of the exploration have resulted? American Bar, Eldorado Bar, French Bar, their names unknown in 1805, but over which Lewis and Clark poled and pushed their boats, are a few of the reminders of the early sixties along the Missouri, when the craze for wealth swept sober men off their feet and made Montana a commonwealth of tented and cabined camps washing the bars and the river and creek banks for gold – gold – gold!

A notable fact in the story of the exploration of Lewis and Clark is, that in their route through what afterwards became Montana, from the Gates of the Mountains to Shoshone Cove, they passed through the very heart of the mineral belt of the region, its treasures all unknown to them.

But in the time of our explorers it was beaver pelts, not gold dust, that men were searching for, and, following their trail, came the trapper, setting his traps in the same Missouri

and its numberless tributaries which meandered down from
the mountains on either side, and across whose snowy summits these pathfinders of 1805 daily saw the sun rise and
set. The beaver meant gold too, until the streams were
depopulated and made barren. Then half a century later,
following the trappers as they had followed Lewis and Clark,
came another army of adventurers, in regiments and bri-
gades, and they shovelled and dredged the same Missouri
and its affluents, taking not beaver and otter, but the yellow
metal itself.

Gold was discovered in Montana in 1852 and the principal
mining camps of the early days were, in the order of discovery and succession, Grasshopper Gulch, – Bannack, –
1862; Alder Gulch, – Virginia City, – 1863; Last Chance
Gulch, – Helena, – 1864; Confederate Gulch, – Diamond City,
– 1865. Smaller placers were being worked on large numbers
of streams, many of them very rich, but the four here named
were those which achieved national renown from the vast
wealth they produced and from various incidents connected
with their rise and fall. In 1876 there were five hundred
gold-bearing gulches in Montana.

Silver and copper first attracted attention in 1864, but
it was some years before copper assumed much importance;
now this is the principal mineral product of the State.

Montana has an area of one hundred and forty-six
thousand square miles. The word itself is an interesting
one. It is of Spanish origin, coming from the Latin word
mons, mountain. An aboriginal word, To-ya-be-Shock-up,
means the same thing – the Country of the Mountains.

The California gold wave reached its zenith in 1853.
What more natural than that the army of miners, with the
decadence of the California fields, should search out virgin
ground? Eastward and northward the conquering legions
swept. Slow but sure was their progress. The gulches

were ravaged and the mountains rent. The exodus from California became the genesis of Nevada, Idaho, and Montana.

When Captain Clark crossed the divide between Ordway's and Pryor's creeks he had at his right hand the spurs of the Rockies about Marysville, where one mine was afterwards to be located from which more than $20,000,000 of gold was to be taken. As he proceeded across the prickly pear plains toward the Missouri, he came in sight of the future Last Chance Gulch whereon Helena, the capital of the State, is located, and from whose auriferous gravels the world was to be enriched to the amount of $40,000,000 more.

From the gravel bars along the Missouri and its tributaries gold dust and nuggets running into millions of dollars have been taken, and the total production from placer mining throughout Montana, including hydraulic mining, from 1862 to 1900 was, probably, not far from $150,000,000, the total gold production from the State being reckoned at about $250,000,000.

On July 23d the narrative mentions a creek "20 yards wide" which they called Whitehouse's Creek after one of their men. This stream was either Confederate or Duck Creek. The two flow into the Missouri near together – the G. L. O. map combines them into one creek. If Confederate Creek – this was the stream where Confederate Gulch was subsequently located some miles above the mouth, in the heart of the Belt Mountains.

This gulch is said to have been discovered by Confederate soldiers of Price's army who, in 1861-62, after the battles of Lexington, Pea Ridge, etc., in Missouri, made their way to Montana via the Missouri River and Fort Benton. On their way to Last Chance Gulch they found "color" near the mouth of this creek. Following up the stream, they found the pay dirt growing richer, and they established themselves in the gulch, naming it Confederate, and within a short time Diamond City, the town of the gulch, was the centre of a population of 5000 souls.

Confederate Gulch was in many respects the most phenomenal of all the Montana gulches. The ground was so rich that as high as $180 in gold was taken from one pan of dirt; and from a plat of ground four feet by ten feet, between drift timbers, $1000 worth of gold was extracted in twenty-four hours. At the junction of Montana Gulch a side gulch – with Confederate, the ground was very rich, the output at that point being estimated at $2,000,000.

Montana Bar, which lies some distance up the gulch and at considerable of an elevation above it, was found in the latter part of 1865 to be marvellously rich. There were about two acres in reality, that were here sluiced over, but the place is spoken of as "the richest acre of gold-bearing ground ever discovered in the world." I quote A. M. Williams, who has made a special study of these old gulches:

> The flumes on this bar, on cleaning up, were found to be burdened with gold by the hundredweight, and the enormous yield of $180 to the pan in Confederate and Montana gulches was forgotten in astonishment and a wild delirium of joy at the wonderful yield of over a thousand dollars to the pan of gravel taken from the bed rock of Montana bar.

From this bar seven panfuls of clean gold were taken out at one "clean-up," that weighed 700 pounds and were worth $114,800. A million and a half dollars in gold was hauled by wagon from Diamond City to Fort Benton at one time for shipment to the East. This gulch is reputed to have produced $10,000,000, from 1864 to 1868, and it is still being sluiced.

Some very large gold nuggets were found in this region. Many were worth from $100 to $600 or $700. Several were worth from $1500 to $1800; one, of pure gold, was worth $2100, and two or three exceeded $3000 in value.

On the night of July 21st, the boat party camped near the entrance – in the direction they were going – of a long and wide valley, a "beautiful plain, ten or twelve miles wide," as Lewis phrases it. The closed-in stretch of river, the cañon feature, was left behind for a time. Just before entering this valley they passed a spot now known as Canyon Ferry. At this point the river is narrow and hemmed in by walls of black rock, and here, in recent years, a superb dam and power-house have been constructed by the Missouri River Power Company, and electric power is now transmitted on wires across the mountains and valleys, to Helena and Butte, where it is used for operating machinery and for electric lighting. A fact of interest in this connection is, that one of the prominent officials of this company, and also a pioneer of Montana, ex-Governor Hauser, is related by marriage to Captain Clark.

This dam is thirty feet high, and the ten dynamos furnish an aggregate of 12,000 horse-power. Another dam is soon to be constructed some miles below this one.

En route to Three Forks, Captain Clark, at some point, added Chaboneau to his little land party, and on July 25, 1805, they arrived at the junction of the three streams, which, mingling their waters within a short distance of each other, form the Missouri. But they were in sorry physical plight. In his anxiety to reach this locality, hoping to find some Shoshone Indians, Clark had been overdoing the matter, with the result that the party was used up.

When they reached the Three Forks, Clark judged that the north – right – hand – fork (the Jefferson) carried more water than the others, and he determined to push on up that branch without waiting for Lewis and the boatmen. He therefore left a note for Captain Lewis – probably at-

365   *Junction of Madison and Jefferson Rivers, Montana. The Madison at the Left, the Jefferson at the Right Centre.*

tached to a pole and fastened in the river bank so that
Lewis could not fail to see it – apprising him of his intention, and then away they went up the wide and beautiful
valley. After a twenty-five-mile tramp, Chaboneau "was
unable to proceed any further, and the party therefore
camped [for the night], all of them much fatigued, their feet
blistered and wounded by the prickly-pear."

Clark was indomitable and, although not well himself,
leaving Fields with the used-up Frenchman, he and another
(Potts?) tramped on up the river twelve miles farther, where
from "the top of a mountain he had an extensive view of
the river valley upwards and saw a large creek . . . on
the right side." Coues makes this "large creek" to be
Philosophy River, but it was evidently Fields's Creek, now
Boulder River. On this tramp he found no "Indian sign."

He now followed an Indian trail down the mountain to
"a fine cold spring."

The day had been very warm; the path was unshaded by
timber, and his thirst was excessive; he was therefore tempted
to drink. But although he took the precaution of previously
wetting his head, feet and hands, he soon found himself very
unwell.

He then retraced his route to where he had left Chaboneau, rested there a while, and the entire party then
tramped over toward the middle fork – the Madison River –
to examine the country for Indian trails. In wading the
Jefferson the water was waist-deep and very rapid, and Chaboneau, who was no swimmer, was swept from his feet and
would have drowned had not Clark been able to assist him.

Pursuing their course to what they afterwards called
Philosophy River, now Willow Creek, all of them worn out
and Clark quite sick from drinking the water of that cold
spring, they camped for the night. Clark was very sick all
night, had "a high fever and chills, accompanied with great

pain," but the following day, July 27th, he persisted in going on until the "Middle branch," the Madison River, was reached, when, finding no trace of Indians, he turned again toward the Three Forks and arrived there at three o'clock in the afternoon, to find that the boat party had arrived not a great while before and were established in camp in "a level, handsome plain" on the Jefferson, a mile above the junction with the Madison.

Clark, "believing himself billious, took a dose of Rush's pills, which we have always found sovereign in such cases," and on the following morning he was somewhat improved, but far from being well.

The band of adventurers had now reached what they themselves well called "an essential point in the geography of the western world." As in the ancient days all roads led to Rome, so here all trails led to Three Forks. From the north, the country of the Blackfeet; the east, the land of the Crows; the south, where the Shoshoni roamed; the west, whence came the Nez Percés and the Flatheads, through the passes of the detached ranges of the mother chain, the Rockies, the trails converged upon this wide, level, beautiful, bountifully watered and verdured valley whence sprang the Missouri. Here was what might well be called the dark, bloody, and debatable ground of the tribes; it "was the immemorial fighting ground of the hostile tribes," and it is almost unaccountable that Lewis and Clark, in their passage through the region in both directions, never once saw an Indian, friendly or hostile.

That the Captains fully appreciated the importance of this beautiful, mountain walled, tri-rivered park region is amply shown in their narrative. They made their "celestial observations" and carefully studied the character of the rivers and the comparative volume of water carried by each. They were in something of a quandary as to how far to carry the name Missouri, and did not come to a conclusion until they were far above the Three Forks, and approaching the Beavers-head. Finally they concluded that as these confluent streams were so much alike, they would apply new names to them, and the narrative reads as if this were done while they were encamped at the Forks, but Gass distinctly states that the time when this conclusion was reached was August 9th, when the party had passed the Bighole and Stinkingwater, or Ruby, rivers.

Their description of the country about the Forks answers equally for it to-day with some exceptions which will be noted. Lewis made the examination about the junction while Clark was away on his long exploring tramp.

When, on July 27th, the boatmen emerged from the cañon of the Missouri and reached the mouth of the Gallatin and found the country suddenly open out "into extensive and beautiful meadows and plains," Lewis went up the new-found river for a "half a mile" and climbed a limestone cliff where, like Selkirk, he was monarch of all he surveyed. From this point he could then, as one can now,

observe its course about seven miles, and see the Three Forks of the Missouri, of which this river [*i. e.,* the Gallatin] is one. . . . During the seven miles it passes through a green extensive meadow of fine grass, dividing itself into several streams, the largest passing near the ridge of hills on which he stood . . . The middle [Madison] and southwest [Jefferson] forks unite at half a mile above the entrance of the southeast [Gallatin] fork. . . . Its low grounds [those of the Madison] are several miles in width, forming a smooth and beautiful green meadow; and, like the southeast fork, it divides into several streams.

Between these two forks [the Gallatin and Madison], and near their junction with that from the southwest, is a position admirably well calculated for a fort. It is a limestone rock of an oblong form, rising from the plain perpendicularly to the height of 25 feet on three of its sides; the fourth, toward the middle fork, being a gradual ascent covered with a fine greensward, as is also the top, which is level and contains about two acres.

Gallatin River and Valley from Captain Lewis's Point of View of July 27, 1805

"After observing the country, Captain Lewis descended to breakfast." They established their camp a mile above the junction of the Jefferson and Madison on the very spot where, five years before, Sacágawea had been captured. In connection with three of the party, Colter, Drewyer, and Potts, the region was, in the future, to prove of peculiar interest.

Lewis must have been greatly impressed, as others have since been, with the beautiful picture presented. The wide-spreading valleys of the three large serpentine streams, expanding fan-like as they stretch away to the horizon and presenting a green, grassy, timbered expanse, with snow-tipped mountains far in the distance, will challenge any one's admiration. The general effect from Lewis's point of view is precisely the same now, but, in the bottom and almost beneath the cliff on which he stood, there are now the remains of a town, Gallatin City, which has come into existence and passed away in recent years. At the base of the cliff upon which the Captain stood there now winds that line of the Northern Pacific Railway which, sweeping down the Missouri whence the explorers had just come, crosses the divide between this stream and Prickly Pear, or Pryor's Creek, to Helena, and then winds on across the Rockies by way of the Mullan pass.

A few miles up the green valley of the Three Forks Lewis could to-day discern another line of the same railway, which follows the very route of the expedition, past Fields's Creek to Panther, now Pipestone Creek, up which it winds across the Pipestone pass of the Rockies to Butte and beyond. A few ranch houses with their wire-fenced fields are now visible, but the essential changes effected in one hundred years are so immaterial as to have caused comment, and some have even asserted that the curse of the Blackfeet lingers upon the spot; if so, it affects not the beauty of the scene.

"Fort Rock" at Three Forks of the Missouri, Montana. Looking South, the Gallatin River at the Left. (From an oil painting by De Camp.)

371

Beyond the point of bluff that limited Captain Lewis's view to the east, the Gallatin River forks and one branch swings northward and eastward in a long sweeping curve, and between it and the high mountains to the south lies the Gallatin Valley, one of the loveliest and richest to be found among the recesses of the entire Rocky Mountain chain. The distance from the mouth of the Gallatin to the confluence of the Jefferson and Madison is given as half a mile; as a matter of fact it is more than a mile.

The Fort Rock mentioned lies between the mouth of the Gallatin and the main stream about three eighths of a mile from the junction. The Gallatin washes the lower end of it and the Missouri almost reaches it on the western side. The eminence is nearly half a mile in length, perhaps a thousand feet wide, and its general appearance is about as Lewis and Clark describe it. It is more than twenty-five feet high at its highest point, and for the purpose mentioned would have been an admirable site in those early days when the Indians used only bows and arrows. But as firearms became improved and the tribes obtained them, it would have become somewhat pregnable, being to some extent dominated by the higher cliffs across the rivers. In a foot-note relating to this rock, Dr. Coues suggests that here is where Manuel Lisa built his well-known fort in 1808. Lisa built no fort here, but did build one in 1807 at the mouth of the Big Horn River, and the Missouri Fur Co. built a fort at the Three Forks in 1810. Lisa was a partner in this Company. The latter fortification, however, was in the open valley a few miles south from this spot — though perhaps in sight from it. The Fort Rock is a somewhat prominent hill, from which a fine view is obtained over the three valleys. I first stood upon this "limestone rock" in 1898, and again in 1902 I was there with Mr. De Camp when he made sketches for his painting. The rock will be

pointed out to travellers, from the railway trains, for
another hundred years, and it is to be hoped that it will
yet be graced by a suitable statue of Sacágawea, the Bird-
woman.

The Missouri Fur Co. post was built early in the year
1810 in the vain endeavor to gain the confidence of the
Blackfeet and Crow Indians, and to establish a thriving
business in furs, for this particular region had the reputation of being the finest fur ground in the West. Lewis and
Clark reported these streams as being dammed in all
directions by the beavers, so that they had difficulty in
working their canoes up the Jefferson.

Manuel Lisa and the early fur men recognized, as had
Lewis and Clark, the strategic importance of the spot, and
they made a determined effort to hold it, but the Blackfeet
would have none of it. Hovering in ambush among the
hills and in the thickets and timber, they attacked the
trappers upon every occasion, and so vindictive and
persistent were these implacable foes that the post was
abandoned in the fall of the same year in which it was
built.

The story of the death of Drewyer, or Drouillard, the
crack hunter of Lewis and Clark, which event occurred later
almost upon the very spot where the expedition is now
encamped, is given in the life of that individual in another
part of this narrative. Drouillard was one of the builders
of the fort at Three Forks, and doubtless his remains found
their last resting-place somewhere in that green and beautiful vale that lies between the two streams named, where
they await the last trump of the Archangel.

This post was located near the present town of Three
Forks. Lieut. J. A. Bradley, 7th U. S. Inf., killed at the
battle of the Big Hole, fought between General Gibbon and
Chief Joseph, during the Nez Percé war of 1877, saw the

outlines of the fort in 1870. Bradley's journal[1] states that from these outlines the fort was

a double stockade of logs set three feet deep, enclosing an area of about 300 feet square, situated upon the tongue of land (at that point half a mile wide) between the Jefferson and Madison Rivers, about two miles above their confluence, upon the south bank of a channel of the former stream now called Jefferson slough. Since then the stream has made such inroads upon the land that only a small portion of the fort-the southwest angle – remains. It is probable that every vestige of this old relic will soon disappear, except the few stumps of stockade logs that have been removed by two or three gentlemen of antiquarian tastes. When Henry abandoned the fort, a blacksmith's anvil was left behind, which remained there for thirty or forty years undisturbed, gazed upon only by the Indians who regarded it with superstition and awe. At last it disappeared and it is said to have been found and removed by a party of white men.

Peter Koch of Bozeman also saw the remains of the fort in the early seventies, and he informed me some years ago that the fort had entirely disappeared.

Lewis and Clark estimated these rivers as being "each 90 yards wide, and so perfectly similar in character and appearance that they seem to have been formed in the same mold."

The Gallatin was the most rapid, the Jefferson the least so, and both the Jefferson and Madison were deeper than the Gallatin. The beds of all the streams were "formed of smooth pebble and gravel, and the waters are perfectly transparent." This is just as true to-day, and the heavy timber of 1805 is a conspicuous feature at the present time.

Roberts, in 1872, measured these streams and found the relative discharges to be:

Jefferson	226,728 cu. ft. per minute
Madison.	160,277 cu. ft. per minute
Gallatin	125,480 cu. ft. per minute

[1] Hist. Soc. Mont. *Contributions,* vol. ii.

Highest Knob of "Fort Rock" at Three Forks of the Missouri from the South

or a total for the three of 512,485 cubic feet per minute. He also adds:

Reducing their quantity to the lowest stage known, there will remain over three hundred thousand cubic feet per minute in the Missouri at this point, which is three times the volume of the Ohio at Pittsburg when at its lowest stage.

As I stood at the junction of the Madison and Jefferson rivers in the summer of 1902, I was convinced that the Madison was discharging much the larger quantity of water of the two. Inquiry and subsequent observation on the upper Jefferson, with some knowledge of the upper reaches of the Madison, confirmed this. One word, a word of but slight significance to us until recent years, but now of tremendous importance to the Northwest, and a word that never entered any one's mind in the days of Lewis and Clark, tells the whole story – Irrigation. This word, or rather the process it represents, has transformed valley after valley traversed by Lewis and Clark from a range for bison, antelope, elk, deer, wolves, and beavers, into orchards, fields of wheat, barley, oats, sugar beets, potatoes, alfalfa, and vineyards.

The greater part of the waters of the Gallatin River are, in the season of growing crops, turned upon the fields of the Gallatin Valley for irrigation, and the same is true, to a great extent, of the waters of the Madison. The irrigated fields of the Jefferson, range, to the knowledge of the writer, from the Three Forks to the Rattlesnake Cliffs of our explorers, a distance of one hundred miles or more, and at numerous points the valley is many miles in width. The quantity of water withdrawn from this stream for irrigation is enormous, much greater than from the Madison, and this explains the reversal of conditions as to the volume of the streams at their confluence.

Before leaving this locality it will be instructive to compare the distances from the mouth of the Missouri to the Three Forks as given by Lewis and Clark with those of the Missouri River Commission:

TABLE OF DISTANCES FROM MOUTH OF MISSOURI RIVER TO THREE FORKS

FROM MOUTH OF MISSOURI RIVER	LEWIS AND CLARK	MO. RIV. COM. MAP	LEWIS AND CLARK OVER	DIS- TANCE BE- TWEEN POINTS	LEWIS AND CLARK OVER BETWEEN POINTS
To	Miles	Miles	Miles	Miles	Miles
Big Sioux River..............	853	811	42	811	42
Fort Mandan................	1600	1507	93	696	51
Yellowstone River...........	1880	1761	119	254	26
Marias River................	2521	2264	257	503	138
Sun River..................	2593	2335	258	71	1
Three Forks................	2849	2549[1]	300	214	42

[1] Brower makes this distance 2547 miles.

END OF VOLUME I.

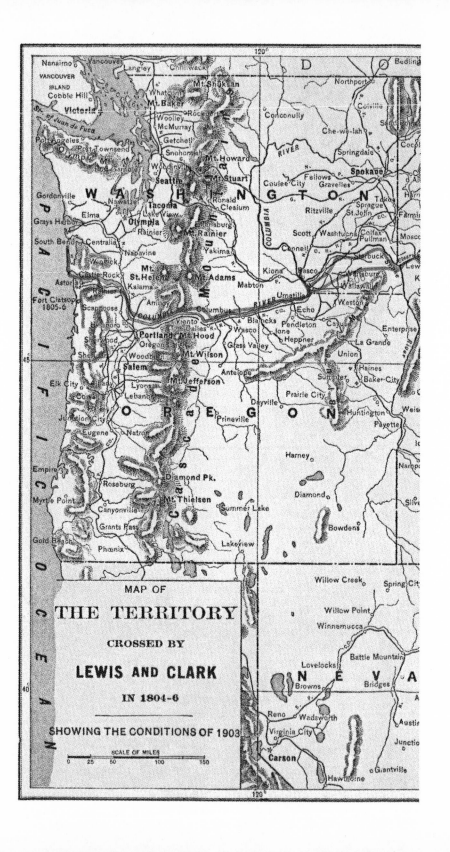

MAP OF

THE TERRITORY

CROSSED BY

LEWIS AND CLARK

IN 1804-6

SHOWING THE CONDITIONS OF 1903

SCALE OF MILES

0   25   50   100   150

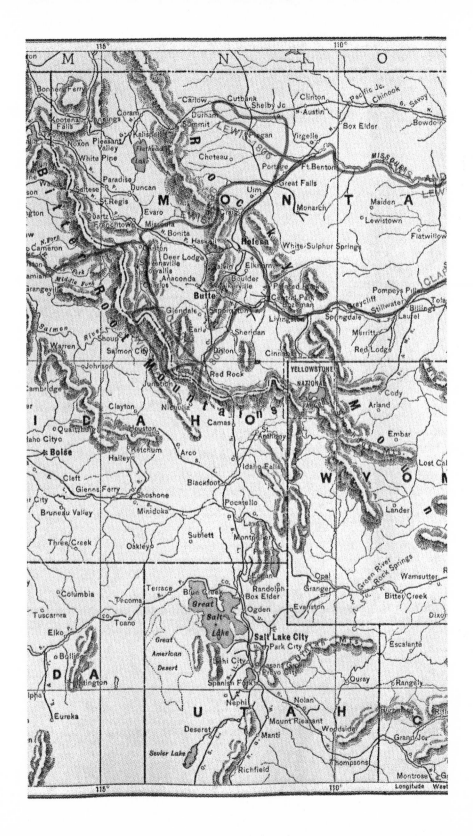

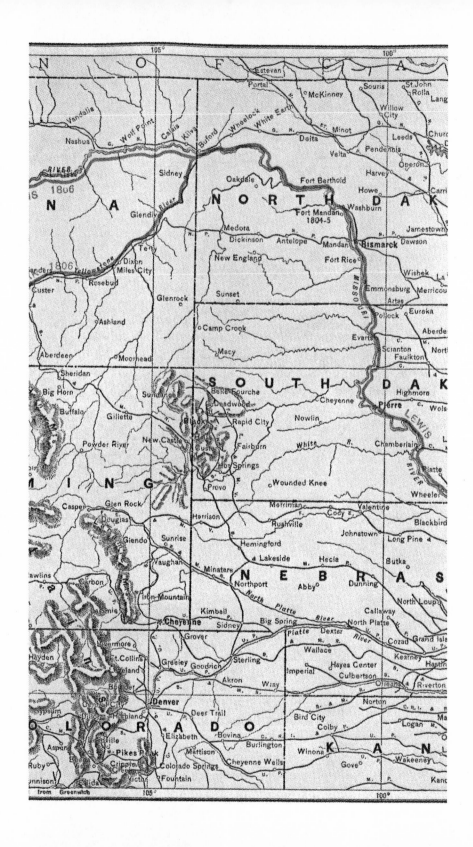

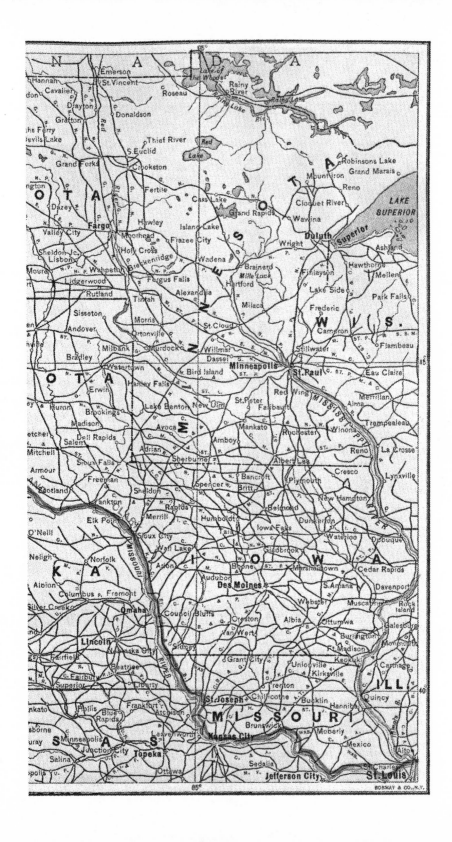

Now back in print
Original Journals of Lewis and Clark
Edited by Reuben Gold Thwaites

Now back in print "Original Journals of The Lewis and Clark Expedition" as published by Dodd Mead in 1904/1905. In preparation for the Bicentennial commemoration of the historic Lewis and Clark Expedition, Digital Scanning, Inc. (DSI) announces the release of their digital reprint edition. The 1903-04 set of **"Original Journals of the Lewis and Clark Expedition"** have been described as the most accurate, work on the expedition. Edited and including an introduction and index by Reuben Gold Thwaites, this set is considered a valuable resource for historians, students and history buffs. This set includes 7 two-part volumes and the Atlas. Illustrated throughout by Karl Bodmer.

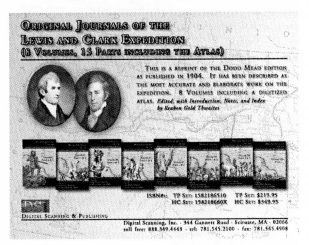

Trade Paper Editions	Hardcover Editions
8 Volume Trade Paper Set 1582186510	8 Volume Hardcover Ser 158218660X
ISBN	ISBN
TP Volume 1 1582186529	HC Volume 1 1582186618
TP Volume 2 1582186537	HC Volume 2 1582186626
TP Volume 3 1582186545	HC Volume 3 1582186634
TP Volume 4 1582186553	HC Volume 4 1582186642
TP Volume 5 1582186561	HC Volume 5 1582186650
TP Volume 6 158218657X	HC Volume 6 1582186669
TP Volume 7 1582186588	HC Volume 7 1582186677
TP Volume 8 1582186596	HC Volume 8 1582186685

Additional Information is available at http://www.Digitalscanning.com or http://www.PDFLibrary.com.

First Across The Continent By Noah Brooks
As Published in 1901

First Across the Continent: The Story of the Lewis and Clark Expedition is presented as a captivating tale. It is drawn from the original journals of the explorers. Noah Brooks uses extensive, carefully selected excerpts from the journals to entice the reader, and then sends the armchair adventurer along on the trek with Lewis and Clark. The detailed description and faithful narratives immerse you in one of the most amazing journeys in history. Originally published in 1901.

Noah Brooks (1830-1903 was a political confidant and personal friend of Abraham Lincoln. A journalist for the *Sacramento Union* during the Lincoln presidency, Brooks was a frequent guest at the White House. After Lincoln's assassination, Brooks moved to the east coast and wrote for other newspapers, including the *New York Tribune* and the *New York Times*.

A great introduction for the young reader, audience 10 to adult.

ISBN TP 1582186820 HC 1582186839 eBook 1582186812

Information and samples available at:
http://www.digitalscanning.com and http://www.PDFlibrary.com

History of The Expedition of Captains Lewis and Clark 1804-1806 by James K. Hosmer

Reprinted from the edition of 1814.

History of the Expedition under the Command of Captains Lewis and Clark is a reprint of the 1814 edition as prepared by Paul Allen, Esquire. This 2-volume set was published in 1903 in preparation for the centennial celebration at that time. The introduction was written by James K. Hosmer past President of the American Library Association.

Volume 1	ISBN	Volume 2	ISBN
Individually		Individually	
Trade paper	1582186979	Trade paper	1582187029
Hardcover	1582186987	Hardcover	1582187037
2 Vol. Sets		**2 Vol. Sets**	
Trade paper	1582186995	Hardcover	1582187045

Information and samples available at:
http://www.digitalscanning.com and http://www.PDFlibrary.com

Other Explorers titles offered by *Digital Scanning, Inc.*

The Life of Dr. Elisha Kent Kane and Other Distinguished American Explorers,
by Samuel M. Smucker
As Published in 1858.
TP: 1582182663 ($19.95)
HC: 1582182671 ($34.95)

The Louisiana Purchase and the Exploration, Early History and Building of the West,
by Ripley Hitchcock
As Published in 1903.
TP: 1582182361 ($19.95)
HC: 158218237X ($34.95)

Our Lost Explorers: The Narrative of the Jeannette Arctic Expedition,
by Raymond Lee Newcomb
As Published in 1888.
TP: 1582182825 ($24.95)
HC: 1582182833 ($39.95)

In the Lena Delta: The Search for Lt. Commander DeLong, etc.,
by George W. Melville
As Published in 1884.
TP: 1582183783 ($24.95)
HC: 1582183791 ($39.95)

Crooked Trails,
by Frederic Remington
As Published in 1899.
TP: 1582182981 ($14.95)
HC: 158218299X ($27.95)

Pioneer Life and Frontier Adventures of Kit Carson and his Companions,
by DeWitt C. Peters
As Published in 1881.
TP: 1582182248 ($29.95)
HC: 1582182256 ($45.95)

Two Years Before the Mast,
by Richard Henry Dana, Jr.
As Published in 1840.
TP: 158218285X ($24.95)
HC: 1582182868 ($34.95)

Trails of the Pathfinders,
by George Bird Grinnell
As Published in 1912.
TP: 1582185964 ($22.95)
HC: 1582185972 ($36.95)

The Making of the Ohio Valley States,
by Samuel A. Drake
As Published in 1894.
TP: 1582184224 ($14.95)
HC: 1582184232 ($27.95)

The Making of the Great West,
by Samuel A. Drake
As Published in 1894.
TP: 1582184380 ($17.95)
HC: 1582184399 ($29.95)

The "Teddy" Expedition (Among the Ice Flows of Greenland),
by Kai R. Dahl
As Published in 1925.
TP: 1582184623 ($15.95)
HC: 1582184631 ($29.95)

The Spanish Pioneers,
by Charles F. Lummis
As Published in 1899.
TP: 1582186243 ($14.95)
HC: 1582186251 ($27.95)

Our Arctic Province (Alaska and the Seal Islands),
by Henry W. Elliott
As Published in 1886.
TP: 1582184585 ($24.95)
HC: 1582184593 ($39.95)

The Story of the Railroad,
by Cy Warman
As Published in 1898.
TP: 1582186324 ($14.95)
HC: 1582186332 ($27.95)

On the Border with Crook,
by John G. Bourke
As Published in 1896.
TP: 1582184461 ($24.95)
HC: 158218447X ($39.95)

Original Journals of the Lewis and Clark Expedition (8 Volumes, 15 Parts including the Atlas),
Edited, with Introduction, Notes and Index by Reuben Gold Thwaites
As Published in 1904 & 1905.
TP Set: 1582186510 ($175.00)
HC Set: 158218660X ($275.00)

On the Storied Ohio,
by Reuben Gold Thwaites
As Published in 1903.
TP: 1582182914 ($19.95)
HC: 1582182922 ($34.95)

**The Expedition of
Lewis and Clark
(2 Volume Set),**
by James K. Hosmer
As Published in 1903.
Volumes 1:
TP: 1582186987 ($27.95)
HC: 1582186995 ($39.95)
Volumes 2:
TP: 1582187029 ($27.95)
HC: 1582187037 ($39.95)

The Mississippi Basin,
by Justin Winsor
As Published in 1895.
TP: 1582186448 ($22.95)
HC: 1582186456 ($34.95)

**The Adventures of
Christopher Hawkins,**
by Charles I. Bushnell
As Published in 1864.
TP: 1582184542 ($17.95)
HC: 1582184550 ($29.95)

The Old Northwest,
by B. A. Hinsdale
As Published in 1888.
TP: 1582186782 ($21.95)
HC: 1582186790 ($34.95)

**First Across
the Continent,**
by Noah Brooks
As Published in 1901.
TP: 1582186820 ($17.95)
HC: 1582186839 ($31.95)

**Life Explorations and
Public Services of John
Charles Fremont,**
by Charles Wentworth Upham
As Published in 1856.
TP: 1582183945 ($17.95)
HC: 1582183953 ($34.95)

The Westward Movement,
by Justin Winsor
As Published in 1897.
TP: 1582186480 ($27.95)
HC: 1582186499 ($39.95)

Lasalle and the Discovery of the Great West,
by Francis Parkman
As Published in 1889.
TP: 1582184909 ($24.95)
HC: 1582184917 ($39.95)

To order any of the above titles:

*Contact your local bookstore and order through *Ingram Books.*
*Contact the publisher directly
(for general information or special event purchases):

Digital Scanning, Inc., 344 Gannett Rd., Scituate, MA 02066
Phone: (781) 545-2100
email: books@digitalscanning.com
www.digitalscanning.com

* Prices subject to change.

Printed in the United States
1173500003BE/2

9 781582 187273